GROWING EACH OTHER UP

Growing Each Other Up

WHEN OUR CHILDREN BECOME OUR TEACHERS

Sara Lawrence-Lightfoot

The University of Chicago Press   Chicago and London

SARA LAWRENCE-LIGHTFOOT, a MacArthur Award–winning
sociologist, is the Emily Hargroves Fisher Professor of
Education at Harvard University. She is the author of eleven
books, including *Exit, The Third Chapter, Respect,*
The Essential Conversation, and *Balm in Gilead,*
which won the 1988 Christopher Award. In 1993, she was
awarded Harvard's George Ledlie Prize for research that "makes
the most valuable contribution to science" and is to "the benefit
of mankind." She is the recipient of thirty honorary degrees and
is the first African American woman in Harvard's history
to have an endowed chair named in her honor.

The University of Chicago Press, Chicago 60637
The University of Chicago Press, Ltd., London
© 2016 by Sara Lawrence-Lightfoot
All rights reserved. Published 2016.
Printed in the United States of America

25 24 23 22 21 20 19 18 17 16   1 2 3 4 5

ISBN-13: 978-0-226-18840-9 (cloth)
ISBN-13: 978-0-226-37727-8 (e-book)
DOI: 10.7208/chicago/9780226377278.001.0001

Library of Congress Cataloging-in-Publication Data
Names: Lawrence-Lightfoot, Sara, 1944– author.
Title: Growing each other up : when our children become
our teachers / Sara Lawrence-Lightfoot.
Description: Chicago ; London : The University of Chicago
Press, 2016. | Includes bibliographical references and index.
Identifiers: LCCN 2015040312| ISBN 9780226188409 (cloth :
alk. paper) | ISBN 9780226377278 (e-book)
Subjects: LCSH: Parent and child—Psychological aspects. |
Parent and adult child—Psychological aspects. |
Learning, Psychology of.
Classification: LCC BF723.P25 L397 2016 | DDC 306.874—dc23
LC record available at http://lccn.loc.gov/2015040312

♾ This paper meets the requirements of ANSI/NISO Z39.48-1992
(Permanence of Paper).

For Our Children
Who Teach Us about
the Changing Shape
of Love

Contents

A Pedagogy Composed
by Children

I WILL NEVER FORGET a moment during a lunch I had with my old friend and colleague Mary Catherine Bateson, a wise, straight-talking woman, an anthropologist whose blend of empiricism and wisdom has always made me see things differently. I had an agenda when I invited her to have hot soup with me on a winter day in Cambridge several years ago. My daughter Tolani—who had jumped into a precocious and volatile adolescence at eleven—was then fifteen, and I was feeling weak and exhausted by the four years of accumulated conflicts at home. Asking Tolani to clean up the dishes after dinner—a chore that was copiously and colorfully spelled out on the family job chart for the week—might elicit an escalation of anger, beginning with excuses that she had no time because piles of homework awaited her, moving on to declarations that I was being unfair and unreasonable, ending in raging accusations that her younger brother Martin had always been my favorite child, her exit from the kitchen—dishes undone—punctuated by outrageous yelling and door slamming. Some battles were protracted, like the long-running struggle over her first tattoo—you had to have parental permission if you were under eighteen, and my fourteen-year-old daughter wanted to have a dolphin carved on her left upper arm—a chronic debate that would simmer for weeks of solicitous, then urgent, pleading and suddenly erupt into a full-blown press of accusations, claiming that I was infantilizing her, theatrically quoting passages from *My Body, My Self.* For the most part, her outrageous behavior was targeted at me and limited to the home front. Out in the world, she carried herself with poise and patience, maturity and aplomb.

As I lunched with my friend, I was also feeling particularly despondent about the years stretching out in front of us that were sure to bring more treachery—a treachery made all the more penetrating because of its tender and loving lining. I thought that Bateson, the cultural anthropologist, might help me see something productive—maybe even redemptive—in our mother-daughter struggles; and I thought that, as a mother of a daughter a dozen years older than mine, she might have some survival skills up her sleeve. Perhaps I was even hoping to be rescued. While my soup got cold in front of me, I spun out my war stories and then waited for her sympathy and support. Bateson listened attentively, never interrupting the rush of emotion that I could not seem to contain or temper. Then she said something surprising. "Your daughter is living on another planet, and she has a lot to teach you about it. . . . Listen to her." Her spare, didactic comment at first felt facile and unsympathetic. She did not elaborate, did not respond to my hunger for her advice. For weeks, I brooded about her take on my troubles, and finally realized that she was saying something powerful and fundamental: that these intergenerational conversations— even the hardest ones—are opportunities for parental growth and insight, and that our children are indeed our teachers, particularly because they are living in a world so different from the one in which we grew up. They are becoming people different from any that we have ever known.

A couple of years later after a huge blowup with my daughter about something that neither of us could even remember or name afterwards—at one of those moments when Bateson's generous perspective had long since worn off—I called a close friend and told him that I was "at the end of my rope." I had no more energy, no more fight in me. I wanted to throw in the towel and admit defeat. His response: "You are nowhere near the end of your rope." And, of course, he was right. Just as Bateson was helping me see that my daughter was teaching me about the world, so too my friend was helping me acknowledge that our sometimes-tortured mother-daughter relationship was offering me the chance to know myself in new ways, that I was developing new capacities, stretching my emotional reserve and repertoire, becoming more patient and forgiving. I was learning a new kind of composure and restraint. I began to understand how important it was to be selective about the timing, and spare in the wording, of my reactions; how I could convey simple respect by really listening before jumping in with my side of the argument; how I might look below the surface tensions to try and figure out the real message underneath. And I now recognize that these same qualities of discipline and perspective — which were wrested from the wreckage of our mother-daughter struggles — became useful in helping me navigate the rocky terrain of many difficult encounters beyond the boundaries of our home.

From a safe distance of a decade and a half, as I reflected on these love wars with my daughter — their fury and their drama, their up-in-your-face attitude — I wondered how those moments propelled me as a learner. I wondered how I was occasionally able to get some distance on the volatile encounters, how I was able to find enough restraint to resist the tit for tat that would typically escalate into pitched battle. How do we as parents have those rare moments of revelation and epiphany? This process of stepping back comes with shifting our role from teacher to learner. It comes with changing the dynamic from adversarial to empathetic, placing ourselves in our teenagers' shoes. It requires breathing deeply — literally and meta-phorically — allowing us the space to listen — a kind of listening that does not assume we already know what our child is about to say, that does not offer up the scripted response but, rather, a kind of listening that attends to the text and the subtext of what is being said. In that moment of listening, empathy, restraint, and stepping back, we begin to take on the role of learner, and we begin to come to terms with the lessons our children are teaching us about themselves and their emerging identity, and about the world that they are inhabiting, the planet that is their perch.

Growing Each Other Up examines the developmental changes in parents that grow out of growing our children, the things our children teach us as we raise them. Most of the developmental literature has, of course, focused on the trajectories of child growth, charting the cognitive, emotional, and social learning that takes place during infancy, early childhood, puberty, and adolescence; revealing the nonlinear path of progression and regression that marks each developmental hurdle; exploring the ways in which parents and caregivers can support and nurture developmental milestones along the way.[1] And this literature has primarily seen parents as the teachers and shapers, guiding and supporting their children's learning and reinforcing the skills, rituals, and values that they believe are important to the child's survival and success in the world. The learning is seen as flowing in one direction, the knowledge passing from the parent to the child. But all of us know that this is a skewed view, one that—in its preoccupation with early development and in its view of parents as the consummate teachers and cultural reinforcers—misses the two-sidedness and adaptive dynamic between parents and their children.[2] It is a static view that is blind to the ways in which parenting requires lifelong learning, a pedagogy that is often composed by their children.

We see the role that children play as their parents' teachers most pointedly in the historical and social science literatures that document the lives and acculturation of newly arrived immigrants or in literary accounts that show the adaptive capacities and rapid learning of the youngsters who must forge and lead the way in the new frontier, dragging their hapless and resistant parents and grandparents behind them.[3] It is the children who first learn the language and must become the translators of words, idioms, and culture; it is the children who make change at the grocery store, ask for directions, and negotiate with the landlords when the rent is late.

In his classic history text, *The Uprooted*, Oscar Handlin writes about the experiences of European Immigrants who came to the United States in the late nineteenth and early twentieth centuries.[4] He focuses on immigration as an experience of interruption, separation, and alienation. The European peasants who made the journey to America had a difficult life, characterized by abrupt separation from the traditions and values of the home country. In adjusting to the American environment, parents relied on the second generation, their children, to be intermediaries, children who from the start, writes Handlin, were "more immediately implicated" than their parents.[5] The children stood at the borderline of the old and the new, and they presented a dilemma to their parents, who yearned for them to retain the culture of their home country and yet knew that to have a better life in the new country, they would have to renounce the old. Beyond the cultural dilemma was a real-life reversal, where parents had to rely on their children for knowledge on how to navigate their alien and difficult environment. Handlin observes that immigrant parents had to accept their role as learners, even as they resented the reversal of the order of things that contributed to their feeling of bewilderment and loss — even as it improved their grasp on the new world.

Although Handlin's book, first published in 1951, was specifically about European immigrants at the turn of the century, more recent accounts, both fictional and nonfictional, of immigrant families arriving from all over the world, chronicle the ways in which the children become their parents' primary teachers, taking on the role of linguistic and cultural translators. These diverse immigrant narratives portray a common theme: the ways in which the asymmetry of knowledge is turned upside down as children race ahead of their parents and parents become reluctant followers, very much dependent upon their offspring but troubled by the ways in which their parental authority feels diminished and their cultural traditions feel threatened. These generational and cultural strains become sites of learning, a role reversal between parents and children that make visible and powerful Bateson's admonition to me.

But even in nonimmigrant narratives, where parents and children are not making huge geographical and cultural shifts, we see that learning is a two-way street and that children are often the teachers and shapers of their parents. Even though I learned to ride a bike when I was seven on winding, gravel country roads in upstate New York, it wasn't until my son Martin and I took to the city streets in Boston that I really mastered the skills of the road. I learned from my six-year-old how to lean into the curves in order to not lose speed or momentum and, as we made our way along the banks of the Charles River, how to balance and steer with no hands on the handlebars. And it was from Martin that I learned everything I know about computers. Over the years, he has sat next to me in front of the screen, patiently guiding my learning, refusing to help when he knew if he waited long enough I would figure it out on my own, relishing his role as teacher, taking on the mantle of restraint and maturity. It was only after Martin's insistent teaching that I finally gave up writing my books longhand — my tools, a sharpened number two pencil and yellow lined paper — and moved, first cautiously and then enthusiastically, to using the computer.

But the more important teaching he did was not skill based; it was not about learning the computer's programs, icons, and buttons; it was not about explaining the mysteries of "the cloud," hovering and unseen all around us. Martin was intentional in modeling an attitude, a way of relating to the machine that was gentle, playful, and unafraid. He tried to lessen my anxieties, get me to lighten up. "What is the worst thing that could happen, Mom?" he would ask rhetorically as he tried to calm the nervousness fogging my mind and fumbling my fingers. So that now that he is thirty-two and rarely around, I can still hear his reassuring, insistent voice telling me that I need to pause, slow down, breathe, and quietly scan the screen for clues. And I can feel his lessons undergirding the way in which I am now able to move past my initial resistance and fears as I approach other things mystifying or intimidating, like designing a website, taking a hip-hop dance class, or driving solo across country.

My daughter, Tolani, has also been my teacher (even during the tug-of-war years). I have, for example, looked to her for lessons on skin care, bath salts, and makeup. It wasn't until she — at sixteen — introduced me to our neighborhood nail salon that I had ever treated myself to a manicure or a pedicure. I neither saw the need for it nor felt that I deserved it. At thirteen, when she made Mother's Day brunch for my mother, my sister, and me — three generations around the groaning board — we realized her culinary skills had outdistanced all of us. After finishing the four-course meal, we grown-up ladies got our notebooks out to record the recipe for a divine pumpkin/spinach soup that she served up, the green and orange liquids magically maintaining their delicate separateness when she poured it in our bowls. My mother asked in admiration, "Where did you learn to cook like this?" and her granddaughter answered, without skipping a beat, "Nana, I'm an artist. This is just like painting."

And speaking of her art, over the years, Tolani has drawn, painted, and sculpted me, creating portraits that have given me insight into how she sees me and who I am becoming. On my fiftieth birthday, she did a large watercolor of me — she called it *The Essence of Mama*. I was stripped of all of my jewelry and combs, a filmy apricot scarf draped around my bare shoulders; my hair, pulled back in a bun, was black on one side and silver on the other. I gazed at the image that did not look like me but seemed to capture my essence and my future. I could see the "me" I was becoming, anticipating a naked-ness and vulnerability that I was still covering up, an unadorned strength that awaited me.

It is not only true that our children may teach us something about ourselves and the world we inhabit, they also often become our mentors and cheerleaders, urging us to take on the next develop-mental chapters of our lives, applauding our efforts that risk change, supporting our new adventures. Many of the folks — between the ages of fifty and seventy-five — whom I interviewed for my recent book *The Third Chapter* spoke to me about the ways in which their young adult offspring helped them find the gumption to leave the routines, habits, and restrictions of their lives and move from the familiar to the strange.[6] It was the adult children who held their par-ents' hands, walked by their sides, watched their backs, and took great pride in their nascent, fumbling accomplishments.

Every morning, for a year and a half, thirty-year-old William trained with Adele, his fifty-eight-year-old mother, in prepara-tion for the half marathon that she was determined to run after recovering from breast cancer. Never before had she even walked a half mile. But with her son's prodding, coaching, and belief in her, she learned to run, first taking tentative baby steps, and finally, just weeks before the day of the big race, finding her groove and pace. She admits that the physical training and strenuous condi-tioning were only a "tiny piece," "the tip of the iceberg" of what she learned from her son. "The learning spread from my body to my mind and heart," she says about the ways that the whole process of learning — "amplified" by her son's tutoring — revised her view of her own emotional resilience and stamina and, at the same time, expanded her capacity to push past the intellectual insecurities and inhibitions that had plagued her for years.

There also seems to be a shift in perspective and purpose for folks in their Third Chapter. Many feel motivated to find a way to "give forward." They want to change their focus from making it up the ladder of success to leaving an imprint on society, from work that is competitive and individualistic to that which is more collaborative and communitarian. Giving forward, making a difference, leaving a legacy . . . these impulses of generosity and service are particularly poignant and powerful for those of us in our Third Chapters. I use the term "giving forward" rather than the more typical notion of "giving back" as a way of reflecting how Third Chapter protagonists sought to develop ways of engagement and service that pointed toward the future. They wanted to resist getting stuck in the anachronisms and nostalgia of the past. In order to be useful, they realized that they needed to find a way of responding to the contemporary context; they needed to be able to envision a future into which their altruism might make a contribution. This required that they listen to the voices and views of their children, an intergenerational discourse that might offer them clues about how they might serve and be useful. Looking back would honor the wisdom and weight of their ancestry. But giving forward — following the lead and teachings of their children — had the chance of being futuristic and transformational, enriching and enlarging those who give and those who receive.

This book examines the ways in which the development and learning of parents are shaped in part by their children, focusing on how those lessons are incorporated into the ways that parents view themselves and their world. I see this work as a challenge and counterpoint to so much of the developmental literature that has centered on the transfer of knowledge, skills, and attitudes from parent to child, documenting the asymmetry of authority and the flow of information from the old to the young, seeing parents as the primary—most important—agents of socialization, the first and last teachers. Instead, I want to document the lessons that parents learn—voluntarily and involuntarily, with intention and serendipity, often through resistance and struggle—from their offspring. I am intrigued by the ways in which these lessons are embedded in evolving relationships and responsive to a rapidly transforming society and world.

There is a good deal of scholarly literature charting the amazingly rapid developmental milestones of babies and toddlers. It speeds by so fast that parents often find themselves breathlessly racing to stay current. Benjamin Spock's classic book seems to be as much a manual on parent education as it is a record of babies' growth.[7] Even the studies of newborns reveal that from the moment they come into the world, they begin teaching their mothers what they need. The now-classic research by Berry Brazelton, for example, documented the first encounters on videotape, showing the initial dance of adaptation—the ways that mother and child try to read each other's gestures and rhythms, the way the mother is being taught by the child about what makes him comfortable, what attracts his attention, what startles and soothes him.[8] The videos show that for some mother-infant pairs the dance is smooth and flowing, and for others it is awkward and edgy, dynamics that often echo through the child's later life—precursors of relational patterns that flow into adulthood. The researchers remind us that the child does not arrive in the world as a tabula rasa on which caregivers make an imprint and mold behavior. Rather, right from the beginning the infant comes into the world with certain qualities, appetites, and characteristics and is active in shaping the behaviors and feelings of caregivers. The infant's development—and the parents' well-being—depend on being able to "read" the infant's moods, desires, and needs.

There is also ample literature on adolescence as a distinct developmental stage and cultural construct that has been stamped into our psyches and written into the social scripts of our families, schools, and communities.[9] It is a time of negotiation and conflict, drama and fluctuation, where there are new alignments in the strained relationships between parents and their teenagers as they take the first treacherous steps towards independence and self-definition. Much has been written about the often painful and difficult journey through adolescence, the parents clueless and humiliated as their children suddenly seem unrecognizable to them. If we looked closely underneath all the rage and heat, there would certainly be charged moments of learning and insight on the part of parents—lessons forged out of the tough teachings by their teenagers.

In the early 1970s, when I was a graduate student studying human development, G. Stanley Hall's classic opus was required reading. His book *Adolescence: Its Psychology and Its Relations to Physiology, Anthropology, Sociology, Sex, Crime, and Religion* (1928) carved out the developmental trajectory and boundaries of the newly emerging, socially constructed concept of adolescence, joined the realms of biology and culture, nature and nurture, and was explicit in emphasizing the volatility and treachery that adolescents brought to the family and wider world.[10] Another standard on our reading list was Erik Erikson's *Identity: Youth and Crisis* (1968), a series of essays that demonstrated the ways in which cultural changes—like social protests and changing gender roles—were bringing on new kinds of identity questions for adolescents.[11] Contemporary texts on adolescence—like Kim Dolgin's *The Adolescent: Development, Relationships, and Culture* (2010)—echo the interdisciplinary themes of Hall and Erikson, underscore the drama and tumult that adolescents instigate, and map the ways in which new shifts in demography, gender roles, and technology shape their identity and experiences.[12] And of course there are bookstore shelves full of self-help books targeted at desperate parents searching for guidance and support in weathering their child's stormy adolescence.

Across time—from Hall's pioneering account to the most recent revisions on adolescent identity and development—one thing has remained constant: parents are presented as baffled and besieged, diminished and confused by their loss of authority and control. The parent-adolescent relationship is tenuous, as the adolescent strives to achieve autonomy by pressing boundaries, and the parent has to calibrate restraint and distance.[13] In none of this adolescent development literature do we get a clear view of what parents may actually learn during their encounters with their young. We do not see how parents are stretched and challenged, even forced to develop new skills, capacities, and perspectives. We do not appreciate how adolescence is riddled with teachable moments targeted at parents.

My interest, however, is not in exploring the way babies raise their parents; nor do I want to focus on adolescence as a distinct and separable life stage. Those developmental sites of learning—highly visible because of their lightning speed and provocative drama—have been under the microscope for a long time; and by now we can anticipate the family scripts. More intriguing to me are the ways in which children become their parents' teachers when adolescence transitions into young adulthood, when the developmental expectations are shifting, adulthood looms on the horizon, and the dynamics of authority are being reshaped.

Recently, researchers have begun to be interested in examining the developmental trajectory and capacities of "emerging adulthood," typically defined as being within the ages of eighteen and twenty-five, or the developmental period following adolescence but prior to adulthood that involves an "extended duration of learning and experimentation before settling into a career and stable relationships."[14] These investigators argue that major shifts in demographic and economic trends and later entry into marriage and childbearing have affected the life course of young people and that eighteen- to twenty-five-year-olds in industrialized Western societies today inhabit a new stage in which they are not adolescents but do not have the financial or educational foundation to strike out as independent adults.[15] This is a time when parents still provide for their adult children, a time when young adults and their aging parents often renegotiate the boundaries of intimacy and distance, autonomy and dependence between them.[16] In *Growing Each Other Up*, then, I shift the lens and landscape as I explore the twenty-year developmental sweep from the ages of fifteen to thirty-five and focus on the lessons that parents learn from their "almost-grown" progeny—those progeny of early maturity who are still figuring out the calculus between distance and intimacy, still negotiating the balance between separation and closeness to their parents. Whether these almost-grown offspring are parents themselves, whether they are living with their parents or not, the relational and emotional bonds continue to be negotiated; the intensity and complexity change but they do not abate. I chose to examine these liminal years of growing adult symmetry because I was interested in the fluidity and complexity of these two decades that I believe defy easy developmental categorization and because I wanted to focus more explicitly on the parent-child relationship as a site of parental learning.

As the research on emerging adulthood suggests, we are living through a time—defined by economic decline, a shrinking globe, technological transformations, and rapid cultural change—when the definitions of adulthood are shifting and the generational alignments are being reshaped.[17] It is not uncommon, for example, to hear middle-aged parents lament the childhood remnants of dependence and irresponsibility that they see in their almost-grown children, or for them to claim that when they were the age of their offspring they were certainly more mature, more competent, more diligent, and more respectful of parental aging and authority. Psychologists have even invented a new diagnostic term—"failure to launch"—a pejorative label that they use to describe the "regressive" behavior of those young people who move back home after college and live under the same roof as their parents, many for prolonged periods of time.[18] How does the increased generational proximity redefine the lessons given and received by parents?

For two years I sought out and listened to parents—most of them in their middle years and most of them mothers—about their experiences learning from their children; about the moments when the tables turned, the "relationship flipped," and their offspring became their mentors and guides; about the learning that felt like long-running plays, with set pieces and vivid dialogue, extended stories with a narrative arc, and the lessons that seemed to appear all of a sudden like an "epiphany." Using what sociologists call a "snowball sample" (asking each interviewee to recommend others who might be interested in joining the project), I searched out parents who were eager to examine the dynamics and contours of their evolving relationships with their almost-grown children, who wanted to reflect on their mutual processes of learning and growth, and who saw storytelling as a vehicle for self-discovery. Even though the developmental and social science literatures have not given much attention to parental perspectives on their children's pedagogy, all of the parents I interviewed immediately nodded their heads in agreement and recognition when I broached the question of their children's teachings, and they usually—without further prompting—launched into a story from yesterday or from twenty-five years ago as they began to draw the scene and capture the mood and the moments.

Occasionally parents needed guidance as they cast around for a place to begin their stories, as they tried to figure out how broad the learning landscape was and whether their reflections offered illustrations of their children's pedagogy. But as one father exclaimed after a stuttering start and some reassurance from me, "There are so many degrees of freedom here . . . and no wrong answers." He then dug into the stories of his children's "impactful and strategic teaching," the ways all four of them have stretched and challenged him to "be a better person and open up to his emotions." During the interviews, I asked only a handful of questions, as parents wove their own narratives, one reflection provoking another as the stories found their gravity and gathered momentum. As I listened, the parents would sometimes look to me for affirmation and understanding; some seemed to be seeking permission to go to the "shadowy dark places."

Even though they were all uniformly generous in telling their stories, occasionally there were tentative and awkward moments when parents worried about exposing their children to scrutiny and judgment. After all, there is nothing more precious to us than our children, and none of us want to be disloyal to them. Our first impulse is to shield them from exposure, present them in a good light, and we want the stories to end well. Some of the parents spoke explicitly about the ambivalence and the tension they were feeling. As one father confessed, "I want to be open and reflective . . . I want to tell stories that are authentic and true . . . but I also want to be protective of and loyal to my children."

The interviews were probing and intense, filled with revelatory moments, expressions of regret and guilt, and proud exclamations of admiration, respect, and love. People wept and laughed and surprised themselves with digging up memories long forgotten or discovering new twists on old practiced narratives. The rich emotional content, however, never felt like therapy even though it was occasionally cathartic. One mother, who claimed she had survived years of individual and family therapy, said with appreciation, "You know when I go to see my shrink, we only look at things that are painful and hurtful, pathological and tortured . . . but here you are asking for the whole story, and I am discovering some good stuff." What she later described as a "benign and honoring experience" was, I believe, related to the ways in which the interviews opened up the chance for people to embrace the inevitable contradictions we live every day, to rehearse their experiences that felt both good and bad, both mysterious and revelatory, both rich and impoverished. Even the chance to tell a story several different ways, creating a kaleidoscope of alternative perspectives and interpretations, all made it possible, for parents to relax into the moment and examine their learning with a fullness and depth that both honored their children and respected their own need to speak the truth as they saw it.[19]

Even though parents often began their interviews with references to something concrete that happened yesterday — a dinner conversation at a family gathering that got tangled and heated, a bike ride through the mountains with their son in the lead — almost everyone quickly retreated to earlier times, to stories about when their young adult children were tiny infants or little children; stories that looked backwards in search of the origins and anchors for more recent developmental tales; stories that captured the long trajectories of parent-child relationships and the shifts in the sites of teaching and learning. Likewise, almost every parent made reference to their own families of origin, to their early upbringing and the ways that the generational echoes resounded in their relationships with their own children, the ways the "ghostly haunts"—both strengthening and undermining—have shaped their own parenting. The interviews, then, moved back and forth through time, recording the past and reporting on the present, skipping years and generations, searching for origins and roots and using those to explain the present and imagine the future.

Although I offered little guidance and asked few questions and was intent upon letting the interviewees determine the focus and shape the arc of their stories, I did always press for details; for a rendering of the context in which the learning took place; for a description of the moments leading up to the learning event and its aftermath; for an explanation of how it felt in the moment; for an interpretation of the meaning-making that both parent and child might have drawn out of the experience. I was attentive to people's vulnerabilities, watching for signs of weariness and wariness, offering opportunities to take a rest or detour away from a reflection that seemed to be causing too much pain. Mostly people wanted to press forward even through the hard passages, courageously pursuing the stories, as one mother put it, "that have always made me restless and scared . . . from which I have always retreated."

Even though the book's protagonists come from diverse backgrounds—in terms of their racial, ethnic, cultural, and religious affiliations—most of them live relatively privileged lives, many are highly educated professionals; in that way they are similar. The majority of people I recruited for this project were, in fact, eager storytellers who anticipated that our encounters would offer them the rare opportunity to reflect on and grow through their parenting; and they believed that tracing their family narratives would be both revelatory and useful to developing deeper, and more benign, relationships with their children. Despite their shared social-class status, however, what is most striking about their stories is not the ways in which they are alike. What stands out—and often surprises—are the complex variations in perspective, expression, and developmental paths among them, variations that reflect differences in their individual character and personality, for sure, but also reflect the ways in which the other sources of their identity—their race, religion, ethnicity, and immigrant backgrounds—sometimes seemed to trump their socioeconomic status and the ways their narratives were often cast as intergenerational stories that cut across educational and social-class boundaries. Those who had grown up in working-class and poor families, for example, could feel the powerful imprint of their upbringing as they raised, and were raised by, their children.

We gathered—at my home or theirs—around our kitchen tables, places that seemed warm and familiar, places where families traditionally come together for nourishment and conversation, over cups of hot tea, coffee, and sparkling lemon water. In addition to having these deep face-to-face conversations, I learned a lot from seeing parents in their own homes, rich with artifacts—photographs, paintings, diaries, unreconstructed children's rooms—that became reference points for launching a story or recalling experiences. In one home, we sat on the sun porch where the easels still stood, where mother and son had—for years—painted side by side, the son modeling a freedom and exuberance in his art that his mother learned to appreciate and absorb. At another, we walked on a path through the woods behind the house where we found a makeshift Buddhist altar that the daughter had constructed out of found objects, the spot where she was teaching her mother to meditate. And I stood at the finish line of a half marathon and watched a mother cross the tape, breathless and victorious, as her son, her coach, cheered her on.

Although all of the insights from my dozens of formal and informal interviews of mothers and fathers, whose children were between the ages of fifteen and thirty-five, resonate in the themes, analysis, and arc of this book, the narratives I collected here were chosen because of their richness and variety, their subtlety and complexity. I have faithfully documented and recorded the voices, experiences, and journeys of the storytellers even though I have— by mutual agreement—altered all of the names and places and a few of the narrative details to protect their privacy and that of their families. Like all good ethnographic inquiries, these stories help us see the strange in the familiar, the exotic in the ordinary, the visible in the invisible. Individually and collectively—in their similarities and differences, their harmony and dissonance—these tales do not allow us to "generalize" in an empirical sense, but they do allow us to glimpse the universal in the particular; and they invite us to identify with the protagonists, to see ourselves in the stories.[20]

The fifteen parent portraits within these pages, then, echo and resonate with the voices of all of the folks I interviewed and reflect the four overarching themes—of witness, growing, intimacy, and acceptance—that emerged as central to the pedagogy composed by almost-grown children and that shaped the development of the book's chapters. Each chapter expresses an essential dimension and gravity of parental learning that grew out of shifts in the contours and dynamics of their relationships with their offspring. The relational themes underscored by the chapter titles also capture the actual words that parents used to describe their children's pedagogy, a language and lens not typically used in the academic or popular literatures to depict parental learning and growth.

When children teach their parents to take on the role of *witness*, they are asking them to listen and observe, not intervene or fix. They are urging their parents to be still, present, and attentive, to notice the subtle changes in them, to resist the impulse to act and protect, and to learn how to "do nothing." It is not only that parents learn through witnessing—really seeing and hearing—their children, they also tell stories about the ways in which their offspring become the inspiration for their own *growing*, the ways in which they instigate developmental changes in their parents through challenge, questioning, and struggle; through leading and modeling; through refusal and resistance; through provocations that are at once inspiring and unsettling. Parenthood itself becomes a mechanism for human development. Part of the experience of growing through parenting is palpably expressed in the contours and depth of *intimacy* that changes as children develop, as they move towards independence, and as they become their own persons. These lessons on intimacy, which parents learn from their offspring, underscore the ever-changing dynamic and process of calculating closeness and distance, connection and restraint between them and highlight the paradoxical, surprising revelation that it is often the growing distance that creates the space for a deeper intimacy to develop. The final relational theme that emerges in the parents' learning narratives resonates with the hard-won, difficult lessons of *acceptance*, the ways in which almost-grown offspring — particularly those who are different from their parents in large and visible ways — insist that their parents see them as whole and worthy, not damaged or compromised, the way they teach them to disentangle their notions of deviance and difference, illness and identity, and accept them for who they are.

It is important to recognize that although each of these chapters focuses on experiences of insight and action that emerge from relational negotiations instigated by our children, they do not represent discrete categories of parental learning. Rather, in the stories of parents, we hear the ways in which one overlaps or bleeds into the next, the way, for example, a narrative about witnessing may also reveal aspects of parental growth and developing intimacy. The learning evolves and is refracted, lighting on a new way of seeing, a reframing of mind, a change of heart, a shift in action on the part of parents who are being taught ever-changing life lessons from their progeny that defy easy or arbitrary categorization.

As I listened to parents weave their narratives, I played many roles. I was the curious ethnographer, gathering the detailed data, carefully observing the action, asking the impertinent questions, and suspending judgment. I was the portraitist listening *for* the story, its text and subtext, relishing the poetic moments, documenting the good, wrapped in a relationship of respect and trust. I was the witness, standing by their sides, watching their backs, and hearing their testimonies. I was also the mother of young adult children of my own, feeling deeply identified and gently implicated, joined in solidarity, resonating with their pain and their joy, their hopes and their regrets. And I was the spider woman, weaving the individual narratives into a larger portrait of learning, tracking the lessons that flow from the young to the old, teaching parents something about themselves and the world that they inhabit—the world that will one day be inherited by their children.

* 1 *

Witness

I wonder how long
Was that violet dancing
Before I saw it?
(*haiku 662*)

The blue of this sky
Sounds so loud that it can be heard
Only with our eyes.
(*haiku 265*)

Only one faint star,
One yellow-windowed ship
And one heaving sea.
(*haiku 324*)

Just enough snow
To make you look carefully
At familiar streets.
(*haiku 521*)

Not even the sun
Can make oak tree leaves as green
As the starlight does.
(*haiku 114*)

RICHARD WRIGHT[1]

THERE IS BEAUTY AND SUBTLETY, detail and precision in this string of Richard Wright's evocative haikus. He helps us focus on small changes, on little differences that make a big difference. He makes us pay attention, readjust our lenses, pause for a moment to smell the roses. He asks us to be present to the slight, almost imperceptible, shifts in the landscape: to the violet dancing, the sounds we hear with our eyes, the snowy streets that do not escape our notice. He suggests that we break our habits, resist our well-worn categories, and be open for surprise as we take in the world around us. He shows us the art and the science of careful looking, the discipline of observation, and reveals his keen appreciation of the ordinary. Wright is the consummate witness, attentive, spare, and exacting as he offers his poetic testimony.

The stories parents tell about their children's pedagogy often refer to the ways they have learned to embrace the "role of witness." Like the lens of a poet scanning the landscape, parents begin to develop a perspective that is watchful, discerning, patient, somewhat removed but fully engaged, a stance that will allow them to learn who their children are and what they need through witnessing them in action . . . observing and appreciating the way their children learn, love, and engage the world . . . noticing the way they build and sustain relationships . . . watching their values and moral judgments made real through their actions. In these stories, we hear the children's voices urging their parents to become observers, asking them to notice the small changes, be prepared for surprise, and be present in the moment. As they take on the role of witness, parents learn to listen, not instruct or fix; they learn to be strategic in their timing; they learn restraint. They learn to back off and create a space that allows them to paradoxically be "in the moment" with their children even as they watch them grow and change over the long haul. They begin to gaze down from "the balcony" rather than get caught in the midst of the fray. They learn to carefully read the ways in which the changing context—social, relational, cultural—shapes their child's character, experience, and behavior. And they learn to give testimony to what they have witnessed, letting their child know that he has been seen and heard.

When parents become discerning witnesses, their views of their children are enhanced by a quality of mind that Ellen Langer calls mindfulness. An innovative researcher and social psychologist, Langer claims that mindfulness can deepen and enrich human experience and propel development and growth. She urges us to "see" and notice the details and subtle changes beautifully documented in Wright's haiku verses; she wants us to become consummate witnesses of our changing world. Langer explains the generative power of mindfulness by comparing it to its opposite: mindlessness. When we are mindless, she argues, we are like programmed automatons, treating information in a single-minded and rigid way, as though it were true regardless of the circumstances. When we are mindful, we are open to surprise, we are oriented to the present moment, we are sensitive to the context, and liberated from the tyranny of old mindsets. Openness, not only to new information but to different points of view as well, is another feature of mindfulness, and "once we become mindfully aware of views other than our own, we start to realize that there are as many views as there are different observers."[2] This suppleness of mind and openness of heart, then, is also a part of bearing witness.

There is, in witnessing, the powerful and quiet relational dimension of "being present," attending completely to what is happening in the moment—sometimes fully engaged, sometimes bearing silent witness, often asking for nothing in return. In my book *Respect: An Exploration*, we meet Bill Wallace, an Episcopal priest, a pastoral psychotherapist, and an AIDS activist who speaks about the witnessing that is core to his work and about how it was his patients who taught him the lesson of "learning to do nothing."[3] As part of his doctoral training at the William Hall Psychiatric Research Institute, for six months Bill was assigned to the ward with patients who had Huntington's chorea, a horrible disease of the nervous system in which people "wither away before your eyes, and there is nothing that you can do to help them." Eventually they die; there is no way of arresting the disease. Bill was the only one on the interdisciplinary team "who could not do anything." The doctors and the nurses could "poke, prod, and give medicines," he recalls. "All I could do was be present." He paints the morbid scene for me. "I'd walk into the day unit. This was one of those so-called well-appointed sixties buildings . . . concrete slabs, turquoise panels, pretty furniture, sturdy carpets . . . and I would find four or five patients sitting in the sunroom . . . just sitting there, not able to talk, drooling, shaking, wobbling, swaying back and forth."

When Bill first arrived on the unit, he would talk to the patients. He even tried to get them to talk to him. He recalls the frustration and disappointment of those few weeks. "I tried talking to them, telling them stories, but it was like throwing green peas at tapioca. I didn't get anything back. They couldn't understand who I was. All they could relate to was my presence. So I just learned to sit with them." Bill is shaking his head as he remembers this "most important learning experience of his life": not talking, not doing anything, just being "present" with the patients. He admits that learning to "not *do* anything" was particularly difficult because he kept on hearing the echoes of his father's harsh admonitions: "My father used to say that if you weren't *doing* something, you were no good."

Once he learned how to "do nothing," the attention that Bill offered the sunroom patients did not anticipate response or reciprocity. They could not return his smiles, his conversation, even his eye contact; and Bill had to discover within himself the selfless, generous gesture that does not expect or demand reaction. This is a rare and difficult discipline. I suspect that we all offer our smiles expecting ones in return. We coo at babies on airplanes because their eager babbling will bring us pleasure. Sustaining attention when you know that no audible or visible response is possible, but when you believe your presence is needed and experienced, is another matter; and it is a crucial dimension of respectful witness.

Interestingly, even though Bill Wallace claims that he initially wished that he was one of the doctors in the sunroom who had skills that would be useful, and perhaps curative, to the patients, who could "poke and prod and give medicine," it may well be that even those people whose job it is to "do" something, need to learn the discipline of witnessing. In his lovely book, *Better: A Surgeon's Notes on Performance*, Atul Gawande claims good medical care requires that physicians practice what he calls diligence. Diligence is more than competence; it is attentiveness to the small changes, to the specific moment, and an awareness of the resources and people that you have at hand to respond in that moment. Gawande admits that diligence can sound boring, dull, even prosaic, especially when we imagine the bold heroics that may be part of rescuing people and saving lives. But, in fact, it is the opposite; it is a readiness to respond, a watchfulness that grows out of genuine caring, "a virtue" that is "moral in nature."

Gawande writes: "What does it take to be good at something in which failure is so easy, so effortless? When I was a student and then a resident, my deepest concern was to become competent . . . as a doctor you go into this work thinking it is all a matter of canny diagnosis, technical prowess, and some ability to empathize with people. But it is not, you soon find out." Diligence is, for Gawande, the first of the three core requirements of good medicine (the other two are "doing right" and "ingenuity"). Diligence is "the necessity of giving sufficient attention to detail to avoid error and prevail against obstacles. Diligence seems an easy and minor virtue. You only have to pay attention, right? But it is neither. Diligence is both central to performance and fiendishly hard." As Gawande describes diligence and the role it plays in making people better, I hear the connections to witnessing and mindfulness, to being fully present.[4] I hear the discipline required to always remain vigilant, watchful, and open to change; I hear the balance of routine and improvisation; and I hear the ways in which it is not necessarily about "doing anything."

When parents take on the role of witness with their children, they need to be able to "see" them clearly; they must not have their sights distorted by faulty or idealized images, inaccurate pictures that might reflect their wishful thinking, their disappointments, their fears, or echoes from their own childhood, ghosts from their past. (Bill Wallace was haunted by the disapproval of his father as he tried to learn the power of being present to his dying patients.) As a matter of fact, cognitive psychologists who study parental development have pointed out that part of the work of parenting is learning how to cast aside faulty, worn-out images of one's children, images that no longer resonate with or reflect who they are. The dissonance between the old picture of the child that is no longer relevant or accurate and the new one that is emerging as real becomes an opportunity for parental growth.[5]

In order to experience the dissonance, however, parents must see and take in the subtle changes in behavior; they must be diligent in listening for the shifts in their children's voices and actions; they must be fully present and ready to not do anything. They must listen for "the sound so loud that it can be heard only with our eyes." "Can I get a witness, oh my Lord" is the first prayerful line of a Negro spiritual. It echoes with the same urgent request children make of their parents every day. Listen to me! See me . . . bear witness to my personhood, my humanity. In this chapter, we hear the pleas of young people asking their parents to listen, to pay attention, to be present; and we see parents taking on the role of witness and testifying about how their clear-sightedness has revealed new, and often extraordinary, qualities and virtues in their children.

Listening

The virtues of witnessing — remaining quiet, still, and attentive — are at first hard for Rachel Goldstein to grasp. She learns her lesson, "the long, hard" way, after years of enduring unrelenting badgering from her oldest daughter, Sasha. By far the most "different and difficult" child of her three daughters, when Sasha turns fifteen, there are fights between them every day — screaming matches that never seem to end. Underneath all of her ranting, Rachel finally hears Sasha's urgent plea. Her daughter is asking her to listen; asking her to pause and take in what she is saying; asking her to not talk over her or come with a prepared script. More than anything else, Sasha wants to hear *herself* talk, and through talking, she hopes to learn what she is thinking and feeling. Rachel has always been the kind of person — and mother — who has wanted to "fix" things, make things right. But her daughter is not asking for her intervention or her guidance; she is not seeking advice or asking her to "do" anything. Rather, Sasha is wishing for an attentive, receptive, quiet response from her mother, a response that is soothing and silent. And it turns out that Rachel also learns to listen to her own inner voice, guiding her toward new spiritual journeys, opening up ways of witnessing the subtle beauty all around her.

At fifty-one, Dr. Rachel Goldstein looks much younger than she is — a youthfulness that reflects her incredible intensity, curiosity, and verbosity. She is a short, heavyset, pretty woman, with long curly brown hair pulled back from her face, bright gray-blue eyes behind wire-framed glasses, a smile that reads as both elusive and welcoming, and an infectious energy that she seems to try — without success — to tame. She is usually dressed in her white dentist coat and flat dancer shoes that allow her to move swiftly from one examination room to the next. But this afternoon, when we meet at the end of her day, she has put on a heavy Nordic sweater and wrapped it over her ample frame. She sits in the kitchen in her office, at a small round table across from me, with her cup of mint tea, eager and ready to talk. She is an "explorer" and an "adventurer" who relishes any opportunity to experience new things and examine things unseen, who seems to be chronically engaged in self-reflection. She is a lifelong learner on a "spiritual quest."

Rachel is also an empiricist who seeks and trusts data and evidence. Many times during our interview she says, "I require proof." Trained as an engineer at the University of Virginia, she went on to study dentistry at Tufts and then do postdoctoral research at MIT. She loves the science and the technical aspects of dentistry, keeping up with the latest tools and techniques of her trade and pursuing the latest scientific advances. She also enjoys the "artful form" that results from having "good hands" and being technically skilled at "making things." She gets great pleasure out of seeking and finding perfection in a bridge well-crafted or a filling expertly executed; and her standards are very high. She works to blend form and function, art and science, aesthetic and technique in her practice every day.

Rachel has three daughters — ranging in age from seventeen to twenty-three — to whom she is deeply devoted and with whom she communicates several times a day, through e-mail and text, Facebook and Twitter. She is a techie who loves the immediacy, spontaneity, and connectedness of the latest tools and appreciates the ways in which these media are transforming human experience. Perhaps she is one of only a few parents her age that might be more of a techie than her children. At one point, for example, she tells me that Facebook has become the "collective unconscious" of our society and world, "crossing boundaries and borders that used to divide us," erasing hierarchies and obstacles that have obscured our paths forward as individuals and as a society.

Her oldest daughter Sasha is a graphic artist and illustrator, now living in Washington, DC, trying to start a freelance business; and when Rachel thinks about lessons learned from her progeny, it is to her firstborn that she turns. Sasha has been the most different and the most difficult of her three daughters. Their differences grow out of their temperaments and orientations, but Rachel boils it down to the bold contrasts. "She is the artist and I am the scientist. . . . I am a type A personality and she is a processer." When Sasha was a young adolescent, she would pick fights with her mother that would last forever despite Rachel's efforts to remove herself. "She would fight on and on, and I would want to stop and have it over. I can't remember what we were fighting about . . . all I know is that there was no escaping her." Rachel had tried to follow the counsel of the dozens of books she had read on adolescence that suggest that parents remove themselves from the battleground. But when she would leave the room Sasha would follow her, continuing her rants. And when Rachel would try to escape to the shower, her daughter would come into the bathroom and draw back the shower curtains. There was nowhere to run, nowhere to hide.

It was many years — years filled with heartache — before Rachel began to hear something urgent and pleading in her daughter's raging encounters. She began to see that Sasha was not asking for her opinion or her guidance; neither was she asking her mother to solve anything. She was simply asking her to listen to what she had to say, without prejudice or judgment. Rachel's voice is almost a whisper as she recalls this hard-won discovery. Her eyes look weary. "I wasn't listening to her. She just wanted to be heard . . . I am a fixer. I wanted to find the solution and have it over and done with." She sums up the critical lesson that grew out of the years of conflict.

"So from Sasha I learned to listen and hear more. . . . Now I try not to stop her from talking and confronting me. . . . I force myself to open my ears and my heart. I even try to repeat back to her what she seems to be saying. . . . I say 'it sounds like this is what you are feeling.'" Rachel is quick to say that, even though she now knows it is important to listen to Sasha hash it out, this is a lesson she has to continue to learn and practice. It requires an uncommon amount of restraint and patience that are hard to come by given her type A personality. So she constantly needs to monitor herself, even though she knows in her mind the best way to proceed.

Just yesterday Sasha called to talk to Rachel about buying a copying machine for her fledgling business. She was trying to decide on the best size and price given what she projected would be the scale of her business and given the space she had for the machine in the small apartment she shares with two roommates. Rachel was pleased that Sasha was seeking her advice and she leapt in immediately with "a million suggestions." She could hear the tone change in her daughter's voice, a tone of withdrawal and dismissiveness, a turning away. "Immediately," says Rachel with frustration written all over her face, "she rejects all of my suggestions out of hand . . . as if my suggestions are an affront to her ego." The conversation closed down quickly as Sasha said the line Rachel has heard hundreds of times before, "What do you think, Mom, I'm stupid?" It turns out—and Rachel only realized this afterwards—Sasha was calling to hear herself talk.

These encounters with Sasha over the years are full of echoes of difficult conversations Rachel has had "for a lifetime" with her own mother. As a matter of fact, she sees that her lessons on listening are directly connected to her daughter's "teaching her to examine the relationship" she has with her own mother. It has forced her to begin to appreciate her mother, her motivations, her experience, and her guidance. This still feels like an "epiphany" to Rachel. "I will call my mother, and she will begin with the suggestions of how I should proceed, suggestions about my business, raising the kids, taking a trip somewhere, redecorating my home . . . but now I hear it differently. Rather than turning off to what she is saying or

putting her down, I assume that—like with my own kids—her intention is hopeful and loving, and now I have begun to listen. I had
always thought her suggestions were intrusive and demeaning, but
now when I actually sit back and listen to what she is saying, she
has some really excellent things to say . . . forward looking, relevant,
thoughtful, and sophisticated. " Now Rachel is throwing her head
back and laughing. "It only took me fifty years to find this out and
I learned it from my daughter!"

The lessons that Sasha has taught primarily grow out of the differences between her and her mother and the conflicts that so often
result; and they feel like ancient reverberations from Rachel's own
childhood. Rachel's relationship to her youngest daughter, Ava,
who at seventeen is still in high school and living at home, has presented different kinds of challenges—challenges that grow out of
their likenesses and similarities. Rachel says it starkly, "With Ava
it's like reliving myself . . . watching myself growing up. It gives me
insight about who I am as a person, but it has the disadvantage of
me being too empathetic with her, identifying too closely with her
point of view." Their "almost twin-ship" makes it hard for her to parent Ava, hard for her to take the grown-up position that she knows
her daughter needs as she finds her own way through her adolescence. She tries to describe the intensity of their relationship in
another way. "Ava and I are very intertwined. With me she is sometimes the mother and then at other times, I become her mother. We
switch roles back and forth." Rachel is quick with an example. After
four years of being separated, Rachel and her husband divorced this
past fall. As the youngest child still at home, Ava suffered the most.
She, in fact, wanted the divorce and urged her mother to proceed
with it. And she was unforgiving of her father and refused to see
him for the first couple of years after he left.

It was only very recently, when Rachel took a professional trip
to California, that Ava agreed to spend the few days that she was
away with her father. It turned out that she actually spent the first
night at his girlfriend's house because she had an extra bedroom
that Ava could use. Rachel did not agree with the plan and knew
intuitively that there would be trouble, but she tried her best to stay

out of it, and she hoped that without her presence, Ava might find a way to reconcile with her father; at least it might be a beginning. As it turned out Ava stayed there only one night. She felt "very uncomfortable and unhappy," and she called her mother to say that she would instead be staying with a friend until she returned from her trip. But Ava was not telling the truth. Their neighbors spotted her car in the driveway; she never went to her friend's and instead stayed at home alone. Now Rachel comes to the punch line; an admission of her "flawed parenting." "No question," she says, "I should have grounded her. She had lied to me . . . she was not supposed to be there alone. But I did not punish her. My impulse was to say, I get how you are feeling. . . . I would have done the same thing."

These obstacles that Rachel has faced with her daughters — either because of difference or overidentification — she now sees as opportunities for growth. Over the years, she has reframed the way she thinks about hardship. "You know," she says, leaning forward intently, "how people always say that we don't get to choose our family . . . well I now believe the opposite. I believe that we choose our children and we choose our parents and that they travel with us through life and teach us lessons." In the past few years, Rachel has embraced a kind of "spiritual foundation" in which she accepts that there will always be hardship and struggle in life, and the tough times stand as "signposts" inviting and requiring your attention. "The universe is saying to me: notice this, learn from this." Rachel immediately translates this approach into her mothering repertoire. "You know, with Sasha, my most difficult daughter who is always questioning and confrontational, pushing the limits all the time . . . I ask, why is she in my life? What will she teach me?" This shift in her spiritual stance has been very liberating for Rachel. She exhales and says, "It takes out the angst of it . . . the conflict forces you to ask what am I being taught here and why do I not like that behavior . . . what does it represent for me?

These spiritual insights certainly grew out of Rachel trying to find a way to make peace with those parts of her mothering that felt most tortuous and troublesome; she wanted, perhaps, to find a safer escape than the exposed place behind the shower curtain. She credits her daughters, particularly her oldest, with escalating the conflict so that she was forced to take notice, examine the "signs," and explore why they were so upsetting to her. But as someone who has always been a "searcher," she has also taken time to explore her spiritual path: reading volumes on psychology and spirituality, attending meditative retreats, practicing hypnosis, and engaging in therapeutic sessions called past-life regression. Her current guru is a Yale-trained psychiatrist, named Brian Weiss, who has written a book called *Many Lives, Many Masters*, which argues that reincarnation actually exists for all of us and that we are surrounded by "spiritual guides" from our past and future lives who will lead the way and protect us, comfort and love us, through the traumas and losses of our lives. Even as she describes Weiss's book with enthusiasm and certainty, she says "Although I find it enormously helpful and beneficial, I don't know whether I buy into it completely." But it helps as she tries to interpret a recent disturbing dream, a nightmare that began to explain the "overprotective" relationship that she has with her middle daughter, Mira. "In the dream, I was a cavewoman and she was my baby . . . we were locked in the cave together, with no way to escape . . . and she died in my arms."

In an interesting twist, Rachel sees this notion of past lives as a way to give more space to her daughters — in her words, an "essential space" that will allow them to develop their independence and stretch their wings. She has always been a hovering kind of mother; she has always verged on the side of being fiercely overprotective, wanting to spare her children from danger and pain. But she now recognizes that this hovering is more damaging than helpful, that it "weakens and diminishes" her children. "You try to shield them and you are actually doing the opposite."

Rachel reflects on a moment when that all became very clear to her. A few years ago, her ex-husband, who comes from a very "crazy and mean-spirited" family, wanted all of them to join his parents on a trip to their ancestral home in Eastern Europe. Rachel refused to go; being with his family just felt impossible. She could not bear the "mess and the pain and the craziness." In the past, she would have gone along, just to protect the children. She would have been their "shield," making sure that they would not be hurt or harmed in any way. But this time, she let her husband take the children by himself, and she stayed at home. "By my not being there," she recalls. "The girls had to face the harsh reality . . . and they became stronger for it . . . they began to discover their own voices, their own way of dealing." But it is not only clear that her daughters became stronger without their mother-shield, it is also that Rachel realized for the first time that they were "capable of being independent, adaptive, and resourceful" when she was not around to protect them.

The Eastern European trip, which Rachel at first saw as potentially dangerous and painful for her children, reminds her of the hardships that she grew up with that she now feels made her a much "stronger person." She is back to the idea of choosing her family; she turns to her own upbringing as the daughter of a mother who was divorced five times, and a father who left the family when she was seven and remarried four more times. Her voice is somewhere between wailing and crowing, sounding pained and proud. "When I was growing up, I lived through five different sets of circumstances, five different households . . . with different values, foods, habits, hobbies, rituals. . . . I used to see the pain and trauma in all of that. Now I see myself as having an amazing life that made me adaptive, strong, and resilient." Even the absence of her father—who was never there for anything, not even her high school or college graduations—gets a benign interpretation. "If my father had been part of my life, he would have inhibited and diminished me. He was a terrible right-wing chauvinist and he would have gendered me . . . made me feel like less because I was a girl. Without him present, I always thought that the sky was the limit for me . . . I never thought of myself as man or woman, and that gave me all kinds of freedom." It wasn't until Rachel was a postdoc working on a big multiyear research grant from the National Institute of Health that she experienced blatant sexism from her mentor who said after her first child was born, "Wouldn't you rather be home taking care of your baby than hanging out in my lab?"

Rachel describes her "new way of seeing the world" as "amazingly liberating," and she believes it makes her more realistic and forgiving as a mother, forgiving both of herself and of her daughters. It is "calming" to be able to see the "beneficial effects of harsh circumstances," or to feel the presence and embrace of your spiritual guides who came before you, or to feel as if you can choose your family, not just suffer the burdens of their legacy. All of this Rachel believes was inspired and provoked by being a mother trying to find a way to love and protect and do the best by her children; a mother trying to find peace and pleasure in the midst of struggle and hardship; a mother who needed to find reconciliation with her own mother. Where Rachel has landed, at least for the moment, is a "work in progress"; she is "strangely enough, in a place" where she has begun to see the connections between her religious heritage and her newly evolving spirituality.

Again her daughters' lessons are central to this new "bridge crossing." All three girls attended a Jewish day school beginning at three years old, a decision that Rachel fought, but one that her husband had insisted upon. "Now," she says, "I think it is the best thing we ever did." Rachel, who grew up in an affluent suburban community outside of Cleveland, hated the idea of going to the synagogue. "It always felt like scraping nails across a blackboard," she says about how much she resisted and mistrusted the institutional dogma. But over the years, her daughters have shown her the power and significance of their faith; they have instructed her in the history, rituals, and tenets of Judaism. They have been trained in "Rabbinics and Tenach," learning the kind of critical thinking and discernment that allows them to "dissect the Jewish laws and guidelines about how to live your life." Rachel says proudly, "I grew up as a superficial Jew and they've grown up as spiritual Jews. Every day, they brought home from school what it meant to them, and they would talk about it at dinner. . . . Their Jewish faith teaches them to be thoughtful, kind, generous, and thankful . . . thankful even for being able to wake up in the morning. This has been ingrained in them since they were three. They are actually living their faith."

Rachel admits that their understanding of and devotion to Judaism sometimes makes her jealous; sometimes she even feels estranged and "marginalized" when she can't fully participate in, or experience the full meaning of, their religious conversations. She wishes she had her daughters' enthusiasm for going to the temple, experiencing those deep religious feelings and celebrating the holidays. But her jealousy is laced with admiration for who they are becoming and a recognition that some of those tenets and lessons of their "spiritual Judaism" have "rippled and transplanted" their way into her life. Rachel can now feel the resonances of her daughters' religious teachings in a different kind of spiritual setting. "Being in the woods does a similar thing for me," she says wistfully. "When I am there I am in the moment. . . . I notice things and take them in. This morning I saw something so beautiful that it was almost blinding. For the first time, I saw a lady's slipper orchid, just one standing by itself. I just stood there for a long time gazing at it. That was my meditative, spiritual moment."

Listening is not something one learns how to do and "accomplishes," like riding a bike or swimming, it is something that is in constant practice, always having to be made and remade in relationship with another person. And the lesson of listening is not bound in time; from her daughter, Rachel Goldstein learned how to listen to her own mother. Listening is also not defined by a particular relationship; it can be a "larger" kind of listening, like Rachel thinking that the confrontations with her daughter are the "universe saying to me to notice this," signs that there is something to be learned. In this larger space, listening becomes a way to learn about, and enlarge, the self, like Rachel's growing spirituality and her ability to regard her own difficult upbringing as benign and strengthening. In learning how to listen, Rachel develops a capacity to see beauty in life — the lady's slipper orchid, the "violet dancing" — and be thankful for it.

Witnessing

Unlike for Rachel Goldstein, witnessing seems to come quite naturally to Elvira Perez. Besides "being wired that way," she gives some of the credit to her eighteen-year-old son Gabriel for teaching her "an approach to the world that is tolerant and calm." Over the years, she witnesses his qualities of peacefulness, patience, humor, and acceptance; his judiciousness and fairness; his capacity to entertain alternative political and ideological positions, resist stereotypes and challenge caricatures; his acuity in offering fresh analyses to well-worn family discourses. Mostly she admires the ways in which Gabriel lives out the values instilled in his family, even the ones passed down across generations. The values are not just delivered as rhetoric, or spoken as moral declarations or abstractions; they are enacted in the world, with family and friends, at school and with peers, in love relationships. Elvira witnesses, admires, and learns from the ways her son moves from "theory to practice," conception to action, from talking about values to embodying them in his life.

When Gabriel was three, his parents divorced. It was an amicable divorce with joint custody and a decision to live within walking distance from each other so that Gabriel would be able to grow up in both households and knit together a wholesome life. Gabriel's parents interpreted the joint custody arrangement in a way that had their son shuttling between their houses every other day. "We arranged the schedule to the best of our knowledge and with good intentions," recalls Elvira, Gabriel's mother. "But the adjustment was difficult for Gabriel . . . whenever he was at one house, he cried for the other. It was heartbreaking." They tried consulting with their pediatrician, school counselors, and a psychotherapist, who all advised that Gabriel—usually called Gabe by his family and friends—would in time get used to the every-other-day rhythm of living in two households. Having endured this arrangement for six years, when Gabe was ten years old, he approached both of his parents and asked if they could make a change, a plan that he thought would work better for him. He proposed that he stay at each home for a week at a time and said that would allow him to better manage all the things—homework assignments, books, athletic gear, projects—that he had to organize for school each day. Elvira remembers his patient and considerate voice as he sat his parents both down, looked them square in their faces, and made his request. They were on board immediately; and the arrangement has been in place ever since; every other week he moves to the other parent's house. By now each of the households have expanded to include new spouses and stepsisters and stepbrothers.

This is the first story that Elvira tells me about Gabe, the first time she can remember "listening to, and learning from, him." Despite all of the contrary counsel from the professional experts, she and her former husband could hear the "urgency and rightness" of their son's request; and it left both of them wishing that they had made the changes in the schedule much sooner. How had they not seen the signs and responded to their son's cries? With the original arrangement, whose lives were they trying to make livable? Whose guilt were they seeking to assuage?

The tale of Gabriel's steadfastness — in living with the original arrangement and choosing the time when he might approach his parents requesting a change — reminds Elvira of another story of her son's long-standing and enduring patience. Gabe was a tiny three-year-old, and the family had gone to New York City for the weekend to see *The Lion King* on Broadway. They stood on line for the half-price tickets in Times Square before the matinee on Saturday; Gabe waited silently, not fidgeting, whining, or complaining. After about two hours he quietly asked his mother, "What are we doing here?" Elvira is shaking her head in disbelief, "First of all here is this little child staying still in line in the hot sun, just waiting to go to a show for which he is too young . . . he tolerated all of it." Elvira does not know whether his "unbelievable patience" — a quality that has "grown up with him" — is an inborn trait (here she does not sound like the scientist she is but, rather, like a mother trying to fathom the mysteries of character in her child), but she knows that he has always been that way. And she also sees this quality as one of the things that she has tried to learn from him, "an approach to the world that is tolerant and calm." "Usually parents are teaching their child to be patient. This has been turned upside down in our relationship."

Born and raised in Barcelona, Elvira makes a bold statement when she enters the room. At about five feet ten inches, she wears high heels and stands tall, her long legs wrapped in snug black leggings, her brocade jacket hugging her curves. Her skin is olive;

her face is framed by a long, full mane of black curly hair, and she smiles easily, often laughing at herself with a gentle self-deprecating humor. Her bright red lips match her manicured fingernails. Her style is European elegant. Several times she refers to how much she loves well-designed clothes and how much pleasure she gets in dressing beautifully. At one point, she laughs at the way she even puts on stylish—"but not fancy"—outfits to work in her garden, and the way her son Gabriel chides her for not dressing like the neighbors in jeans and sweatshirts, for sticking out in a way that sometimes embarrasses him. At the same time, her son also admires his mother's elegance and aesthetic and is proud of the way she carries herself in the world. As a matter of fact, Gabe's sense of European style and taste—very different from his American adolescent peers—seems to be a direct inheritance from his mother and his architect uncles in Spain. Their love of "the aesthetic" is one of the places where "our lives meet."

Elvira balances all of this attention to outward decorative appearance with a heady, rigorous intelligence and a big, demanding career. She has her PhD in astrophysics and has spent the last twenty-five years working in various fields of science, most recently in biomedical research. After completing her undergraduate degree in Barcelona, she did her graduate work at Cornell University, followed by postdocs at Stanford and MIT. She is now in her second marriage. Both times, she says without apology or regret, that she has chosen scientists as partners, men who, in fact, pretty much fit the stereotype—"nerdy and emotionally reserved." Her personality and background are a vivid contrast. She describes herself as a humanist, as someone who enjoys, and is sustained by, relationships; and she loves being surrounded by family, by lively conversation, by good food and fun.

Even though Gabriel at first cried a lot for whichever parent he wasn't with when he shuttled back and forth after the divorce, Elvira reflects on some of the ways in which over time living in two households has been central to defining their relationship and been a "source of learning and growth" for her. It turns out that the two households have "very different political and ideological views." Elvira comes from a family that is very liberal. They were part of the socialist, leftist party in Barcelona; they lived under the Franco dictatorship until 1975, and when he died, they celebrated for days. Elvira also points out that Barcelona, where she was born and raised, is a very independent, separatist part of Spain where Catalan, not Spanish, is the official language, and where she went to a "progressive school which had a humanistic, collaborative view of education" that spawned in her a commitment to socialist values. Elvira's views on health care, immigration, gun control and the wars in Iraq and Afghanistan reflect her early socialization in her family and school "whose views were deeply aligned"—views that fall squarely "in the liberal, progressive bucket."

Gabe's father's household, in contrast, is politically conservative. They are, for example, staunchly against gun control and against Obamacare (his father is a physician and a medical researcher); and "they talk a fairly straight Republican line." "At my house," says Elvira, "it is staunchly no guns . . . at the other family's, they claim that guns are important for protection in case an intruder comes into your house . . . they say, why is going to the shooting range for sport and pleasure any different than playing baseball?" Over the years, Elvira has watched her son negotiating these opposing political discourses, listening to, and participating in, these contrasting conversations around the two dining room tables; and she has seen the way in which his response has been measured and discerning. "Gabe refuses the dogma whether it is from the left or the right . . . he seems to take each political issue on its own terms, weighing the pros and cons," says Elvira admiringly.

Although she admits that her politics have changed very little since she arrived in this country as a graduate student—she holds fast to her liberalism—Elvira also says that one of the things that her son has taught her is the value of "considering the complexity and singularity of your ideological stance," not being driven by the either/or polarities that his parents represent. As he shuttles between the two families, he is the unscripted one; the one whose positions and assertions feel unpredictable and often surprising; the one who is most likely to patiently consider the alternative positions before he jumps in and takes sides. Again, Elvira sees Gabe's patient temperament as the source of his open-mindedness. "His willingness, at three, to stand in line for two hours to buy tickets to the theater is connected to the way he now patiently tolerates different views . . . the way he listens, considers, and waits."

Gabriel also has another quality that helps him navigate the often-heated exchanges at the dinner table. "He has a sense of humor," says Elvira smiling, "and perfect timing." When an argument threatens to escalate out of control, it is almost always Gabe who will cut through the tension with a humorous aside. "Everyone in the family says that this is something that defines him," says Elvira, not able to think of a specific example because "it is so much a part of his repertoire." Then she remembers a conversation in the car a couple of weeks ago when the family was driving up to her husband's extended-family gathering—a scene where the tensions always run high—and Gabriel turned to his mother with a mock whisper and said, "Remember Mom, you and I have the role of making peace."

As she talks about Gabriel's temperament—his gentle patience, his ready humor, his respect for difference—she begins to see him as a "teacher and leader." He is the one to whom the family turns for the surprising reflection, the impertinent question, the witty aside that cuts through the rising tensions of family debate and argument. She has learned so much from the way her son is "in the world." Elvira contrasts those temperamental teachings with the lessons her son has taught her that grow out of his "obsessions." Gabriel has two big obsessions—cars and music—and over the years he has worked very hard to introduce his mother to the skills, pleasures, and artistry of both. Despite his best efforts, Elvira has not learned to fully—"or even minimally"—appreciate his love of cars, but she admires his laser focus, his technical skills, his deep knowledge, and most of all his passion. Both his father and his step-father are mechanically inclined and will work for hours with Gabe out in the garage, building and fixing cars, and Elvira admits that "the fathers' devotion and rapt engagement" give her an excuse to retreat from something about which she is mostly disinterested.

Currently, Gabe owns a 1995 Impala that he bought with money he earned working after school and that he has rebuilt from scratch, ordering the parts online and painstakingly putting the pieces together. When she speaks about her son's obsession with cars, Elvira smiles at the ways in which Gabe's efforts to teach her "that stuff" have largely fallen on deaf ears. She is just "not that into" cars, even though she enjoys the patient way he instructs her through hands-on experience and admires the ways he has challenged himself over the years and become a real expert mechanic.

Gabe's second obsession is music, and here Elvira has not been a reluctant learner. In fact, when he was about five, and she spotted his love of music, she was quick to find him a piano teacher who had a new approach to working with kids that was both "demanding and fun." A couple of years later, Gabe took up the guitar on his own, and since then he has worked hard to become a skilled and expressive rock musician in the "Jimi Hendrix and Janis Joplin" mode. He has become a serious student of music, learning theory and composition, exploring the historical contexts of various musical periods and styles and the life stories of the significant musicians in each era. He has also become a sophisticated listener, able to hear the subtle tonal shifts, the chord progressions, and the shape of the musical arc.

Elvira sounds like a nascent, fumbling student as she searches for the musical terms that he has taught her. "He teaches me about the chords . . . the beauty of the melody . . . shows me the baseline and the rhythm." Often she and Gabe will sit down together and watch a documentary on the life and work of a musician — Charlie Parker, Thelonious Monk, or Billie Holiday — and he offers a running commentary alongside the film's narrative that always "enlarges and enriches" his mother's understanding of the film and the music. This obsession is one that Elvira loves to share with Gabe. "It is such a big part of his life, and it exposes and expresses the more sensitive part of him."

In fact, when Elvira thinks about the "sensitivity and sympathy" that are evoked in Gabe's music, she is reminded of the ways in which she has always tried to nourish the "masculine and the feminine qualities" in her son, and how she has been drawn to the ways that he comfortably balances the male and the female. "As a parent, I always had an approach of not thinking about things as male or female. . . . I was comfortable, for example, with his learning knitting, and I taught him to knit when he was a teenager. It is the same thing with my love of design and clothes, which I have passed along to him as well." But it is in the music that Elvira feels the "feminine in him that transcends" anything that he might have inherited from her. Through the music, their "hearts can touch" in ways that Gabriel himself orchestrates. The learning is "composed by him," and it touches his mother deeply. Recently, Gabe made a CD for Elvira's new car, and when he gave it to her, he told her that he chose each of the songs because he could see her in them. Elvira is throwing her head back and laughing at the surprising experience she had when she first listened to the CD on her way to work the next morning. "It was really the other way around, I could actually see Gabriel in the songs!"

These reflections of the feminine and the masculine and the ways they are balanced and expressed by Gabe through his music make Elvira recall a conversation one evening at the dinner table when her son was about fourteen. His three stepsiblings were there, and the moment was obviously planned and staged by Gabe. He announced — without fanfare or drama — that he thought he might be gay and waited for his family's response "which he knew would be accepting." It was his oldest brother who did most of the talking; assuring Gabe that "over time he would figure it out"; that "it was a process of discovery"; and that he was "happy that this could be a conversation with the whole family." There were no sparks or drama in what turned out to be a short-lived conversation. To Elvira it all seemed "completely natural." In fact, she was surprised and a little disappointed when she called her mother in Barcelona ("who is very liberal and open-minded") to tell her about Gabe's announcement, and her mother seemed worried and resistant. "Maybe they are teaching them too much about homosexuality in school," her mother had said, "and maybe that is influencing him."

One of Gabriel's best friends, it turned out, had recently come out to him. In fact, Gabe was the first person he told, fearing that his parents would not be accepting and that he might be bullied or humiliated in school if he shared it more broadly. And Gabe had kept his secret, offering him support and asylum until he was ready to tell his parents and a small circle of peers. Even though there continues to be some secrecy and fear around being out and gay in their school and community, Elvira is struck by the ways in which societal norms have changed. "This becomes part of the norm, not the exception," she says with some relief. "It is not considered pathological; it is seen as healthy."

There was a brief period—when Gabe was fifteen or sixteen—when he said that he was bisexual, when he would often talk to his mother about "sexuality as a spectrum; to some extent we are all bisexual." When I ask Elvira how he identifies his sexuality now, she smiles broadly and says, "Well, he has a lot of girlfriends." About a year ago, just after Gabe's seventeenth birthday, she remembers him coming home one afternoon and reporting that he had had his first sexual encounter. She can recall the three questions that immediately popped out of her mouth. "First I asked him whether he had used protection . . . second, I asked whether the person was a boy or a girl . . . and third, I asked whether he was respectful to him or her." It turned out the person was a girl; they had used protection; and Gabe had said that there was mutual respect between them. In fact, the next day, Gabe told his mother that she had "handled the conversation very well." He appreciated, he said, that she did not react with a lot of drama, that she did not interrogate him or ask for a lot of details. "All you cared about," Gabe said gratefully "was that I was okay and she was okay."

The level of intimacy between mother and son seem rare to me, and I ask about Gabe's disclosure of his first sexual encounter. Was the conversation really so straightforward and calm? Did Elvira worry at all about how Gabe might respond to her three queries? She is silent for a while, seeming to measure how much of the ease between them might be related to "the times" and how much probably reflects their "special relationship." "I think that Gabe's disclosure was unusual, but much more usual than it used to be," Elvira says thoughtfully. But she admits that theirs is a "rare intimacy," a mother-son bond that she believes — perhaps counterintuitively — has emerged out of the space that has always been between them. Their closeness comes in part, she believes, from their not being together all the time. "Living in the two houses has made both of us value our time together," she says definitively, "and the fact that I have always worked full time has made Gabriel appreciate the time when I am at home and can devote myself to him . . . it has always made us talk more together." Elvira recalls a recent comment by Gabe that immediately made her tear up with gratitude. They were watching some documentary about women choosing family *or* career and its implication for their child-rearing and their satisfaction and self-esteem as women; and Gabe said, "Well Mom, you have always chosen both . . . family *and* career." In that pronouncement Elvira heard her son recognize that "all along he had been my witness"; all along, he had felt chosen by her.

The ease of the conversations between mother and son, and the intimate expressions of appreciation and respect, cause me to finally ask whether Gabriel's adolescence has been completely conflict free, whether there has been none of the typical drama or fraught explosions that usually go with the territory. Her stories have sounded so modulated to me, so full of calm and mutual admiration. Elvira seems surprised at my surprise, but then admits that for the most part, yes, Gabe's adolescence has been mostly without major trauma or turbulence. She can think of things that bug him about her behavior, but she obviously sees these moments of frustration and friction as "trivial stuff." "He does not like it when I keep on texting him to find out where he is when he is out too late. He does not like it when I ask him to fold the laundry or empty the dishwasher, and I keep on repeating it because he does not get to it fast enough . . . and he does not like it when I garden in the yard in my fancy clothes or when he thinks I am too dressed up when we are going to the other family's house . . . sometimes I have to change my clothes twice before he thinks that I am appropriately dressed." But even as she lists these encounters that "ruffle feathers occasionally," her voice is light; it is clear that they do not rise to the level of adolescent rebellion in her eyes. "No," she says finally, "Gabe's adolescence has not been defined by conflict . . . the teenage years have been wonderful."

As a matter of fact, Elvira and Gabriel have just been through one of the most typically treacherous times of late adolescence. He has spent the last year applying to colleges, and he has just been accepted for early admission into the college of his choice. Elvira had girded her loins for what she anticipated would be a hard time of redrawing their relationship during this time of major transition. She says gratefully, "Even though everyone warned me that there would be huge drama in the transition to college, it hasn't been that way for us. . . . Thinking of him going has not been sad for me at all . . . you see I don't feel that I am losing him. We will still be very close." She puts her hand over her heart to signal that Gabe will always be with her, in her.

For much of the interview, Elvira has been trying to give language to something "subtle but very important" that she has learned from her son. At one point, she wonders out loud whether she is having difficulty finding the English words, whether her inarticulateness might in fact be a language problem. But when she switches to Catalan, she shakes her head in frustration once again. Just as we are about to end our time together, she discovers the feeling and the language, and says tentatively, "What I have learned from Gabe is that the values that I have held theoretically, conceptually, he has found a way to enact, to live in his life . . . part of that is who he is and part of that is that he is a product of his time, his generation." Gabe has, in essence, taught his mother how the values she professes — and has professed in their many conversations around the dinner table, listening to music together, knitting side by side, watching documentaries — have embedded themselves in his everyday encounters and choices. "It is not just theoretical . . . you spend years breeding that in him . . . then you see it lived by him in a way you could not have predicted, and that feels so good."

She searches for an example of this "theoretical translation." A few months ago Gabe had come home and said that he had "fallen deeply in love" with Tanika, an African American girl who is in his class at school. Elvira had always told Gabe that she "would be open to biracial relationships," but she herself had never experienced that in her own life. As Gabe described the nature of his relationship with Tanika, it turned out that he had mostly fallen in love with her sturdy and confident sense of self, not with her exotic African Americanness. He explained to his mother that after meeting Tanika, he had discovered that there are actually two types of girls. "The first type are incredibly dependent and self-centered . . . they need to hang by your side all the time, and be told over and over again how great and pretty they are . . . they need to be petted and admired to feel good about themselves. . . . The second type have so much going on in her lives . . . they are independent and self-sustaining . . . you see the beauty in their substance . . . you love them for that and they get more and more beautiful every day." Tanika, said Gabe, falls squarely into the second group of girls. His discovery of why his love for her is so compelling, why it seems to grow deeper and deeper, makes Elvira extremely happy. "He is appreciating the woman who has a lot going on . . . these are the kinds of things we have talked about at home theoretically . . . then you see it happen in his life . . . it is a revelation, a living lesson for me."

We see the mutuality and reciprocity in Elvira and Gabriel's witnessing, their close watchfulness of one another, and we hear the mutual admiration in their testimonies. Elvira Perez's stories—of her son asking for custody arrangements that make sense, of his making peace at the dinner table, of his cutting the tension at family gatherings with his ready humor, and of his offering generous assessments of people's character—all point to a deep admiration of her son; she admires not only how he *is* in the world, but what he is able to *bring* to the world. Likewise, Gabriel sees his mother clearly and offers his appreciation. He compliments her on the way she handles the conversation about his first sexual encounter; he compiles a CD of music that speaks to her heart and soul; he conspires with her to join him in "peacemaking" before a tense visit with his stepfather's family. Elvira is a scientist and a humanist, and it almost seems as if she sees Gabriel as an enrichment to her world, a presence through which she can witness what is important and special to her, those values that make the world a better place. The lack of conflict and drama is a different facet of intimacy, an intimacy no less deep for its lack of fire. Their intimacy allows for this clear witnessing of life as it should be.

Observing

Like Elvira Perez, Jacob Simon is temperamentally inclined to look to and listen to his three children as they make their way in the world, and he relishes the role of witness, observing qualities in each of his offspring that he greatly admires and wants to emulate. He, like Elvira, sees them as models, guides, and teachers who don't just talk the talk—about justice, service, respect, and kindness—they walk the walk. He draws lessons of love from his daughter Rebecca, love that is multifaceted, tough and giving, self-protective and vulnerable. He observes, and gathers wisdom from, the "ethical caring" of his son Paul, his daily habits of empathy and service that make Jacob see the difference between rhetoric and action. And he observes his oldest son, Luke, with whom he is deeply attached and enmeshed, pulling away from him as he enters adolescence, as he insists on his own space. Jacob feels hurt and abandoned at first, an inner turmoil that smacks of "narcissism" and is reminiscent of Rachel Goldstein's struggle to let her three girls find their ways in the world without her protectively shielding them. But over time, and by observing *himself* more closely, Jacob learns the lesson of seeing his child as a separate being; he begins to value Luke's autonomy and growing independence.

When Jacob Simons talks about the lessons he has learned from his children, it is with some reluctance, a reluctance I believe born out of his wanting to protect them and the sanctity of his father-child bond, but also from his wanting to not seem immodest. Several times during our interview, he says with some shyness, how much he admires his three offspring—Luke who is twenty-four, Paul who is twenty-one, and Rebecca who is eighteen—and the stories he tells are mostly focused on how each of them has modeled a way of being in the world and in relationship that he seeks to emulate. It is through being attentive and observant that he has over the years seen certain qualities grow up in his kids—qualities that were evident very early, engrained in their characters and personalities and that have been reinforced and enhanced in the intimacy of their family and in their experiences in the world. He says about all three, "I have learned a lot from all of them. . . . I have learned partly through observing the way they are in relationship to me. They have modeled ways of being in the world that were not in my repertoire."

Jacob is a child psychologist, a clinician, and a professor and he sees his children through the trained and discerning eyes of an experienced practitioner and through the deeply devoted, loving gaze of a father. Sometimes he speaks about "overthinking" the former and being "blinded" by the latter. As we talk together, Jacob is deeply thoughtful and unscripted. His musings are meditative and his words come slowly. Often he finds it hard to move from an abstract thought—using the language and concepts from psycho-therapy and psychoanalysis—to a concrete story. He apologizes when he notices that the abstractions are difficult for me to follow and understands why I press for the details of the story, but he sometimes finds the "specifics hard to deliver."

As he surveys his mind (and heart) for those things he has learned from his children, he takes them one by one, starting with the youngest, and "working his way up." About Rebecca, he begins with a simple, unadorned statement. "She has taught me about love and about how to love." "Rebecca," he says in a husky voice overcome with emotion, "is an unusually loving person. She loves purely and deeply. I tend to be a much more critical person . . . then I watch her, and see the ways that she draws out this capacity in others." A freshman in college, she was just home for the winter break; and Jacob witnessed his daughter do her "loving thing" with one of their friends, a woman who Jacob and his wife Susan find very difficult, someone who actually drives them both crazy. "Difficult in what way," I ask, and Jacob answers reluctantly. "This is a woman who is self-involved, who talks too much, and is incredibly needy." Her husband, Jacob's best friend, died recently, and Jacob feels a special obligation to support his widow, even as he has suffered with the loss himself. But when she dropped by for a visit last weekend—her neediness at an all-time high—it was Rebecca who reached out to her, listening attentively, indulging her narcissism, patiently protecting her. "And Rebecca is not making it up," says her father incredulously. "There is no artifice there . . . and it is much more than her taking one for the team . . . she is actually able to find things in her to love."

This story of how Rebecca is at eighteen reminds Jacob of another tender moment when his daughter was just four. Jacob's father had died, and he and Susan were trying to decide whether Rebecca was too young to attend the burial. They finally decided that it was best to bring her along. When it came time for Jacob to shovel the dirt on top of the coffin at the gravesite, Rebecca slowly walked over to him, looked into his face, and told her father she wanted to shovel with him. They clutched the shovel together, an act of intimacy and closeness that sticks out more than any at that time of such great sorrow. "She is very supportive of me. She wants to be there for me. . . . I have seen this from a very young age. It is a part of her character."

Rebecca's capacity to love—a gentle, nurturing tenderness—seems even more powerful in the midst of some of her other qualities, which strike me as edgier and more self-protective. "She doesn't take any shit from anybody," says her father proudly. "She is a fiercely loyal and loving friend . . . she can let herself be vulnerable and wounded, and still stay in the fray." Jacob smiles reminded of how her toughness is sometimes unleashed on him at home. If she hears Jacob giving Susan a hard time, if she feels her father is treating her mother unfairly in any way, Rebecca will speak up, usually with chutzpah and humor in her voice, sometimes with an edge of sarcasm, "Well aren't we in a good mood today, Dad."

When I ask Jacob whether he believes that he has had some part in nourishing Rebecca's outspokenness, her ability to balance the gentle and fierce parts of her temperament, he admits to always being aware that she was a girl in a "male-dominated family," and he wanted very much to encourage her "feistiness." "I'm a feminist," declares Jacob out of the blue. Even though he knows that feminism is a label that has become soft and muddled, he also knows what he means in this case. In raising his daughter, he has wanted to support her strength, independence, and self-knowledge. Recently, Rebecca wrote a letter to her father from college, thanking him for being a feminist, for "giving her space to find her voice." "These were qualities that I didn't just build up in her," says Jacob about his role in developing Rebecca's beautiful blend of lovingness and protective strength. "These were qualities of something she had." He has learned from Rebecca how to love — "she has modeled that for me" — but he has also learned that the tender love can coexist with something tougher, feistier, and more self-protective. In fact, these qualities side by side create a colorful "dialectic."

There is another part of Rebecca that can be "theatrical and overly sentimental," qualities that Jacob sometimes finds hard to take — qualities that remind him very much of his sister. "That's my sibling transference," says Jacob smiling and sounding like a psychotherapist. In fact, one day his sister with whom he has had a complicated and sometimes fractious relationship, said to Jacob, "You know, Rebecca's a lot like me and that must drive you crazy!" His sister was right, but not entirely. Yes, his sister and daughter share these qualities of "sentimentality," but Jacob has learned that the generational echoes do not have to bring up the same response in him. "As a parent," says Jacob, "you have to learn about transference. I could have responded more angrily to my daughter if I was blinded to the transference going on." Hearing and understanding "the ghosts" from his childhood allows Jacob to not distort or obscure his relationship with his daughter. He can see her separately and clearly.

"Now we are getting very deep here," says Jacob tentatively. "Seeing these qualities in my daughter makes me revisit my relationship with my sister, which was so conflicted . . . but knowing what is going on generationally, I am able to develop a relationship with my daughter which is unconflicted." His eyes look into the distance as he asks an unanswerable question that he says comes to him from time to time. "What would I have done if my sister had been my daughter?" As he speaks the question out loud this time, he seems to have a new insight. It is not so much the qualities shared by his sister and daughter that drive him crazy, it is that his sister's "sentimentality and overdramatization" seem to reflect something deeper, perhaps a "profound narcissism" that made it hard for Jacob as a child to feel loved and seen by his sibling.

Next Jacob turns to his middle child, Paul, who has been his teacher in "important and profound ways." If Rebecca has taught him how to love, it is his son Paul who has been his "moral compass." "Paul is a mensch," says Jacob proudly, his eyes misting over with tears. "He is a very ethical human being . . . generous and kind and good. He is a popular kid, but he is willing to take on his friends if they say anything that is racist or sexist or hurtful to another person." Jacob remembers going to a parent-teacher conference for Paul when he was in the fourth grade and hearing his teacher talk about his fairness and sense of justice and the ways in which he intervenes if there is any bullying, if other children are being threatened and excluded. The teacher said that she had learned from Paul "how to resolve conflicts in her classroom." At twenty-one, Paul's goodness is manifest in large and small ways. As a social activist, he is very attentive to the harms of privilege; he has always volunteered for nonprofit, service organizations, working in tutoring, and peer mediation programs. Along with his older brother Luke, he has just returned from a year in Guatemala, working in a juvenile detention center there.

At home, Paul is attentive and protective of his parents. "He doesn't want to see me go out to breakfast or dinner alone," says Jacob. If he spots a couple fighting on the street, he insists that they pull the car over to try and be helpful. And when Jacob's best friend died of a malignant brain tumor, it was Paul who met him in San Francisco and stood by his side at the hospice to say their final farewells. "It was so hard to see my friend unresponsive, skeletal, looking the way he did," recalls Jacob. "I was really spooked by it all. But Paul was not spooked." He was a calm, attentive presence, and when they left, they sat down and wept together.

"There are times when I feel I talk the talk and Paul walks the walk," says Jacob about the authenticity of his son's ethical caring, and how he constantly learns from him about the distance between rhetoric and action. "Paul is modeling things for me. He has a deep moral awareness, a keen moral radar. When I witness it, I feel I have to raise my ethical game." Again, I am curious about whether Paul was born with his moral radar—a temperamental quality that has always been there—or whether Jacob has seen it grow up in him over time. He pauses for a long time before he answers tentatively, pointing to Paul's place in the family, the second-born child, the younger brother. "I was extremely close to Luke, his older brother, who was three when Paul was born. Although I was thrilled when Paul arrived, it was a more mixed experience for me. My instinct was to be protective of Luke, who was very unhappy with the newcomer. Perhaps my not being as close to Paul made him have to fight to be in the family . . . eventually leading to this lovely quality that reaches out and cares for people. In some sense, he had to earn his place in the family." But even as he tests out this hypothesis, Jacob thinks that most of Paul's ethical awareness was "part of his original character."

We move on to Luke, the oldest, the son who captured Jacob's heart—"completely and intensely"—when he arrived, and for several years afterwards. "The big issue was being very close . . . perhaps too close to Luke," Jacob says pensively in what feels like an understatement to me. Jacob was thirty-two years old when Luke was born, and right from the beginning they had an intimacy that was "so pure, so uncomplicated, so joyful." Jacob remembers especially those years when Luke was between five and ten, when being with his son was his "favorite place" to be, when hanging out together was his "greatest pleasure." But when Luke hit adolescence, the relationship shifted: he no longer wanted to spend as much time with his Dad; he usually chose the company of his peers. Jacob remembers feeling abandoned by his son: "devastated and rejected." After weeks—maybe months—of moping around and feeling hurt, Jacob was told by his wife Susan, "in short, to get over it." At first he responded defensively to his wife's blunt refrain, but it did cause him to begin to question the magnitude and power of his response. "It set off my thinking . . . in a relationship with your child, it's got to be about your child," says Jacob. His voice still sounds surprised at how far wrong he was. "How did I confuse his needs with mine? How can I begin to see his needs lucidly?" Jacob remembers struggling for a long time with the answers to these questions, trying to learn from his son's strides toward independence and self-definition how to renegotiate a relationship with him.

One day, as part of his work serving as a consultant to a mentoring program, Jacob was speaking with several incarcerated women about how they would like the mentors to guide and communicate with these women's children. The response of one of the women surprised and amazed Jacob. Most of the other mothers said that their children needed someone who might fulfill the role of father figure or grandparent. But this woman said without defensiveness or accusation, "My daughter needs a place to talk about how much she hates me . . . I betrayed her . . . I was a drug addict . . . I was not there for her." Jacob, who had been struggling with something so much "milder" — his son pushing him away so he could get on with his adolescence — found a "huge lesson" in this woman's words. "I was amazed that this mother was able to parse what her child needed to do even if it meant her child hating her. It was so clearly not about her. I said to myself, I want to be that kind of parent. If Luke needs to separate, *he* needs that. It's not about *my* being wounded."

Jacob, the psychologist and clinician, sounds a little embarrassed that all of this came as such a surprise to him and that it seemed to require the intervention of someone whose circumstances were much harsher, but whose perspective was so much clearer than his. "This was my sister's narcissism coming through," says Jacob wearily. "I did not want to inherit that in my relationship to Luke." But even though the testimony of this mother in prison caused a "kind of epiphany" in him, Jacob understands that the lessons about navigating closeness and distance with one's children requires constant rethinking and struggle. "On a weekend, when you want your child to hang out with you . . . which he should do from time to time . . . and he wants instead to be with his friends the whole time . . . what do you do? And on spring break when you want to go away on a trip with the whole family, and your kids want to stay behind in the city . . . what do you do?" These calculations — so full of emotion and vulnerability — continued to confuse and exhaust Jacob. He admits, "My ability to judge that was so muddled." Susan was often helpful in drawing the boundaries of distance, and he gives her credit for her restraint. "My wife was not so thoroughly enmeshed." But he also believes that parents often need someone "outside the system" — for Jacob his close friends occasionally play that role — to observe the dynamics and speak up about what they are seeing. Over the years, Jacob thinks he has gotten better at observing himself and his son from some distance, standing above the fray, or, as he puts it "being on the balcony looking down."

Luke's temperament and character have also helped Jacob manage the tension between intimacy and distance. "He teaches me," says Jacob again. Luke has a "discipline, determination, and self-knowledge" that is rare in a young person, a sturdy sense of his own capacities and of what he needs to forge an independent path. Perhaps most important, Luke is "unruffled and not easily slighted." If somebody — including his father — says something hurtful, he will not be undone by it. During Luke's adolescence, as they navigated the dynamics of closeness and separation, Luke's steadiness brought some clarity to his father's angst and confusion, some balm to the wounds, and has since paved the way for a relationship between them that now feels open-hearted and reciprocal.

Jacob Simon's work as a child psychologist is to be a discerning observer and diagnostician, and so it feels especially poignant that the "blind spots" that he occasionally experiences are ones that blur his vision of his own children. His lessons are in seeing — really seeing — his children's virtues, working to incorporate them into his own repertoire. He sees how his daughter loves and he takes her love as an inspiring model and as a cautionary insight about the conflicted relationship and distortions of love he experienced in his own family of origin. With his middle child, he observes his unerring "moral compass" that underscores the distance between rhetoric and action, and may mark the distinction between his "theories" of human behavior and the "practice" of everyday life. With his oldest, Luke, Jacob learns about the separateness of his son's needs and his own, and the primacy of the former. There is distance required in witnessing, watching "from the balcony looking down," observing and making sense of the observation.

Introspection

In Hannah Fairchild's relatively smooth and benign relationship with her son—who was until his late adolescence a very "easy child"—she has always felt a current of tension between "letting go and holding on." The tension always felt the strongest as she observed him seeking out his role and space in the various places around the country where the family moved for her husband's work, and now as she sees the ways in which her son and his wife negotiate the demands of their careers and the responsibilities of child-rearing. Witnessing her grown son and daughter raise their families and manage their work lives—with complexity and fluidity, with chaos and exhaustion—causes Hannah to become deeply introspective. Like Jacob Simon, watching her children makes her observe herself and her own past more closely. It makes her revisit and examine the haunts she has inherited from her own upbringing in a fiercely authoritarian home where her parents' views and values went unquestioned, where there were strict gender roles carved out by her physician father and her homemaker mother. As Hannah speaks about trying to learn to "hold her tongue" when she observes and judges her children's parental choices, she begins to see that understanding the ancient echoes from her own family of origin might help her give her children the space and respect they deserve to walk their own path, to raise the next generation.

It is a long drive down a gravel road in southern Vermont; the frigid weather and icy conditions make the trip feel longer. I try to keep the mountains in view to keep myself oriented as I search for numbers on the snow-covered mailboxes. All the while, I try to imagine what it must be like to live through a hard winter in this remote place. I wonder how I would deal with the isolation and loneliness. Would I learn to be quieter, more self-reflective, more self-sufficient? Hannah Fairchild's contemporary house, painted a soft rose color, comes into view, and I slip-slide across the ice to her front door. She welcomes me into a cold study that leads to a warm living room with a crackling fire and a magnificent view of the mountains. The back of the house is all glass, and I am treated to a sweeping panoramic view of this beautiful setting. We sit at the dining room table and start with Hannah's homemade butternut squash soup with salad. The simple repast matches Hannah, who immediately strikes me as warm and generous, spare and simple. Later on, when she tells me that her mother was a Quaker and that she went to the Germantown Friends School in Philadelphia, I am not surprised. She has a Quaker-like way about her, a quietness and clarity, a simplicity that I have seen so many times before at Quaker meetings and retreats, at Swarthmore College where I was an undergraduate. At seventy, Hannah is both lean and solid, with all white hair that she wears pulled back in a bun, and eyes that are gray-green. Her outfit is understated and functional, dark burgundy corduroy slacks, a red sweater with layers underneath; tiny silver earrings and her wedding ring are her only decoration.

Married to Peter, a public-health doctor, for almost a half century, Hannah has always been primarily a homemaker and "stay-at-home mom" whose life has been filled with volunteering and public service. Many times she tells me how much she has loved her life of raising children and serving the community; how she feels privileged to be able to be "taken care of" by her bread-winning husband; how she has always enjoyed being in charge of "managing the home front." Although I believe every word she says about her pleasure and satisfaction in her chosen role, I think she also feels she needs to find a way to explain and justify her choices to me whose life, she knows, has been so different. In an effort to explain her choices (she definitely sees these as ongoing choices), Hannah tells me that she is just like her mother, who was also the wife of a physician — a high-powered surgeon — and a stay-at-home mom with six children, three girls and three boys. Like Hannah and two of her sisters, her mother was a Bryn Mawr College graduate, who loved reading, travel, and art and sent her children to fancy private schools. Hannah's mother was always a role model for how a woman could enjoy an abundant life, raise her children, take care of the home front, and at the same time fulfill her own passions. Having her husband as the breadwinner did not diminish her mother's power; neither did it squash her adventurous spirit and self-respect. Hannah's two children — a son and a daughter — who are both in their early thirties, and married with children, have chosen a different kind of family-work balance, and many of the lessons Hannah has learned from her children refer to coming to terms with those generational contrasts.

One of the reasons Hannah saw her full-time mothering role as essential to the family's well-being is because of the many moves they made because of Peter's career. With each move, it was Hannah who had to scramble to find schools and pediatricians, go house hunting, redecorate their homes, and help the children acclimate to the new environment. The biggest move, the one that required the most dramatic cultural shifts for the family, was the transition from Charlottesville, where Peter had held a faculty position at the University of Virginia, to Birmingham, Alabama, where he served as dean at the state university. The move felt huge, a vast cultural and psychological distance from a place where they had been surrounded by good friends who were, like them, fairly liberal and academic, to a "totally different environment" of conservative folks who were born and bred there. "We were a total aberration," explains Hannah. "Everybody went to church on Sundays, and we were not churchgoers. We didn't belong."

Hannah begins our conversation with memories of this transition, and wonders out loud whether she was attentive enough to what this move meant for her son, Walker, who was then in sixth grade. "I did not understand what was going on underneath the surface with him all the time," she says somewhat apologetically. It is a kind of musing — lacking in drama, regret, or hyperbola — that

I hear many times during Hannah's interview as I try to figure out the depth and meaning of her subtlety. She admits that Walker, who had always been a happy, easygoing child, "laid back, outgoing, and sociable," "had a sadness underneath" when they moved to Alabama. He went from a public school in Charlottesville where "he was on top of the world" to a private school (that Hannah had some questions about, but was a far cry better than the public school alternative) where he was an outsider; "marginalized and called—with derision—a Yankee" (she says "Yankee" with a southern twang that makes it almost indecipherable to my ears). Because Walker had always had a "logical, easygoing way" about him, because he had always been a mellow child, Hannah reckons in retrospect that she and Peter assumed he would get along in the new environment, that he would find his way without much trouble. He did, in fact, adapt well to the academic demands of school; he shot quickly to the top of his private-school class. But he never felt he belonged, and "belonging was important to him." Hannah's normally modulated voice is filled with intensity as she recalls going to school events and seeing her son on the sidelines. "I was aware he was peripheral, and it broke my heart," she says of his loneliness and isolation, and, I believe, of the way in which her pain about his sadness never rose to the level of conversation.

What finally saved him was a friendship Walker had with another boy a couple of years older than him, who was on the tennis team with him. He was also a transplant from another place—hailing from Oklahoma—and they were two outsiders drawn together. One friendship was enough to make life better, more bearable, "even though he was still not in the thick of things." But two and a half years later, when Walker had "cemented his friendship with this boy" and found his "identity as a tennis jock," Peter found a job in Hanover, New Hampshire, and the family was moving again. I ask how Walker said goodbye to his bosom buddy, and Hannah laughs. "Well you know adolescent boys, there was some grunting and pushing off of one another . . . no real emotional expression." Peter and Hannah had both grown up in the Northeast, and they felt relieved and thrilled to be returning home. But Walker had never lived in the Northeast and took the news sadly but stoically. "We pretended," remembers Hannah, "that the children had input into the decision to move, but they really didn't.... We tried to convince them that they would find more kids on their wavelength in Hanover ... that they would be less lonely."

In the Hanover public schools, the world seemed to be divided between the jocks and the geeks, a separation and cliquishness that seemed unbridgeable to Walker when he arrived on the scene. Hannah watched in dismay and displeasure when Walker chose to bond with the jocks. "In retrospect, I really do think that Walker wanted to do well academically, but all the cool kids were jocks, and he did not want to be a geek." So he underplayed his academic prowess, refused to join the honor society when he was elected in his junior year, and grew more and more sullen and distant from his parents. There is a hardness to Hannah's voice as she says succinctly, "I was not pleased with his choice of friends." She missed the boy Walker had been: "easygoing, sociable, and logical." He had disappeared. "By senior year, my cheerful, easygoing son was nowhere to be found ... he was not happy with himself, with his parents, or with his world." Hannah surmises that "it was vintage adolescence" and describes the mix of conflicting feelings that she had to examine within herself as she tried to respond to her son's teenage struggles.

"We were not unduly upset," she recalls from a distance of more than a decade. As a former pediatrician, Peter was aware of the dramas of adolescence and professed to not being worried, preferring to just ride it out; and Hannah understood enough psychology to tell herself that she should not take all of this "personally." But underneath her exterior calm and restraint, she struggled with conflicting feelings and huge ambivalence. "The part of me that is like Walker, sociable and outgoing, felt sympathetic with his wish to be in the in-crowd ... his wish not to get stuck on the periphery. On the one hand, I was anxious for Walker to be who he wanted to be ... but on the other hand, the person he wanted to be, I felt, was not so good." She tries to explain her paradoxical feelings another way. "I knew that it was wrong to project all of my thoughts and feelings onto my son, but I also felt very strongly that our values were important to convey to him and imprint on him." The learning was often painful for Hannah, coming from a place of ambivalence and uncertainty and arising out of a struggle that was rarely talked about explicitly, evoking little heat or drama in the household. She missed her son and their easy intimacy; she knew that he was experiencing the normal struggles of his adolescence, and she needed to let him find his space, his place. But she also knew that she had to be engaged in this struggle; she had a role to play as a responsible parent, even though her son seemed to want her out of the way. This "letting go and holding on" led to a great deal of "introspection," a kind of self-questioning that Hannah had never really had to practice much in her life.

When she thinks of the ways in which Walker's adolescent struggles forced her to be introspective, she reflects on her own upbringing in a family where her parents were the ultimate authorities, where she and her siblings were never allowed to question their rules, routines, and decisions. "There was never any question," Hannah says with certainty, "about what was right and what was wrong with my parents. By contrast, Peter and I were open for discussion . . . we tried to show our children that they had a point of view worth listening to, that we were willing to listen. Some things, of course, were nonnegotiable." "Like what?" I ask. "Well drinking and driving," she shoots back. "That was not acceptable, even if you need to call us at 3:00 in the morning to drive you home." But even with these certainties, Hannah was aware of the observant and discerning antennae of her children, the ways they became watchful "witnesses" of their parent's edicts and noted the discrepancies between what they said and what they did. To the "no drinking and driving" rule, they asked, how come you parents have a cocktail before going out to dinner? That is clearly drinking and driving. Hannah laughs at herself remembering the way they sort of dodged the adolescent accusations — "well we monitor our drinking very carefully, and we are much more experienced . . . we are not under any pressure from our peers" — and then proceeded to do what they had always done. But it was during these exchanges, when her adolescents would point out the hypocrisies in their parents' behavior, that Hannah, for the first time, "realized that they were paying attention, that we were being watched and monitored, that they could see the inconsistencies."

Even as Hannah has consciously worked on developing her introspective capacities as a parent, she recognizes how far she has come from the household in which she was raised, and how haunted she still is by the ghosts from her past. Her father had grown up in a very "uptight Presbyterian family" where there was a "moral rigidity that reigned over the household"; and her mother came from a Quaker background where the rigidity seemed softer and mellower but where the righteousness—the surety about what values were best, what rules were unassailable—was palpable. "You inherit these stereotypes," says Hannah about the authoritarianism and rigidity that were imprinted on her by her parents, even as she works to be a more flexible, listening parent with her own children. She immediately thinks of another trait that she has inherited from her folks, one that her kids have noticed and call her on from time to time. "We grew up comfortable at home," she recalls, "but my parents were as tight as they could be. . . . My parents never understood the Depression was over, and that was a terrible burden that has been hard to get over." She sees her parents' tightness in her own frugality, which even to her can feel like "stinginess." "I am my father's daughter in this way," she says dryly.

Her watchful children have gently prodded Hannah to "lighten up" and take it easy, to splurge for a change, to enjoy the abundance of her life. But the "burden and heaviness" of her frugal inheritance are always in the wings threatening to bear down. Recently, Walker went out with his six-year-old daughter to buy the groceries for a family gathering, and when he returned, Hannah asked out of habit and reaching for her wallet, "How much do I owe you for the groceries?" Walker shrugged her question off with a smile. "No worries," he said lightly, knowing that it would take a long time to train his mother to cast off the burden of her tightness and enjoy her grown-up son buying food for the family. Hannah also tries to monitor her "compulsive" qualities when she is visiting her daughter Caitlyn's family, but it is hard for her not to do a little straightening up when the house is so messy. Last time she was there, she found herself, almost without knowing it, picking up a sponge to clean up the bathroom counter. Caught in the act, Caitlyn asked her to stop. Her frustrated voice seemed to say "give it a rest, Mom." "I'm sorry, but that is not worth my time to do," her daughter said, leaving the room. "Even though both of my kids have a bunch of compulsiveness in them that they have inherited from me, they are asking me to loosen up," says Hannah admiringly.

The generational contrasts are even more vivid in the ways that her children are raising their families and living out their own work-family balance. Both of them are academics on a publish-or-perish trajectory, navigating the expectations and pressures of anticipating tenure reviews. And both of them are parents of children and married to spouses with full-time careers. As Hannah watches them juggle their many obligations and commitments, she tries very hard not to be judgmental; she tries to appreciate — and learn about — the "flexibility of roles within their families," and the ways in which they are "adapting to and negotiating the new world where gender roles are much more fluid, where families need two incomes to survive." Caitlyn, for example, is the primary breadwinner in her family, with a job at the university that is extremely demanding, and a disposition that makes it hard for her to say "no" to the endless requests that she take on new projects, chair committees, and teach additional hours. Her husband Sam, a "calm and reassuring presence," stayed at home for a year after their now five-year-old daughter was born and resumed part-time work as a school counselor when she was two. He continues to be the primary caretaker, the one to whom their daughter turns when she needs comforting or wants a play partner. "Caitlyn acknowledges that little Nora will go to Sam first," says Hannah about an arrangement that "seems to work for this family." But although Sam does a "huge chunk" of the parenting, Caitlyn does all of the housework. "Being in the kitchen is not Sam's thing," Hannah says with a laugh. "He is one of four boys raised by a stay-at-home mother and that is not a stretch he can make."

Even though Hannah sees the domestic balancing act and role reversals as admirable, she finds it more of a challenge to keep her judgments "at bay" when she observes her children's parenting. Talking with me, she begins by expressing admiration for them. They are "wonderful adults and caring and committed parents" who are devoted to their children. But she also admits that it has been hard to "learn the most important lesson of keeping my mouth shut." She is clearly in the midst of this struggle "to stay out of it," and she claims that in all of her thirty-five years of parenting, she finds this the "hardest letting go of all." The frown on her face mirrors the degree of difficulty. "They don't want my insights . . . and I am by temperament too interfering . . . I'm way out there." Her efforts to "temper" herself (Peter is much more "circumspect and tactful") are ongoing, accompanying every conversation, Skype encounter, or family visit. She smiles wearily when she recalls Walker's early warning to her when his wife was pregnant with their first child. "He said something about letting us raise our own children. It made me extremely conscious of their not wanting my input." And now that their firstborn is almost six, and their second is approaching two, Hannah has had a lot of experience trying to hold her tongue and practice restraint, more or less successfully. "It is an imperfect art," she says about trying to monitor herself and respect her children's wishes to raise their own in the ways they see fit.

Many examples spring to her mind, ordinary moments of frustration, missteps that are likely to be part of the flow of life when the two generations get together. When Walker's youngest was just a year, his parents were preparing to go out apple picking with their older child, and they asked Hannah to care for their son. She shakes her head remembering the exasperating scene. "The baby was not behaving well at all. He did not want his parents to go and he was pitching a fit," Hannah recalls. "Finally, with huge effort, I got him to calm down . . . when his parents swooped in and made a huge deal about saying goodbye to him." Their big farewell, of course, made her grandson erupt into more screeching and crying, more begging to go along with his parents. Hannah shot her son a look that said "how could you?" and he responded, without apology,

"We always tell our children when we are leaving . . . we never sneak out!" "Give me a break," Hannah screams out to me remembering how the baby got "all wound up again" and she had to start all over trying to calm him down. I shake my head sympathetically. She tries to summarize the ways in which these generational differences cause friction and demand restraint. "My grown children and I are not agreeing on procedures, not on the same page about childrearing . . . but neither did I agree with my parents whose shadow of authoritarianism I am still trying to escape."

Hannah Fairchild's son's difficult adjustments to the different schools and communities, social circles, and friendships during his teenage years provoked a kind of "introspection" in her, "a kind of self-questioning." She questioned the way she and her siblings buckled under the rigid values and rules of her authoritarian parents; she began to notice and question the inconsistencies between what she told her children and what she actually did; she began to see the uptightness inherited from her family of origin that she had trouble shaking free of with her own children. Perhaps, she is also questioning—even as she defends it—her own life as a stay-at-home mom, as she observes the flexibility of domestic and gender roles in her grown children's families. Hannah is learning to let go of her urge to influence her children's parenting life; she is "holding her tongue and keeping her mouth shut," in an effort to respect their priorities and choices. Perhaps her "letting go" is connected to her "holding on" to her own upbringing and her deeply instilled habits, which introspection—itself a reserved, quiet process, befitting her personality—can help.

2

Growing

Parenthood gives us an opportunity to refine and express who we are, to learn what we can be, to become different.

DAVID GUTMANN, "PARENTHOOD"[1]

IT IS NOT ONLY that parents learn through witnessing, observing, and seeing their children—from a perch that is somewhat removed—they also tell stories about the ways in which their children become the inspiration for their own growth, the ways in which they experience changes in their own identities, their own emotional repertoires, their own perspective taking and worldviews as they navigate their relationships with their offspring. The parents speak about how their children instigate their growth through challenge, questioning, and struggle; through cheerleading and modeling, through refusal and resistance; through long suffering. Sometimes the learning is slow, incremental, and barely noticeable, often retreating and reversing its direction, but quietly, over time, taking hold of the parent's consciousness. Other times, the learning arrives like an "epiphany" that feels like a "growth spurt"—a sudden awareness of something fundamental that has changed, a new insight or revelation, a shift in a well-worn habit, the development of new ways of being and seeing oneself. Whether the growth feels fast or slow, abrupt or evolving, many parents see its imprint when the parent-child roles become reversed and turned upside down. Parents begin to be aware of the parenting in their children's pedagogy, and they speak about resisting or embracing the new shifts in authority and maturity. "It feels like we have traded places," says one father who claims the role reversal with his twenty-five-year-old son is both "disquieting and inspiring."

While developmental research that concerns parents mostly focuses on the ways in which adults socialize and guide their young, there is a small but growing body of work on parental development as a concept or phenomenon—the idea that parenthood itself is a mechanism of human development. Although echoing many of the narrative themes that we hear in this chapter, this literature differs in that it describes parental development through the articulation of discrete stages, and it does not tend to focus explicitly on the pedagogy of children or on parent-child relationships as sites of teaching and learning. Jack Demick, a developmental psychologist who has extensively summarized the stage theories of parental growth, claims that "parenthood is a powerful generator of development."[2] He traces the evolution of parental development theory, starting with its first conceptualization in psychoanalytic theory by Therese Benedek, who proposed that relationships with children can cause advances or regressions in the parent's personality. Even though the parent's role is certainly to guide and nurture the child's development, in the process, the parent cannot help "but deal with his own conflicts unconsciously, and by this, normally achieve a new level of maturation."[3] In the tradition of psychoanalytic theory, Benedek's observations focus largely on the unconscious, subterranean shifts in the parental psyche and on the conflicts and anxieties that provoke them.

Benedek's proposal that parenthood is a specific stage in development is closely aligned with Erik Erikson's influential theory, which articulated eight life stages across the life span, each reflecting a tension between a positive and a negative force—between moving forward and being pulled back—that must be negotiated successfully if the person is to ascend to the next stage.[4] It is not that the positive wins over the negative; rather, the manner in which these crises get navigated and resolved influences the development of each individual. Even though there is a downside to each of Erikson's turning points, he sees each developmental crisis as potentially hopeful and productive. In his view, the struggles, the contesting forces of progress and regression, are inevitable and necessary for propelling growth. It is Erikson's penultimate stage — generativity versus stagnation — where he locates the developmental strains of parenthood, because as he sees it, the primary task at this point in the arc of adult growth is to give to another person. By generativity, he is primarily referring to the impulse within us to nurture and guide the next generation.

More recent stage theories of parental development track the ways in which the parents' growth is seen in their increasing distance and differentiation from their children, in their awareness of the societal and cultural forces that shape their interactions with their young, and in their ability to see their children as individual and separate — not merely as appendages or reflections of themselves — while still maintaining a connection to, and relationship with, them.[5] We notice the increasing complexity and breadth of the parental lens on their children reflecting their own development as human beings. Parents grow from a stage of looking inward and fulfilling their own needs to looking outward at the forces beyond themselves that shape their children. Psychoanalyst and lifespan researcher George Vaillant, in his masterful and exhaustive account of adult development, makes the most powerful claim for the relationship between children's pedagogy and parental growth when he suggests that the best predictor of successful aging is how people answer the question, "What have you learned from your children?"[6]

These various stage theories, focusing on parenthood as a generator of human growth, capture the plasticity of learning across the life span and the ways in which child-rearing is a powerful provocateur of development. Conceiving of parental growth in "stages" also helps us recognize the sequential process — one stage building on the next — and the tasks, challenges, and preoccupations that present themselves to parents as their children grow up. However, like most theories that articulate discrete stages, there is little reference to the messiness, missteps, and minefields that are part of any trajectory of human growth — the unexpected turns and detours that interrupt the smooth path forward. The theories do not help us notice the reversals, repetitions, and regressions that may distort and impede the developmental journey. And we do not get a glimpse of what kinds of challenges and struggles are being waged with children that provoke developmental shifts in parents, that insist that parents "grow up."

Finally, and importantly, the stage theories do not capture the patterns of parental growth when children are "almost grown." They cease recording the stages just past the strains and struggles of adolescence, suggesting that the development of parents is no longer formative, that their learning is essentially complete. But the growing-up narratives in this chapter reveal a much longer, more complex and layered journey of identity formation, perspective taking, and meaning making, as parents continue to navigate their relationships with their children in the twenty-year span from fifteen to thirty-five years. The dance of adaptation and mutual accommodation that Brazelton so vividly documents in his videotapes taken during the first hours and days after the child's birth—as mother and infant try to read, and accommodate to, each other's gestures and rhythms—seem to have echoes decades later as almost-grown children continue the dance, often taking the lead in teaching their parents the new—and often more difficult and subtle—steps.

In his beautiful and evocative memoir, *Father's Day*, Buzz Bissinger captures the messiness and the minefields, the repetitions and the regression, as well as the passion and poignancy of parental growth, a growth that is deep and cathartic, slowly simmering with rage and suffering but also arriving like a bolt of lightning—a sudden, overwhelming epiphany.[7] Bissinger recounts a cross-country road trip he took with his twenty-four-year-old son Zachary, who at birth had been given a diagnosis of "pervasive developmental disorder," accompanied by limited cognitive functioning, severe learning disability, and verbal and physical tics. Because of brain damage sustained during childbirth, Zachary has the comprehension skill of an eight-year-old; he also has an incredible memory for dates, places, and people, excellent navigation skills, and a sociable, easy personality. His father loves him deeply but suffers the feeling of not knowing him and the belief that he never will. "It is strange to love someone so much who is still so fundamentally mysterious to you," Bissinger writes. "It is the most terrible pain of life."[8]

Bissinger yearns for a conversation with his son, one that would help to make Zachary more open and self-aware; he wants the road trip to bring on epiphanies and revelations, "to crack through the surface" into his son's soul. As the trip goes on, however, Bissinger becomes more aware of *his* own reality, the surfaces and depths of *his* own soul. They spend long days together, father at the wheel, son navigating with the maps in his head; father trying to initiate new ways into conversation, the son offering up the same repetitive, disjointed phrases. They are together and bonded, yes, but the liberation is of the father, not the son. In witnessing how Zachary sees the world literally and concretely, without the spin of a self-imposed agenda, Bissinger critically reflects on his ambitions. Watching Zachary try his hardest to control his tics, endure an uncomfortable car ride, and never complain or lose his temper, Bissinger thinks about his own character. Observing Zachary's kindness and honesty, Bissinger comes to reflect on his own identity. He writes: "I lived inside my head and I could not get outside. Work and the pursuit of success formed my only true identity. I was terrified of what I would be without it. I had always been scared. My self-confidence was a come-on. I hid my insecurity and fear behind a barrage of angry outbursts at editors and friends and wives and waiters."[9] As Bissinger tries to focus on what Zachary can do instead of what he can't, he starts to wonder about his own capacity to see and appreciate the positive, his own potential to liberate himself from a consistently negative outlook that he uses as protection against disappointment and pain. As the trip drags on, Bissinger begins to release his goal of greater togetherness and understanding of his son. The intimacy of the hours on the road, in the company of his adult son, begins to reveal his own limits, his own deficits. "I have an impairment, an emotional impairment, the anger of what happened, the helplessness, the forever haunt of watching my newborn son through a hospital window, bloody and breakable." And it is his son's gentleness and ability to connect that repairs him. After blowing up, cursing and screaming because they are lost on the road, when they finally stop for dinner, Bissinger hears his son ask him to buy an ice cream. He watches as his son eats the ice cream "in a complete wash of his happiness" and writes: "It is a question he asked me when he was five. It is a question he will ask me as long as I am here with him. At this moment, I feel neither pity for him nor self-pity. I feel gratitude. Zach knew how to save me."[10] For the first time, Bissinger is able to move beyond anger, frustration, and depression. His son moves him.

Later in the trip, they visit an amusement park where Zachary convinces his father to try the bungee jump. This experience becomes the moment of epiphany, though not the one that Bissinger imagined. The next time he is overtaken with sorrow and pain about his son's life, during a conversation when he realizes that Zachary knows that some of his aspirations will never be realized, Bissinger remembers the bungee jump. This is what he learned: "The quiet sets in. I refuse to default to extended brooding over what my son will be, won't be, should be, should not be, would be, will never be. The exhilaration of the bungee jump is still within me. I cannot forget his arms clutching me, needing me. Needing each other. Nor can I forget the liberation I felt, which occurred only because of his resilience in making me do something I never would have done without him. He stood firm even when I confronted him with the possibility that he would *die*."[11] In a reversal of the usual pattern, where the parent comes to know the child or the child comes to know the parent, the parent comes to grow and know something else entirely. It is the father who grows in capacity, provoked by his son's resilience and unfettered faith.

In this chapter on growth—its unlikely origins and unexpected consequences—we hear four mothers describe the years and moments of provocation when their children's presence or teachings aroused in them new identities and expanding capacities. We see the long-term evolution in parental development described by stage theorists, the ways in which the children's growth propels and guides the parents' growth, and the ways in which some of the lessons learned are resisted as the parents wrestle with the tensions between regression and progression that will allow them to get to the next stage. And we listen to the shifts in roles, interpersonal relationships, and intrapersonal dynamics that shape, and are shaped by, the new parental growth. Bissinger's narrative of learning in response to the teachings of his impaired son—whose cognitive and social capacities are severely limited—gives us a more nuanced and complex portrayal of parental growth, of the rage that distorts his seeing and hearing his son, of the hard-won insight that emerges out of his struggle, of the love that grows out of his suffering, and of the learning that is ongoing and never ending. Each of these frames—the stage theories that chart the sequenced unfolding of parent development and the father's memoir that captures the darkness and the light, the detail and the nuance, the losses and the liberation of lessons benignly taught by his son—helps us hear and interpret the "growing-up" stories—of evolution, adaptation, and survival—that follow.

Evolution

"Authenticity" is Margo Lockwood's favorite go-to word. She uses it to refer to the ways in which she has evolved as a human being and the ways in which her evolution has been provoked in large part by her daughters, now in their thirties. By "authenticity," she is speaking about becoming more open-hearted and less judgmental, more spontaneous and empowered, more collaborative and respectful, more spiritually tuned in, and more loving. As she describes her evolution towards authenticity, Margo talks about the lessons she has learned from knowing her daughters deeply—lessons she has absorbed from experiencing their contrasting temperaments, intelligences, and the different ways they each engage the world. She also identifies the moments of learning—arriving like "epiphanies"—when a momentary interaction with one of her daughters sparks growth within her . . . her older daughter's refusal at eight to take her hand crossing the street was a lesson on love . . . her younger daughter's refusal, at fifteen, to do her homework was a lesson on the negative application of power and control.

When Margo Lockwood declares—referring to herself in the third person halfway through our interview—that "Margo at fifty-five is ten times the Margo she was at thirty," she is primarily describing her "journey towards authenticity," a journey that continues to offer her lessons in knowing, and being true to, herself. Most of the lessons that she has learned along the way, she credits to her "primary teachers": her daughters Angelica and Lena. Now at thirty-three and thirty-one years old, respectively, they have been her most important and inspiring companions, her biggest cheerleaders and provocateurs, her source of greatest pleasure. They are the ones, who through their example, their intentional guidance, and their strong and contrasting personalities have given her "windows into myself and windows onto the world." Some of their teachings she remembers as dramatic moments of epiphany, after which the world suddenly looked and felt different. Other teachings seem to flow from who her daughters are and who they are becoming, from the way Margo has watched them etching their own unique self-definitions over the years. And now that they are both in their third decade, she sees them very clearly, admires them as "independent, intelligent, creative, and powerful women," and enjoys describing the ways in which they have nourished her growth.

When the girls were three and one, Margo and her husband divorced after four years of marriage, and until she remarried Jens a decade and a half ago, Margo was a single mom and the three of them were a tight family unit. Although she says little about the reasons for the dissolution of her first marriage—except to briefly admit that her Pakistani husband was very controlling and at times abusive—Margo hints, from time to time, about the ways in which the divorce had an impact on the wariness and self-protectiveness that she and the girls might have suffered, as well as on the fierce closeness that the three of them share.

Margo describes her daughters as "polar opposites," "as different as night and day, and yet wonderfully complementary." Angelica, a journalist who has also worked in public relations and is currently the director of communications at the University of Pennsylvania, is tall, beautiful, and light brown, with long black hair and almond eyes inherited from her father. "My girls got my height and stature and their father's coloring," says Margo as she digs in her pocketbook and proudly shows me their picture; both are gorgeous young women with radiant smiles and a confidence that is palpable even in the still and static photograph. "Angelica is very smart, very independent, and has traveled all around the world," says Margo about the autonomy and adventurousness that she "purposely spawned in them."

"I used to always tell them, let your twenties be yours. I want you to have choices and options. I don't care what you ultimately do, but I want you to get a good education so that you can choose . . . Once you are married, there will inevitably be compromise. Take your twenties to make authentic decisions." Certainly Angelica has taken her mother's insistent teachings to heart. She has traveled everywhere, often with her sister, and their global sojourns are always spiced with adventure, exploration, and surprise. "They are not tourists," says their mother admiringly. "They travel close to the ground, meeting the local folks, hearing their stories, eating the food, staying in neighborhood places."

Angelica's independence — so encouraged by her mother over the years — can sometimes be intimidating. "She has strong opinions and she expects you to have opinions . . . she wants to have rich and productive conversations, and it can sometimes be intimidating for people who are less sure than she is." Margo lets out a loud laugh and admits, "She sometimes even intimidates me." There is hint of sadness in her voice when Margo tells me that Angelica — despite the fact that she is "popular, beautiful, successful, and smart" — is not currently connected to anyone. She surmises that her older daughter has had about "half a dozen boyfriends over the last dozen years," and the relationships have all followed the same pattern. After Angelica dates someone for three months, she introduces the young man to Margo — not asking for approval, just wanting her mother to know who is in her life. Then six months into the relationship, she does an "assessment"; and at least so far, no boyfriend has survived her high standards and evaluative criteria.

I ask Margo why she thinks Angelica decides to break up with these "perfectly wonderful guys" each time, and why there seems to be this repetitive pattern of approach/avoidance, and she says, tentatively, trying to be "authentic" but loyal to her beautiful daughter, "She just doesn't feel like she loves them enough. She feels like there should be more. She knows that she will not change them and she does not want to waste their time or her own continuing on in a relationship that is not satisfying and will not endure." Sometime, it seems as if Margo's early message to her daughters, of avoiding the compromises of marriage in their twenties, has and will extend far into Angelica's thirties. But Margo also believes that part of her daughter's reluctance to commit to a long-term relationship must be related to what she describes as "the scars of our divorce." "Because of the divorce, I think that there are vulnerabilities that she fears exposing. She has a wall that is hard to get by. . . . Someday there will be a crack in the wall and someone special will meet Angie, the little girl who is delightful and charming and sweet . . . they will see the child in Angelica."

In all ways "big and small," Lena is so different from her big sister. "Angelica is organized, strictly scheduled, intimidating, and Lena is very spontaneous and improvisational." They are each other's best friends, Angie's yin to Lena's yang. The younger sister's approach to people — young and old — is always one of listening and being receptive. There is not a "judgmental bone in her body." Margo remembers when Lena was a sophomore at Pomona College in Southern California and was flying East on her school vacation, first to see her sister in Austin, Texas, and then to visit her father who was in New York. On the day before her flight, Margo asked her about her travel plans — what airline she was taking, when the flight was scheduled to depart — and her daughter "had no idea; she was nonplussed." "That is Lena's style," says Margo smiling proudly, "Her attitude is always, well let's see what happens . . . let's figure it out as we go along. It excites her to *not* know, to see what evolves organically . . . naturally."

Although Lena's spontaneity sometimes drives her mother crazy — Margo's basic temperament is much more "controlled and organized" — she loves her daughter's spirit and believes that it was from Lena that she has learned "authenticity." "Over the years, Lena has taught me to give up all the meticulous planning and let go of the need to control. She has helped me learn to leave room for the powers that be . . . what I call the Holy Spirit." And unlike, her older sister, Lena has made room for a long and "continuously evolving relationship" with a wonderful Argentinean guy that she met at college when she was a freshman and he was a senior. Over the years, they have lived apart and together, pursuing their independent dreams and "connecting in a deep and loving way," making it up as they go along. Lena has been able, somehow, to embrace her mother's admonition; she has had choice and commitment, independence and relationship, authenticity and compromise.

Margo describes Eduardo as an "unusual man who has captured Lena's heart, but not insisted that she shape herself for him." "He is a wonderful, caring, and gentle person . . . I think they refer to men like him as metro-sexual. He's not the tough guy and he is not effeminate. He uses hair products, does yoga, and reads poetry to Lena. . . . He's not afraid to be a whole person." Witnessing Eduardo and Lena's ever-changing and deepening relationship has been a "lesson in love" for Margo, a lesson that inspires her to see the freedom and autonomy and mutual respect that is possible between a man and a woman, where neither person is in control, neither person dominates.

Not only does she credit Lena with teaching her the lessons of authenticity, Margo also vividly remembers a moment when her daughter taught her about the "depth and breadth of individual power." Unlike the learning that seemed to grow out of who her daughters are/were — their beings, characters, and personalities — the lesson on personal power seemed to arrive like "an epiphany": all of a sudden and with great clarity and force. Lena was about fifteen and a sophomore in high school when she stopped doing her homework. Both girls were straight-A students, the kind of students who scored off the chart on aptitude and achievement tests, the kind of class leaders who were well liked by their peers and admired by all of their teachers. But one day, Lena just stopped doing her homework; she went on strike. She thought homework was for the kids who didn't get it in school and needed time to practice and improve at home. The problem was that homework was a third of the grade and not doing it would compromise her academic record. Margo had always required that her girls come home and spend two hours on their homework before doing anything else; and they had been pretty dutiful about obeying the house rules. So when Lena suddenly went on strike, Margo just became more insistent, requiring that she go up to her room until it was done. One afternoon, after they had battled about this for a few weeks, Margo went up to Lena's room to check on her progress. She found her daughter quietly sitting on her bed, "carving her lipsticks with a straight pin, sculpting miniature statues." "It was very artistic," recalls Margo wryly, "but it was not doing her homework."

Lena showed no surprise or guilt when her mother caught her carving the lipsticks, her homework completely untouched. She just looked up at her mother and said "clear as day," "You can lock me up . . . you can take my phone away . . . you will not control me. You can't make me be anyone but who I want to be." Margo remembers that her daughter's voice was not menacing or threatening; it was positive and strong. "At that moment, I realized that she was right, that she was in control of her . . . that her choices were hers." For a moment, Margo stood still as she absorbed Lena's lesson, then turned on her heels and walked out the door. But Lena's voice and determination stuck with her, a "real wake-up call" that kept on reverberating and having an impact, "a gift that kept on giving."

Interestingly, although the clarity of Lena's teaching made a "huge imprint" on Margo, the days and weeks that followed were filled with small negotiations between them, mother and daughter each softening and giving in a little, Margo backing off and Lena quietly—and stealthily—getting her homework done. It was almost as if what mattered to Lena was not the principle of abandoning her homework, nor was she out to prove that she could prevail as an excellent student without doing it. Rather, she wanted her mother to cease infantilizing her, to stop trying to control her, to let her feel her own power; and once Margo got the message and retreated, Lena did not have to hold her ground so dramatically.

At the time, Margo was working as an independent consultant to high-powered corporations, giving executives and their staffs' guidance on organizational health and innovation. Almost immediately, she noticed the imprint of Lena's teachings on the ways she began to do her work. She was "fully conscious" of the ways in which her daughter's lesson — "you don't have control over anyone" — resonated in her interactions with, and expectations of, her colleagues. "The whole idea of power shifted in my mind. I really changed. I began to see my work very differently. I started setting up teams, being more collaborative. I became a facilitator and guide, not 'the boss.' . . . I began asking questions rather than making statements." And as her approach shifted, as she learned to share power, Margo became much more successful with her clients. She also felt herself becoming a "better person," "happier with myself, my life, my interactions . . . with my God."

Margo recalls wistfully the same kind of sudden and surprising learning — another "epiphany" — at an unlikely moment when Angelica was eight-years-old. They were crossing the street, and Margo instinctively grabbed Angelica's hand. "You don't need to hold my hand," said Angelica withdrawing from her mother's grasp. "But I love you," was Margo's quick, unfiltered response. "If you loved me, you would let me walk across the street on my own," Angelica persisted. Margo remembers the exchange vividly and recalls the mix of feelings — frustration and surprise, rejection and revelation — that were a jumble within her. Even though she was just trying to get the two of them safely across the street, a most typical maternal instinct, Angelica's response made her question her impulse and forced her to think about "the meaning of love." "I began to understand," says Margo thoughtfully, "that love is defined by the person receiving it, not by the person giving it . . . loving my daughters is not about telling them what to do . . . not about making 'the face' to indicate my displeasure at something . . . not about being judgmental." Eight-year-old Angelica withdrawing her hand was, in fact, an early signal to Margo about "the changing nature of love," about how it is important "not to get stuck in the part you have played before." Margo pauses for a long time, seeming to consider whether she wants to probe this idea of "an evolving love" any further. Finally she says slowly, "I wish I had understood all of these things I learned from my daughters about control and love back when I was married the first time. We might have had a better relationship although in the end we were probably just much too different." Her voice drifts off.

She does, however, believe that these ongoing lessons on love have been helpful in shaping and sustaining her relationship with her second husband. Margo and Jens, a Swedish engineer, were married when Lena was fifteen and Angelica was eighteen, after Margo had "mostly survived" the "many fertile lessons" learned as her children were growing through their adolescence. She traces the big lesson of her now fifteen-year marriage back to crossing the street with Angelica at eight. "I have learned with my second husband about letting him define what love is to him. . . . I've learned not to push my version of love onto him, and I have tried to teach him to do that too . . . continual learning for both of us."

She cites the typical male-female emotional barrier. "You know when the woman starts to cry, the man freezes and withdraws." This was certainly the case between Margo and Jens when they started out. "But over time, my husband learned that when I cried—which I almost never do—I needed comfort. . . . He needed to just sit down next to me and put his arms around me until I felt ready to talk. We continue to try to communicate what we need in a calm and rational way and to make an effort to satisfy the needs in the other person." Margo says that because love changes, this is an ongoing process of empathic negotiation, and they have learned together to hear and see the signals—explicit and oblique—when they are "not on the same page"—when a conflict is brewing. "A sharp retort from one of us is the signal that we need to deescalate. We may part and come back together after we have calmed down enough to talk and listen." Margo says these last sentences with a kind of straightforward simplicity that seems to belie the effort and sensitivity, the emotionality, the compromises, and adjustments that I am sure have been, and continue to be, part of love's redefinition for them. But her last line is full of gratitude, emotion, and no small measure of pride. "We have even learned to be loving in our anger."

There are echoes of Angelica's "outspoken truths" and teachings in so many of Margo's vivid recall of specific moments. She remembers when Angelica was fourteen or fifteen, and Margo was insisting that Angelica do something—like clean her room or make her bed or call ahead to tell her mother when she would be home—that she kept on neglecting or avoiding. In exasperation, Margo screamed, "But I keep reminding you to do it and you never do," rehearsing a sentence she often used when she was frustrated with her daughter's inaction. But this time, Angelica shot back at her. "You are not fair when you use those words, 'never' and 'always.' . . . It is not true that someone never does something or that somebody always does something. When you say those words, it makes me feel like you don't notice when I do the things you want me to do." Like so many of Angelica's declarations, this one stopped Margo in her tracks, and she listened hard to the truth and subtlety of her words. Yes, it was true that to say she "never" cleaned up her room was patently not true; sometimes she did even if too often she didn't. But the way it played out when Margo began yelling in exasperation was a blanket statement that didn't recognize those times—however few—when her daughter was doing the right thing and being responsible. Ever since then, there has been a house rule that no one is allowed to use the forbidden words of "never" and "always." Adhering to the rule makes a difference; there is much less hyperbole carelessly "flung around." As a matter of fact, when Jens moved in after marrying Margo, he was immediately informed of the family rule. These words were not to be spoken in the house.

The lessons about authenticity, power, control, and love that Margo recalls with such clarity—both the moment and the change in attitude and behavior that followed—all seem to be related, in one way or the other, to her daughters' developing independence. They seem to be teaching their mother to give them space, to grant them autonomy, to see them clearly for who they really are, to simply hear them. These lessons about space and boundaries are woven into many of the daughters' clear and uncompromising declarations about hand-holding, about inflexible language, and about not doing homework.

By the time Angelica and Lena reached college, one at the University of Texas, Austin, the other at Pomona College, they were far away from their mother's powerful orbit; they had earned their independence. And Margo sat at the other end of their weekly telephone calls feeling mostly pleasure in the ways in which they were taking on their worlds and carving their paths. She made peace with being on the margins, not at the center; peace with the kind of restraint and boundary setting that did not come naturally; peace with the chronic feeling of missing them. Her imagery is compelling. "Calling them at college each week was like tuning into your favorite Dallas soap opera. You are not an actor in the show. You are watching, a spectator. . . . You want to say, 'don't open that door' . . . then they open it. It is, after all, their life. When you finish the conversation, it is like turning off the TV." She brightens with a smile, remembering the welcome moments of reprieve that sometimes followed. "Every once in a while, you get an invitation for a cameo appearance. They ask for your opinion about something; they ask for your help, and it feels so exciting!" There is excitement in hearing the request for guidance and assistance; but there is an even deeper pleasure in witnessing the ways in which her daughters are now ready to take on the world. "They are launched. They have found their paths. It is nice to see that you can walk away." Margo takes her gratitude a step further, moving on to a statement about the purpose of life and the responsibilities of parenting. "As parents, we replace ourselves with people who are going to be an active part of the world. That is our work made visible."

Margo connects the deep pleasure she feels as she witnesses her girls becoming women and defining their own paths with her own developing spirituality. Her philosophy and practices are grounded in religious tenets continually being searched and reinterpreted.

Once a month, she meets with her spiritual guide—a Lutheran minister—who "walks beside her" probing the layers of religious meaning and interpretation. "I began to develop my own personal vision of things like 'eternal life.' . . . I see it as what happens right here on earth, your influence in the world after you are gone. You want to know that your energy hasn't died . . . it lives on through other people you have impacted." Just as "eternal life" does not refer to some distant heavenly place, so too Margo sees the "Kingdom of God" as "what He created here." It is the story of God's reconciliation with mankind. "The Kingdom of God is not concrete. It is not something you see. It is more like something you feel and experience. It is a wonderful feeling of love, joy, and genuine caring." Her words do not sound didactic; she admits to uncertainty and the need to "continue exploring the meaning of these things." And she talks about this "lifelong learning" as springing in part from challenges her daughters voiced, when as adolescents they stopped attending church on Sundays and began to ask "what religion could be instead of rules and rituals."

Again Margo credits Angelica and Lena with helping to give meaning and purpose to her efforts to lead a godly life. "Through conversations with my skeptical daughters who asked probing and irreverent questions, I began to develop different interpretations of religion, of God." As a matter of fact, it was Lena who about three years ago saw the posting of the job—as global ambassador for an international peace organization—that Margo now has and urged her mother to apply. It is the perfect job for this point in Margo's life; and it requires above all that she "live the lessons of authenticity." Traveling all over the world—over the course of fifteen months, she has been in fourteen different countries—Margo goes to impoverished, underresourced, and oppressed communities and tries to connect with people "on the ground" who are doing community organizing, leadership development, and capacity building around human rights violations. As global ambassador, she is able to offer some financial support, but mostly she is focused on giving spiritual nourishment and encouragement. "The work is trying to get people invested in sharing, celebrating, community building, and listening to each other . . . developing agency, initiative, and collaboration."

I hear Margo, a tall, ample, straight-backed woman of Irish Scottish heritage, with cropped black curly hair, who seems to be an American standard through and through, tell me how she leaves her "cultural baggage at home" when she travels to Iraq or Gaza or Syria or South Korea or the Sudan and makes every effort to stand in the shoes of the indigenous folks who she is there to help, not save. I imagine her sitting close to the ground, face-to-face with "ordinary people," mostly listening. Margo calls this work the "Good News of Christ," and it is all about "reducing infant mortality, educating young girls, and creating better conditions for poor people, not about saving souls." It is deeply spiritual work, but it is also practical and political.

As she sits and listens to the people's stories, she often pictures — actually she feels — the ways in which her younger daughter, Lena, has always listened to people. She has, her whole life, modeled this way of being in the world and her mother has been her "consummate student." "Lena is a people person. She is amazing in the way she relates to the very old and the very young and everyone in between. She is truly attentive and absorbs what people are saying . . . she builds trust . . . she lets people know that they have been seen and heard." So as Margo travels the globe and sits with people, Lena is close by; she actually feels Lena "in" her. "To be invisible is hell," says Margo with great feeling. "I meet with marginalized people every day in my work who feel not cared for, not included . . . and I carry the resources and lessons I learned from my girls, who insisted that I see them and listen to them, as I try to make the folks I meet feel recognized and heard."

Margo Lockwood's epiphany, brought about by her daughter's calm refusal to do homework, that "you don't have control over anyone," is a way of thinking about one's place in the world. Over who — or what — do we have power? It seems that the only power we have is over ourselves, in how we want to be in response to the world. That way of being is evolution: a responsiveness to situations, contexts, circumstances, and people; a realization that others' desires and ways of being are not one's own; a questioning of current habits of mind and being so that one does not "get stuck." Margo's love for her daughter evolves as she learns that love "is defined by the person receiving it, not the person giving it." Her work evolves as she learns that there is more power in facilitating and guiding her clients than in directing them. Even her relationship with her second husband has evolved, as Margo learns to continually redefine how to give and accept love. Evolution is the ban on the words "always" and "never" because life is changing, always in flux, always a bit of something, never absolute. Evolution needs space, a space defined by boundaries and a willingness to observe, rather than participate. And evolving means being attentive — truly attentive — to others on her journey, truly seeing and hearing the people with whom she works and lives and seeking to understand them.

Always Growing

The evolution towards authenticity, that slowly takes hold in Margo's work and family life, in her moral and spiritual anchoring, in her witness and service to oppressed people all over the world, takes place against a benign backdrop of ordinary life experiences, made more precious by her discernment and notice. By contrast, Stella Robbins's story of "always growing" as she is mentored and led by her four adult children captures the hard-earned learning that follows an unspeakable tragedy. A horrific diving accident that paralyzed her older son Tony became the moment when Stella turned to Max, her youngest, to take the lead, to respond to the crisis, to organize the troops, to deal with the doctors, to stay strong and remain hopeful. Max came forward and Stella followed, filling in the places where she was needed, seeking solace and encouragement when she was losing strength. Stella's story, of recognizing and admiring the mature capacities of her grown children — "of backing off and letting go," of giving them the space to spread their wings and find their ways in the world — is made all the more poignant as her paralyzed son becomes increasingly independent and self-sufficient, as he lets his mother know—respectfully and gently—that she no longer has to hover or help. Stella feels that the incremental steps of "letting go"—vividly recalled in subtle detail—are an invitation for her continued growth, liberation, and new sense of autonomy.

Everything changed in that moment. It was a sunny afternoon in late July and the whole extended family and close friends were celebrating the marriage of Stella's oldest daughter Maya. The wedding the day before had been a small and simple affair, with only a few witnesses. The informal reception at the grandparents' house by the lake was fun filled, with swimming and canoeing, hotdogs and hamburgers, and a chocolate wedding cake. A bunch of people were already in the water when Tony, Stella's older son, came sprinting out of the house at full speed and dove from the low dock head first into the water. Stella's husband, Will, was the first to notice that things were not right. Tony seemed to be struggling, his body limp and slow in the water. Will said to Stella, "Look over there, Tony's behaving strangely." As she stood up to get a good look, Stella heard Tony say, "I can't feel my legs." She shouted for Max, Tony's younger brother. "That was the first word out of my mouth. I screamed Max's name," recalls Stella as the first of many tearful moments blur her eyes, and as she tells me how she counted— "intuitively and involuntarily"—on her younger son to be the leader in this crisis.

Max immediately jumped into the water and instructed four other people to hold Tony still. "We learned afterward that holding him immobile in the cold water was the single most important response to his being able to survive the injury . . . keeping the spine cold to keep the swelling down," says Stella. Max took over, letting his wife Alice and his sister Emma, both nurses, "call the shots" and directing other people in a coordinated effort that felt as if they had all "practiced for this moment all their lives." The call went out to 911; ambulances and emergency vehicles came through the woods within minutes and took Tony to a medic helicopter that landed in a field several miles away for the flight to the hospital. Max, Stella, and Tony's girlfriend, Caroline, were right by his side; the rest of the family followed in their trucks and cars. "It all worked smoothly, like clockwork," remembers Stella about how "no one panicked" and "everyone pulled together"; about how it all felt like "slow motion and lightning speed"; and about how Max's favorite saying "Let's go and let's get it" seemed to carry them forward through all the trauma and danger.

As Stella tells this story—which she has told hundreds of times before—her words feel both practiced and surprising to me, as if in the retelling she is discovering something new. She moves from tears to laughter smoothly and quickly, cycling up and down like a well-oiled roller coaster. She tells me that laughter is her "salvation," and she always seems to find lightness and absurdity in the midst of the pain. As sixty-two, she is strong and energetic, short and stocky, with long auburn hair that she casually pulls back in a ponytail. She leans over the table and looks me square in the eyes, a piercing gaze that demands my attention. For twenty-five years, she has owned a successful interior design business in Portland, Maine, that struggled through lean years for the first decade and is now prospering. Stella is fiercely entrepreneurial, a business acumen that is always delivered with a motherly touch. She has built a loyal customer base, is a prominent civic leader, and has a well-earned reputation as a generous employer. At one point during our interview, when Stella was describing her efforts to "let go and step back" as a mother to her grown children, she said in mock exasperation, "How can I do that? I mother everyone!"

When the surgeon, looking weary and dazed in his scrubs, found them in the waiting room, he walked toward them and asked, "Is this the family?" He seemed to be looking through them, not at them, as he delivered the news, a perfunctory, unadorned one liner. "He will never walk again; although over time he should gain some use of his arms." With that, he turned on his heels and started walking away, as they stood there in stunned silence. Max was the first to recover his voice. "You don't know my brother!" he shouted at the surgeon's back.

Stella begins with this story as she arrives at our interview after accompanying Tony on his Monday morning appointments at three rehabilitation facilities. I open the door and her story pours out, without apology, artifice, or hesitancy. It is now a year and a half after the accident, and her life is measured in increments — often invisible — of progress and in life "before and after" Tony's injury. We both know that there is no way to talk about her mothering, about her children, or about the teaching and learning that has shaped their path forward without beginning with this "life-transforming experience." It is not only the "biggest thing" in all of their lives, but Stella also sees it as a "great backdrop" for reflecting on the ways in which her children have emerged as her "leaders and inspirers," as her adult teachers.

Stella is proud of all four of them — Maya thirty-six, Emma thirty-four, Tony thirty-two, and Max thirty — proud of who they are, and "who they are becoming," a pride that allows her to admit their struggles and vulnerabilities. She begins by speaking about traits they all share. "I have raised very independent children . . . they are smoke and drug free . . . they all have great jobs, and all have their ups and downs but they appear to be able to work through the down times . . . they are self-motivated wonderful kids." She pauses for a minute, and then identifies a concern that flashes through her mind from time to time. "Every once and a while, I say, 'Now when are you going to go off and have some fun?"

Her youngest, Max, seems to be the most driven, the one who has the most crowded and stressful life that leaves little room for fun. Occasionally, Stella will talk to him, gently, about his "plate being very full," and he always responds the same way, "Well, then I'll just have to eat faster." As a second grader, he was diagnosed with dyslexia, a condition that he has "overcompensated for," by now earning three postgraduate degrees. When he was diagnosed with diabetes at fifteen, he was overwhelmed with disappointment because it meant that he would not be able to fulfill his life dream of joining the Navy Seals. His disappointment turned to anger, a chronic seething rage that hung around for a few years during his late adolescence, until he set his sights on becoming an arborist. "Of all of my kids, he is probably the most positive and self-motivated, but he is also the one who can get crushed most easily," says Stella about his mercurial temperament, which cycles between incredibly energetic, purposeful, and sustained work—after only three years of teaching, he is the head of his department at a large regional agricultural high school—and brief moments of "crashing" when he faces obstacles in his path. He is, for example, the assistant basketball coach at school. The head coach, an important mentor and good friend, recently left for another job and was replaced by a man who Max has found lackluster and lacking in leadership skills. "For a few weeks, he hit the wall, furious he had been put in the position of having to take orders from a guy he considered lazy and unskilled," Stella recalls. She listened to her son's ranting and complaining, knowing he would get over it. She has learned that Max's drive and ambition are partly fueled by his explosions of displeasure: the chance to vent from time to time, the chance to climb back on top of his game.

It was Max's name that Stella called when Tony broke his neck when he dived into the lake. It is Max, her youngest, who became the leader through the crisis, who rallied the troops, coordinated the rescue effort, and warned the surgeon that he had no idea who he was dealing with when he said his brother would never walk. When Stella recalls what she has learned from Max, she says that he teaches us "determination and optimism." "He keeps carrying us forward," she says gratefully about a temperament that they share but one that her son "continually enlivens" in her. Right after hearing the surgeon's prognosis, Max turned to his family as if he was a quarterback in a huddle calling the next play and said, "Okay, let's figure this out." A plan was made for who would stay at the hospital, what jobs needed doing, who needed to be contacted, and how they would communicate with one another. All of it led by Max. Sometimes when Stella gets discouraged, weighed down by the worry or weary from the fight to stay positive, she actually "channels" Max, even though she knows that he, too, has to crash from time to time.

Tony was in the intensive care unit for three days, when the family—at the urging of his wonderful male nurse—requested that he be moved to a rehabilitation hospital in Boston. It is very rare to move a spinal injury patient so quickly out of intensive care, but his nurse could already see something in Tony—"his willingness to always do more than was asked of him, his cheerful, upbeat demeanor"—that made him push hard for an early transfer. The ambulance ride into Boston was excruciatingly painful. After arriving at the hospital, Tony made his one and only request: that he never be left alone. In the spinal injury ward, there were forty patients, thirty-eight of whom were men between the ages of eighteen and thirty-five—"daredevils wired like Tony for risk and danger," says Stella shaking her head. For the next several weeks, Stella, his girlfriend Caroline, and his three siblings took rotating turns at the hospital. Stella recalls the ways in which they all grew closer through this time: "We monitored the medicine, treatments, and progress very closely, communicated everything we saw and noticed to one another . . . it brought us so much closer." Now tears are streaming down her face. "As mothers, we want our children to love each other . . . to be best friends. This tragedy cemented some of that, and I am grateful."

The way they all came together—including Caroline—reminded Stella of another painful and traumatic time when they bonded together as a family unit, when love and belonging were the benign consequences of seeing their lives torn asunder. She gives a detailed account of how she met her first husband Jay at Oregon State University—when she was a fresh-faced and naive freshman and he was a handsome, sophisticated, and well-traveled masters student—and she was "swept off her feet" by him. They moved back East, to Portland, Maine, when he finished his masters, and had Maya, their firstborn, five years later. Jay balked at the thought of becoming a parent and asked his wife to have an abortion, a painful and puzzling request that Stella had never anticipated from the man she loved and thought would be a good father. But it turned out that his reluctance was related to the anger and pain he had inherited from his own "dysfunctional" family, and one of the first signs of his incapacity to "process things" in his life, his unwilling-

ness to "slog through the mud like all the rest of us." He was a brilliant, self-centered man with no patience for taking care of other
people.

When Stella, still feeling very young and vulnerable, went to
Jay's mother to tell her that her son was pushing for an abortion,
his mother was unfazed. "Well, all men are boys until they have
children and are forced to grow up," she said as she urged Stella to
have the baby. When Maya arrived, she was her Daddy's "angel";
Jay was "over the moon." Three other children followed, each two
years apart, and Stella watched her husband become increasingly
overwhelmed, depressed, and isolated from his family as he moved
through long periods of unemployment. A few years later, when Jay
had just turned forty, they received the diagnosis that he was in the
early stages of Parkinson's disease; and everything seemed to fall
apart as his emotional and physical ailments conspired to "take him
down completely." "The scene was stressful and chaotic as I tried
my best to hold it together," Stella remembers wearily.

When they finally went to see a therapist at Stella's desperate urging, the therapist told Jay that until he was willing to work on himself and take on his own demons, there was no way to save the marriage. Jay refused and things began to deteriorate further. "When
people are out of control," says Stella leaning forward intensely,
"then they become even more controlling." As Stella struggled to
keep the family financially afloat and take care of her four small
children, Jay grew more "childlike and irresponsible," often exploding into rages and shouting mean accusations. Stella knew that
her marriage was over, but she kept talking herself out of it. "I was
raised in a normal middle-class family. I came from healthy stock
in the Northwest country. We were taught to work hard, do our
best, and be cheerful. When there were family reunions, eighty-four
people would gather and we would all know one another . . . I had
no sense that there could be a reality that was so dysfunctional. I
was still blinded by this view of perfect, caring families who stayed
together."

Finally, she took refuge in therapy, the only place where she
could "feel her feelings" and hear her "own voice." For a year and a

half, she resisted the dissolution of her marriage, remaining "stuck and fearful." The same image kept washing over her every time she would talk to her therapist. "I feel like I am in a box and all these chains are keeping me bound up," she kept telling him. And then one day, out of the blue, Stella "saw the light"; it was "instantaneous and very clear." "I think I just let myself out of the box," she told her therapist, who smiled and responded: "I have been waiting for you to say that for a year and a half." Stella still shakes her head in disbelief about how long it took her to come to that decision. "I knew then that I could separate from Jay. I thought, yes, I can have one less child to take care of now . . . yes, I can keep my four children safe from the chaos . . . yes, I can be independent and self-sufficient." Max, her youngest was three at the time. Determined that she and her children would survive, and that it was her responsibility to rescue them, but still feeling the vestiges of guilt about leaving her sick husband, Stella gathered up her four offspring and took off for rural Oregon to stay with her parents for a few months.

Even though the battles around divorce and custody continued for a few years after their return to Maine and they all have scars to show for the trauma that the children endured, Stella points to the "shreds of goodness" and the lessons learned from this difficult period. First, she learned that she could break the chains that were imprisoning her in the box, that the decision was ultimately "intuitive": it required listening to her heart, not overthinking and rationalizing a bad situation. Second, she discovered that out of the chaos she and the children could prevail. If they "clumped together" and watched each other's backs, they could find a togetherness that was healthy, strong, and intimate. Together, they could survive and even thrive. Both of those potent memories—of listening to her inner voice and surviving trauma together and making something beautiful out of it—have echoes, she believes, in the way the family has come together since Tony's accident. "We feel it and we move forward . . . with no second guessing." Only now, it feels like her adult children are mostly leading the way. They are the guides, the inspirers; they are calling the shots.

At the center of the reclamation efforts is the patient who says clearly and often to his mother, "If I need something, I will ask for it." He is an amazingly disciplined and determined young man who always does more than he is asked, who pushes the limits, and gains the admiration and respect of his doctors, nurses, and therapists. He also refuses to be seen as disabled and helpless. I gaze at a photo of Tony taken yesterday. He is sitting in a wheel chair with a harness around his body getting ready to ascend a rock-climbing wall at the rehabilitation facility. He has a huge smile on his handsome face, a skullcap on his head, and bulging biceps on the strong frame of his muscular body. I cannot help feeling his positive energy as I exclaim to Stella, "You know it is hard to feel sorry for this guy." She laughs, "That's exactly right . . . that's how he makes everyone feel." Every day, it seems Stella learns lessons from Tony about "letting go," lessons that have "rippled into" her relationships with her other three children. "It has been a difficult journey," she says about how her impulse has always been to do too much for her offspring. Tony's lessons are small, almost gestural, but cumulatively they make the point. Stella offers a few examples from the past twenty-four hours.

Last night she had driven into the city to have dinner with Tony and stay overnight at his apartment before making the rounds with him to his morning rehabilitation sessions. His girlfriend Caroline was away for a couple of days visiting her parents. Stella and Tony made dinner together. She had thought she would buy food on her way into town, and then fix the meal. But Tony texted her to say he had purchased food for dinner, and when she arrived he fixed the chicken, vegetables, and rice, as she stood alongside him at the counter preparing the salad. When dinner was over, and Stella began to clear the table, Tony told her to keep her seat. Then he put the plates in his lap and wheeled over to the dishwasher to deposit them. I ask Stella—who is sporting a brand new Ford SUV—whether she drove Tony to his appointments the next morning. "He is now driving," she says proudly, her voice still filled with astonishment. He gets himself from his wheelchair into the driver's seat by using his immense upper body strength; and once in the driver's seat, he dismantles, folds, and stores the wheelchair in "less than thirty seconds." "It looks like ballet," says Stella about his moves, which are graceful, strong, and spare.

Tony's independence seems to be fueled by a cheerfulness and work ethic that is infectious. "Honey to the bees," says his mother about the ways in which the physical therapists, doctors, and nurses are drawn to the patient who makes them feel successful and gives them reason to hope. It is not that Tony always takes their advice — in fact, he does not always believe what the medical people tell him or accept the limits they want to put on him — but rather that they welcome his positive energy, his fierce determination. As Stella has watched — and learned from — his "declarations of independence," she has begun to believe that he gathers his drive and energy in part from the way he reaches out to and helps others. Stella had just witnessed one of these typical gestures of generosity that morning when Tony was doing his rowing exercises in the gym. A young woman, eighteen years old or so, came into the gym, filled only with "sweaty ex-jock" men working at their rowing machines — a real macho scene. She had only been rowing for two months and she looked tentative and afraid. Tony was the first person to greet her and offer her help and encouragement. And Caroline and Tony have together befriended other couples who they have met in re-hab, who are struggling with how to put their lives back together after their spinal injuries. The other night, for example, they took dinner over to a young wrestler and his wife. "Tony reaches out and mentors other people," says Stella admiringly. "He always says, 'We have to be part of something bigger.'" Interestingly, Tony is also very discerning about whom he chooses to help; he seems to know he has to reserve energy for his own strengthening and healing. "He seems to understand who will move with him and who won't," says Stella about a calculation she has noticed in her son. "He goes through a process of evaluation and commits to those people who will use his help well." Again, Stella sees a lesson in her son's careful discernment. She sees herself as someone who has tended to "give it all away," using herself up in the process. As she watches Tony, she notices ways she might take care of herself even as she generously gives to others.

Tony's lessons in helping his mother learn to "let go" of her maternal instincts to hover and help have carried over into her relationships with her other children. When early on a conflict developed between Tony's youngest sister, Emma, and his girlfriend, Caroline, Stella's first instinct was to try and repair the rift, to quickly make it all right between them. Right after the accident, Emma, a nurse, felt that she was being pushed to the side and that Tony's girlfriend was assuming a place of honor and responsibility that she didn't deserve. Caroline was stung by Emma's competitiveness and disrespect. For months there was a complete standoff, as the two avoided all contact and felt wounded when other family members seemed to take sides. Stella admits that it "sadly may never be resolved between them." But she has taken herself out of the middle of it, a restraint and discipline that she finds both "unbearably hard and a big relief." "I need to stop meddling," she says with great force, as if she still has to convince herself. "I need to step back and let the sparks fall wherever they will. If I do their bidding then they will not have to face each other." Stella has already noticed a little bit of progress, a "melting down of the icy relationship," at least from Caroline's side. "She is learning to let it go . . . learning not to relive the negative things. Now Emma has to find a way to say that she is sorry. If she can do that, it will set her free."

Sometimes the letting-go lesson comes in the form of a "blunt kind of truth telling," in the moment when one person says to the other "just get over it." For months after Tony's accident, his sister Maya, the bride, was bereft with guilt and sadness. She would say—to herself and anyone who would listen—"if I had not gotten married, this would not have happened." "In fact, she still feels so guilty," says Stella weeping. After trying to gently assuage her guilt and empathize with her pain for the first few months after the accident, Tony finally told his sister to "just get over it!" He repeated a mantra that has always defined his approach to life: "If you're not living on the edge, you're taking up too much room." This courting of danger—whether it is downhill skiing on the most harrowing slopes, or mountain climbing to the highest peaks, or racing his Harley motorcycle—has always been "his pattern since he was a little kid," says Stella. "That is how he is wired." As she listens to Tony's impatience with Maya's tears, Stella says she is learning how to "not get stuck in the grief." She is learning that in order to move forward you have to "quit second guessing . . . you have to find the path that will set you free."

It has been a long and intense afternoon, but Stella still seems vigorous, as if telling "the story" gives her new energy. Before we stop, she wants to distinguish between two kinds of learning that have been inspired by her kids, "lessons that are alike but different." "I have been talking to you about my children giving me lessons in 'letting go' . . . but I have also been learning the lesson of 'backing off,' which is slightly different." "How so?" I ask not hearing the difference or understanding the distinction. "Well backing off is recognizing that I do not have to know everything about my kids' lives . . . understanding that they have a different journey . . . letting them have a more independent life." When I ask for an example, she has several. "I do not need to know that Maya is going off for a weekend . . . I do not need to be alerted about when they return home safely from their travels." This "backing off," she realizes, has important implications for the new path that she is trying to forge. For the first time, she seems to shift her sights to Will, her stalwart husband of twelve years, and to the beginning of a "long overdue conversation about retirement." "For so long it has been a story of me and my four children, surviving, teaching, learning, and moving forward." "It is," Stella says tenderly, "time to nest with my spouse. I no longer want to sit at home and wait for my kids to need me."

I am struck by the way that Stella Robbins describes her children—all in their thirties—as growing towards their full maturity, as being proud of "who they are becoming." Perhaps it was Tony's accident that led to this perspective, her refusal to accept what he "has become" because of the tragedy as a finite limit, an ending of sorts.

Stella survived the traumatic dissolution of her first marriage, not allowing that to stop the growth and togetherness of her family and not letting it fill her with bitterness and grief. She then let her children guide the family as they dealt with the accident, not allowing it to dissolve Tony's future and making space for his independence and perseverance. In accepting Tony's growing autonomy, in admiring his "balletic" grace against the odds, and in relinquishing her desire to "fix" her other children's challenges, Stella makes space for growth in her own relationship with her husband. She "backs off" to make progress, to keep on growing.

Adapting

Stella Robbins's account of her growth, provoked by her adult children, who took the lead following Tony's horrific accident, echoes the family crisis of a bad divorce fifteen years before when they all "clumped together" and drew strength from one another. Surviving the traumas together, "with optimism and determination," Stella and her children plotted a path forward. In contrast, as if they are protagonists in a long-running play, Althea Powell thoughtfully describes the teachings of her twenty-three-year-old son Amari as subtle lessons ("set pieces") in "adaptation," a trajectory of learning that requires ongoing and patient calibration—a trajectory very different from the avalanche of learning following Stella's "life-transforming experience." As Althea raises her older son, whose temperament and appetites and whose experiences and upbringing are so different from hers, she learns how to attentively listen, how to frame her questions carefully, how to push but hold firm. She calculates when it is time to stop waiting patiently for his self-corrections, when it is no longer smart to sit still. Althea feels the constant adjustments that she must make as she witnesses and responds to Amari's "zigzag" journey through life (her path has been much more traditional and straightforward) and strives to give him the space to learn and fail. Althea is also adapting to raising two black sons in a predominantly white, upper-middle-class suburb very different from the all-black, lower-middle-class neighborhood in the Deep South where she was raised. As she mothers, she knows that she has so much to learn and so much to teach, adapting to the new cultural context of her sons' lives, accepting and honoring their choices, while she works to protect them from the ancient dangers — of being young, black, and male — which remain as lethal threats in the world they now inhabit.

Even before we begin our afternoon together, Althea Powell tells me that mothering is her most precious work. The other parts of her busy life, other people can do; she is not irreplaceable. But mothering her two sons — who are now twenty-three and twenty-one — is her most important role; nobody else can do it. Althea, a striking, elegant fifty-five-year-old African American woman with light brown skin, a gorgeous crown of silver hair, and colorful threads of exotic fabrics, is a clinical psychologist with a full and eclectic professional life that she has carefully composed. Only once in her life — for exactly one year — did she have a job that required that she show up every day at the same place for five days in a row. She much prefers to put lots of pieces together — "a colorful quilt" — which allows her autonomy, freedom, and variety. She works as a school psychologist, with her office on the "main thoroughfare," with a door wide open to the children, teachers, and parents in her care — not in "the basement behind a boiler so people have to sneak down" to see her. She does training for postdocs who plan to do clinical work with multiethnic and multiracial populations, and she has a thriving consultant practice that frequently requires travel out of town. In the midst of all that peripatetic movement, Althea is a serene presence, who listens attentively, speaks slowly and thoughtfully, and smiles easily.

Althea was born and raised in a lower-middle-class African American family in Jackson, Mississippi, where her neighborhood, church, and school were all black. Several times during our interview, she refers to her roots in the Deep South and her anchoring in the black community, and she makes clear that even though she has lived in northern California since 1977 — more than half of her life — she is still very much a "Southern girl"; she knows, and is proud of, the ancestry from which she comes.

When Althea arrived for her freshman year at Stanford University, she stood alone at the edge of the campus with her suitcases and trunks piled up all around her and felt she was in some place very foreign. When she arrived at her room, she was thrilled to discover that her roommate — who is still her best friend in the world — was also black and was sitting on the edge of the bed, fixing her hair with a straightening comb, a familiar and comforting sight for Althea. And all through her four years at Stanford, all of her close friends were black. "My world at college had no white friends . . . we students of color were arm in arm, had each other's backs, were there for each other. Together we marched through the morass of indignities and challenges to our intelligence." Althea offers this preamble as a way of orienting me to her "deep sense of self" that is steeped in her Southern, middle-class blackness and, I believe, in order to help me anticipate the ways in which her sons — living in white suburban communities close to San Francisco and attending predominantly white schools — have known a different reality, one that has forced Althea to adapt and learn from the generational shifts in identity and perspective. "These are different times," she says many times, "and a different generation."

Althea does not begin her reflections on mothering focused on matters of race or the generational differences between her own sense of black identity and that of her sons. In fact, her starting point is the long-winding tale of her firstborn son, Amari, who "right from the very beginning" was always a "challenge" to his parents. When he was just three-years-old, Althea and her husband Gregory used to ask him in mock seriousness, "What do we always say about you?" And he would respond with a smile, "You tell me that I am a challenge." He has always been the child who took the "zigzag path"; always the one to "make a bold statement"; always the "expansive, big thinker"; always the "creative, artistic force"; always the one to "act out of impulsivity." Many of these attributes of her firstborn are rendered in bold relief when Althea compares him to his younger brother Chinua, who is a self-proclaimed "mama's boy" and who approaches the world much more "rationally and methodically," who follows the straight path, and whose way of thinking and seeing the world is more like his mother's.

For Althea, the challenge of mothering Amari has always been trying to find a way not to "stifle" his creativity and imagination while at the same time striving to get him to be more "realistic and purposeful" in making his life choices. This tension—between supporting and celebrating his artistic appetites and reining him in—has always felt like a difficult balancing act for Althea who is "built very differently" than her son. "I am much more methodical," she admits. "I measure twice and cut once. Amari has always been a challenge in that he moves through the world very differently." The challenges that Althea has experienced with Amari have always been "sources of struggle" and "sites of learning" for her.

The lessons Amari has taught Althea, then, largely originate in navigating the differences in their temperaments, appetites, and approaches to their lives. And these contrasts have been revealed most dramatically when Amari and his parents have been making decisions about his schooling. It was in these moments of difficult decision making—about which schools to attend and which ones would be the best match for Amari . . . about whether and when to leave when the choices turned out not to be good ones—that Althea discovered "how to listen," how "not to go toe to toe" with her son, and how to ask questions that would "not offend or cause him to resist." It was also at these moments that she learned how to "hold firm," when "to draw the line," and how to endure what she and her husband called "the tribunals" they staged at home when it was time to have a come-to-Jesus conversation.

There were many twist and turns in Amari's journey through school. His first school experience was at Brookside, a fancy white independent school in Menlo Park, California. By the third grade, his parents had pulled him out of Brookside—which had high tuitions and required a long carpool ride—and put him into their neighborhood public elementary school. "The public school did not have all the fancy physical features and expensive tools and equipment that Brookside had, but we discovered that what was going on in the classroom between the teachers and children was just as rich and interesting," recalls Althea about a move that still seems to have been made "for the right reasons." By the time Amari had finished ninth grade, both he and his parents felt that he needed a more structured and demanding learning environment than the public high school offered. He transferred to the Latin School, an all-boys elite preparatory academy with a reputation for high academic standards and a fairly rigid and prescribed curriculum. As Althea looks back on Amari's experience there, she wonders out loud about whether the rigidity of the place was actually a "disservice" to her creative, free-spirited son, whether his three years there were complicated and difficult because his teachers "never really got him," never fully appreciated his gifts.

After graduating from the Latin School, his choice of Skidmore College — "a much more artsy, progressive, creative place, a former women's school" — was clearly a reaction to the rigidity and strict structures of his all-male high school. After the euphoria of the first several weeks at Skidmore — where he enjoyed the autonomy and freedom that he had missed so much in high school — Amari began to feel rudderless, confused, and in need of some direction and structure. "I think he had swung too far the other way," says Althea in a voice that seems to say "be careful for what you wish for." Amari struggled through his freshman year, feeling a chronic unease, but holding fast to what he believed were the benefits of "living his beliefs about himself and the institution." After all, Skidmore was the kind of school with an educational philosophy and culture that he had always fantasized about, a school that would encourage and reward his aesthetic and his creativity, a place that would honor his wish to carve an independent path. He held fast to the school's reputation and rhetoric even as he became increasingly confused and unhappy.

Despite the difficulties of his first year there, Amari decided to return for his sophomore year, unwilling to give up his tenuous attachment. But by the end of his first semester, his grades had plummeted, and it was apparent to his parents that he was wasting his time and their money. They insisted that he return home rather than stay at the college "flailing around." "We said, 'Come on home and let's figure it out,"' says Althea in what seems like her characteristic understatement of the anxiety lurking underneath these important and difficult choices that required that her "independent and stubborn" son "enter into deep dialogue with his parents." The conversations were hard and demanding, concluding with Amari's reluctant withdrawal from Skidmore and his transfer, after a semester at home, to Williams College in Williamstown, Massachusetts. Right from the beginning, Williams seemed the perfect match: "artsy and creative but with a frame and structure." Amari flourished, majoring in sociology but also taking courses in architecture, painting, and design. He loved the "thinking and exploring" that was required by the liberal arts curriculum. "Williams did right by my son," says Althea with relief still ringing in her voice. "He grew and blossomed . . . he responded to the rigor . . . he branched off in unexpected directions."

Althea's praise of Williams, and of her son's capacity and determination to thrive there, remind her of his surprising decision to enroll in French courses when he got to college, after "barely managing to pass French" at the Latin School. As a matter of fact, his struggles with high school French had compromised his academic record and had almost gotten him thrown out of high school. The Latin School required three years of language training in French and Latin, and because of the timing of Amari's transfer from public school, he had to do three years of language classes in two years. He struggled mightily. "It was a brutal, difficult experience for all of us. Just the worst. That is when we introduced the 'tribunals' where we slugged it out together . . . real truth telling, real tough exchanges," recalls Althea about the ways in which Amari and his parents were often locked in battle about what appeared to them to be a lack of focus and motivation on his part. Even his French teacher seemed to be giving up on Amari when she said to Althea and Gregory at a parent teacher meeting, in a tone that seemed to hold a threat, "Does he even want to be here?" When things got really bad and failure seemed imminent, Amari's parents offered him "an out." "We told him, if you want to push the eject button, you can leave . . . that is all right with us." But Amari persevered, struggled, and prevailed; he worked very hard, got lots of tutoring, and barely passed. Althea believes that Amari simply "refused to fail." "My son is gutsy and stubborn," she says about the way he digs in when people tell him he can't succeed. "They thought he couldn't do it, so he was going to show them that they were wrong. It was amazing but very painful to witness." She also feels that there was something within him that wanted to understand the source of his struggle, "something told him he should have been a stronger French student."

When Amari decided to study French at Williams, he was hoping to settle an old score and he was more determined than ever. During his senior year, he found a tutor, a French exchange student, who was at Williams for her sophomore year. They worked and played together, his French improving by leaps and bounds. By the end of the semester, they were officially boyfriend and girlfriend, and Amari was quietly hatching a plan to travel to Paris after graduation. "We wondered how much was this about becoming proficient in French, and how much was about the girlfriend," says Althea slyly. By the spring semester, Amari had added another element to his plan. He decided to enroll in an intensive English as a second language (ESL) course at Columbia—three weeks of full-day instruction—so that he could be certified to teach English in Paris. "We supported the ESL training knowing that it had some income potential," says Althea, signaling their early concern that their son become more financially independent after paying the hefty college tuitions at Williams.

As Amari anticipated his move to Paris, however, he imagined that whatever he decided to do, he would still be receiving substantial support from his parents. "He thought we would be thrilled to support him in Paris, and we kept saying that we were not prepared to do that . . . if he wanted to live like an adult person, then he had to have a plan about how to support himself. We kept insisting that now that you have graduated, we can't be the whole of your plan," recalls Althea about how their insistence on his having a realistic plan erupted into pitched battles between them, with Amari claim-

ing that they "didn't want him to go" and "they were not being supportive" and with Gregory and Althea insisting "we are on your
team . . . we believe in you, but you need to bring us a plan." Many
"tribunals" followed as Amari expressed his disappointment and
frustration with his parents' point of view and his outrage at the way
they refused to budge from their hard stance. Finally—after what
began to seem like daily, difficult, contentious disputes—Amari
"got it," and the "toxicity in the air around us that had consumed
us for months" vanished. "To his credit," says Althea proudly, "this
young man came up with a plan."

The plan was not one that either of his folks would have ever
predicted. He signed up with an international agency that matches
American au pairs with European families, and almost immediately he was matched up with a French family—with two moms
and three young children—living in a suburb on the outskirts of
Paris. The moms had wanted to hire a man, and they hoped that he
would teach their children English. The interview was Skyped, and
Gregory and Althea got in on the tail end of it as the moms took
them on a virtual tour of their house and tried to make them feel
comfortable about their son living and working there. Even though
Amari struggled with the language for the first two months and
worried that he would never feel comfortable as a French speaker,
and even though he found the children surprisingly freewheeling
and undisciplined, and even though it was initially hard for him to
figure out the limits of his authority as a hired caregiver, it turned
out to be "an incredible match." The moms and the children adored
Amari and they took care of him like he was family.

By Christmas time, when Althea, Gregory, and Chinua, Amari's
younger brother, flew over to Paris to visit him, he had become
a "French-speaking phenom." "It was a magical experience," says
Althea tearing up, "to see your son not as a child, but as a young
man . . . mastering the language, navigating his environment, negotiating everything, building new relationships, caring for the children, guiding and teaching us about all the new things we were en-
countering." She looks back at his struggles and near failure at the
Latin School and feels "awed" by the way her son fought back and

proved himself. Mastering French feels, by now, like a metaphor for so much else: for Amari's overcoming adversity with stubbornness and courage; for his choosing an unlikely path, the "zigzag route"; for his showing the world that he was smarter than they thought; and for his parents, engaging the conflict and standing their ground with him in a way that felt impossibly hard at the moment but ultimately forced him to take control and forge his independent path. Althea smiles at the "happy ending which isn't an ending at all, but the beginning of his discovering his manhood." As Amari confidently guided them around Paris, his parents "kept saying to him, you should be proud of yourself for making this happen. You were the one to figure it out."

There is irony as well in his Paris experience that Althea is quick to point out. Amari always said that he never wanted to have any children. "He was adamant about that . . . figuring that he had been such a big 'challenge' to his parents that he did not want to have to suffer that with his own kids." But now he has taken a job that requires that he nurture, care for, and teach his young charges, he has discovered that it is demanding but he is enjoying it and that he feels good about the love they return in good measure. This has forced him to rethink his child-free plans and to reflect on and appreciate the way he was parented. "Now he calls," says Althea, in an "I told you so" voice, "with gratitude and appreciation for the way we raised him."

Althea reviews the twists and turns in Amari's long "French narrative" and underscores the lessons she has learned along the way, lessons about patience and trust, restraint and listening. She almost seems to be looking down from above and observing her relationship to her son from a distance where she can see the progress that often eludes her when she is "in the midst of the struggle." "Amari taught his mother that I have to sit back and not assert myself. I try to keep my feet on the ground, not go toe to toe with him . . . I try to plant the seed, saying 'maybe this is something that you might think about, or what would it look like if you did this or that?' . . . Then I back off and work hard not to let my ego get mixed in," she says thoughtfully. "But even before I plant the seed and ask the questions, I have had to learn to really listen to him." She looks into the future, when all of her efforts at patience and restraint might yield a definition of a "new kind of distance" between them. "I want to be out of a job for being the person Amari needs. I want to know that he will not be afraid to move forward on his own, that he won't be too timid or tentative . . . I want him to want to be near me, but I don't want him to need me."

It is when Althea mentions Amari's recent trip to Morocco that I hear her first references to her son's racial identity. He and his French girlfriend had taken a two-week getaway to Morocco, his first trip to Africa, and it had been a "transformative experience" for him. Afterwards, Amari told his parents that he felt immediately "welcomed and embraced" by the brown-skinned Moroccans who would call out to him in the market with "brotherly familiarity" and who thought he was French — not American — because of his excellent French accent. "Amari was giving his girlfriend entrée," says Althea about the role reversal that they both noticed in North Africa. "She did not get the same kind of deference that he did . . . and this registered in his psyche." When he returned to Paris after the trip, Amari called his parents and told them that his trip had been "brilliant and transformative," and he admitted that he might have had an even better time if he had traveled alone. Soon after, Amari broke up with his girlfriend. Their relationship had slowly deteriorated and cooled since his arrival in Paris — she had returned full time to the university and would visit her family several hours outside of Paris on the weekends — but the Moroccan trip seemed to seal his desire to "go solo." To Althea, his voice sounded lighter during their weekly Google hangouts, as if the breakup was something of a relief for him; he seemed to feel freer and less encumbered. "He was ready to focus on himself and get himself launched . . . he was not wanting to be coupled," says Althea with some relief in her voice.

When I ask Althea whether her sons have ever dated young women of color — a question that she seems to expect from me — she pauses as she scans the handful of girlfriends who have been in the picture the last few years — all white women "without melanin," a few with international pedigrees from Russia, Spain, and Sweden. Althea's tone seems to blend hopefulness with resignation. "I've had to breathe very deeply on this one . . . if I were to be totally honest, I would say that I hope that by the time my boys are ready to settle down, they will choose a partner who is some version of brown . . . that they will settle on someone in the brown spectrum." Her next statement seems less cautious. "Amari is a good black man . . . and I would like him to find a good brown woman. . . . After all we have invested and poured into him, that would be my wish, my deep desire . . . I have never said that to him explicitly, in a direct way. That is not my place, and if he did not make that decision, I would not want him to be worried on my account. But I wish for a woman of color in my heart of hearts." I look at Althea as she reflects on the mixture of feelings welling up inside of her . . . her earnest, heartfelt desire that Amari will settle down with a brown skinned young woman; her determination not to burden her son with her real feelings because that would not be fair to him and that is not her place; and her willingness — actually her intention — that whoever he ultimately chooses, she will learn to love her. She seems ready to stop struggling with these complicated feelings, as she gives emphasis to a "summary sentence." "Ultimately, I will love whoever he chooses just so she is a good woman and loves my son."

Althea wants to make sure that I do not wrongly interpret her sons' record of dating white woman; dating white women must not be taken as a sign of a conflicted or weak black identity. "Both of my sons know exactly who they are," she says with a Black Power raised fist and a defiant smile. Right from the beginning, she and her husband Gregory have been very "intentional" in letting their sons know they are black. They have "consistently and persistently" underscored the responsibilities, challenges, and vulnerabilities of being born "black and male in this culture." Althea takes us back to her own roots in the Deep South where her whole world—her school, church, and neighborhood—was black; where she never saw—or yearned for—diversity until she came to California for college. But her sons have had a very different reality and been raised in a "much more diverse world," and Althea and Gregory have worked very hard to both hold onto the deep threads of race and culture that they knew growing up, while at the same time finding a way to honor and appreciate the world that has opened up for their boys, a world still marred by racism but also one with more opportunity and access for blacks.

Even though they chose to live in a predominantly white suburb, for example, they carefully selected a family day care run by a Jamaican couple who are still, twenty years later, "very much woven into" their lives. They joined an all-black AME Zion Church in San Jose and traveled from the suburbs every Sunday to attend services; they enrolled their boys in the only Afrocentric preschool in East Palo Alto; and they gave them both African names when they were born. Again, Althea says, "There is no confusion about who they are!" Even their hair announces their identity. Amari has long dreadlocks that cascade down his back, and his younger brother Chinua, who is a few inches taller, has grown out his Afro, a bold, black halo reminiscent of the sixties.

When the boys were still in elementary school, Gregory and Althea—in their most "intentional" effort to be in the company of other black families like theirs—would get together on Sunday afternoons once a month with five families, all of whom lived in nearby white suburbs, all of whom were dual-career, professional families. They would gather for the afternoon at each other's homes, the host family doing the cooking, and preparing a lesson that they wanted to teach the children. The subjects ranged widely and usually reflected the vocation or avocation of the host parents. For one of the moms, an academic and economist, there was a lesson about the stock market; for a father who loved fly-fishing, there was a demonstration at a nearby river; for a father who was a musician, there was a lesson on the blues; and for a mother who was a history buff, there were lessons on slavery and the Civil War. Although the lessons were always informal and fun—designed to be different from the pedagogy and content their children were receiving at school—the social-relational benefits of these gatherings were, by far, the most important thing. These black parents, most raised in all black communities, wanted to give their children a taste of what it felt like to be in the company of folks like them, a "safe space" that contrasted with the tokenism and "hypervisibility" that their children experienced in their neighborhoods and schools.

I also hear in Althea's description of the Sunday afternoons a wish to introduce her boys to other middle-class, professional black folks: people who were making it in the world as doctors, entrepreneurs, lawyers, and academics, people who might become role models for her children. "For more than a decade we gathered, and it worked wonderfully," recalls Althea, "It was a terrific experience for my boys and it was great for the parents, too. We loved being with each other, and we shared our stories about what it meant to parent black kids in a still-racist society . . . we looked to each other for support and guidance." It was only when the kids "rose up and said they had had enough" that the parents reluctantly decided to end the ritual Sunday gatherings. As Althea looks back on the "trail of Sundays," she now sees that the parents were engaged in "collective learning" as well. The mothers and fathers were teaching lessons to their kids — on history, fishing, food, geography — but they were also "learning lessons from them" about the ways in which their offspring were navigating race in their own lives, the ways in which they were acting out a kind of "racial fluidity" and "improvising on a new racial landscape."

When Althea speaks about watching her sons move across racial lines with their friendships and romances, she also wants to stress that, despite this "fluidity," her boys "absolutely know who they are." "Yes," she admits, "they have taught me to be more open and accepting . . . but I have insisted that they know the world in which we live, the harsh realities in which black males are still the most vulnerable. My antennae as a mom of black males are always alert and ready, and knowing when and if to act is hugely emotional and exhausting. . . . We have had all of those black male conversations . . . what to do if you get stopped by the police . . . when the white policeman is not aware of his unconscious racism, and does not know that this is a beloved, well-educated young man and treats him with disrespect . . . or maybe even decides to kill him because he looks at him funny." Althea's naturally serene face is now lined with worry and rage; her voice is ringing with defiance. I can see her lioness, protective stance kick in. "My heart is in my throat when my sons go out at night . . . I'm trying to keep them alive . . . we take great pains to see that there is no bulb out on their car that will give the police an excuse to pull them over."

Gregory and Althea have never second-guessed the need to teach these defensive and protective strategies to their sons. They know that whatever racial fluidity and openness their sons possess, that others will always just see them as ordinary, scary, black men: thugs walking down a dark street. It is a relief to Althea that her sons have been able to get the double-edged message, a message that is alert to their own vulnerability and victimization but also one that does not rob them of their humanity. It is a delicate balance, but Althea believes that Amari and Chinua "get it completely." "They do not reject it, even though they would like the world to be different . . . and it does not cripple them or make them afraid."

"Different times and different generations" is Althea Powell's repeated refrain as she refers to the racial fluidity that characterizes the shifting cultural landscape and to her efforts to understand the path and choices of her son Amari. Adaptation is a constant adjustment, learning when and how to listen, to ask questions, to not push, to not go toe to toe — calibrations that seesaw between past and present and are always about the child's future. Adaptation is sometimes about staging "deep dialogues" and "tribunals" when tough issues and irresolvable differences have to be confronted directly, when it is time to go to the mat and exert parental authority. Adaptation, for Althea, is about not letting her ego get mixed in — even as her ego, her very self, might deeply desire something for her son that he has not yet (and might never) choose. Adaptation is about knowing the risks that exist for her sons in the world, even as the world has become almost unrecognizable from the one she knew. Althea has learned to protect her child in *his* world.

Surviving

Sometimes the lessons our children teach us are far less subtle than the calibrations and maneuvers that Althea learns as she adapts to her son's zigzag journey. They may, in fact, be dramatic and dangerous lessons in survival, lessons in self-defense, in protecting oneself against rejection, betrayal, and violence. When Juliana Jordan and her husband Jake decided sixteen years ago to adopt three young siblings—who had been horrendously abused by their biological family—from a Russian orphanage, they had to learn to survive their children's violence and assaults, their running away and suicide attempts, their drug and alcohol addictions, their driving-while-drunk violations and incarcerations. Survival meant learning to live with fear, loss, and chronic disappointment, learning to erect protective barriers, learning to go underground and hide out. Juliana has had to survive for her children, who have themselves survived unspeakable trauma. And in learning to survive, she has "grown in humility" and found glimmers of hope in the suffering. After all, as long as her children are alive, there is reason not to give up; the script remains unfinished.

When Juliana Jordan searches for a way to begin talking about something she has learned from her children—Darya, Viktor, and Lev who are twenty-four, twenty-three, and twenty, respectively—she comes up with an "extraordinary recent experience" that sounds completely unremarkable to me. She clearly wants to begin our interview on a high point, with some good news, some promising "sign of possibility." It was Labor Day weekend, and Juliana and her husband Jake's twenty-five- and twenty-three-year-old nieces were moving together into a third-floor apartment in West Philadelphia. When they rented the apartment, they had no idea that their cousin Viktor, Juliana and Jake's older son, whom they had not laid eyes on in at least five years, had a place on the first floor of the same building. But when Viktor made the discovery, he rallied his sister and brother, reached out to his parents, and offered to help with the move. He called his parents and asked, "Can we help our cousins move in?" He suggested that he could use his car, his brother Lev could bring his truck, and Juliana and Jake could help out by renting a U-Haul. "Many hands would make light work," says Juliana casually, barely masking the surprise in her voice.

In fact, Juliana and Jake were stunned — "actually blown away" — by the offer of help; they had never heard any of their three children speak to them kindly, never heard them offer anyone in their family support or help of any kind. In fact, the overwhelming experience of raising their children had been one of being "rejected, threatened, lied to, and abused." "We would not have expected that offer," says Juliana. "This was completely out of character for them. . . . For the first time in the sixteen years since we brought them back from the Russian orphanage, the children seemed generous, warm, participatory, engaging with their family. . . . It was actually delightful . . . so normal." The word "normal" lingers on Juliana's lips as if never in a million years would she have expected to be able to say it, as if "normal" has always seemed incredibly remote and unattainable. And she says it cautiously, as if she doesn't even dare to believe that it is real or sustainable.

Juliana remembers the words of warning from one of the scores of psychiatric specialists that they have consulted with over the years, who have worked with severely traumatized patients suffering, like her three children do, from reactive attachment disorder. The doctor had said that if their children were ever going to accept them, if they were ever going to be able to form even the most tenuous attachment, that it would likely not happen until they were in their thirties. But here they were, all three in their early twenties, doing what had seemed "unthinkable and inconceivable" to Juliana. They were reaching out to their parents and reconnecting with their cousins; they were offering their help.

Even though Juliana definitely felt anxious as they coordinated the plans for the move, and even though she held her breath for most of the day as they packed up the niece's stuff and loaded the U-Haul, everything went off relatively smoothly. No one talked very much; there was no banter back and forth, no laughter, no break hanging out over a pizza, just the steady, somber, efficient movement of boxes and furniture. But it was still an "amazing" day that definitely caused stirrings and questions in Juliana's heart, a "tempered, cautious optimism" that made her feel that her children might be "moving forward slightly," that this might be a significant developmental moment. She offers me the lesson she learned on that extraordinary/ordinary moving day. "As a parent, you always need to keep an open mind. You cannot, and should not, be writing the script in advance."

Juliana wants me to know why her opening story—of cautious hope—is amazing. She knows that I won't really understand its importance unless she gives me the "backdrop of history." Only then will I appreciate its full significance. When Juliana and Jake were told by the Russian agency that they had three perfectly healthy siblings that were being recommended for adoption, they were at first reluctant to move forward because they had actually wanted to adopt two siblings and did not know whether three might be too much to take on. But they were assured that the children were "healthy and happy and deeply bonded with each other; that they had no physical or emotional problems; and that they were in need of a family because both of their parents had suddenly died." And the pictures that the agency sent of the children revealed them to be very small and somewhat malnourished—at seven, six, and three years old—but they otherwise appeared to be quite sweet and bright-eyed. In fact, it turned out that their life before the orphanage had been brutal and horrific and that the adoption agency had lied to Juliana and Jake because they desperately wanted to get rid of the children, who had come to the orphanage traumatized and damaged.

The children had witnessed their biological father's murder at the hands of his alcoholic mother; he bled to death in five-year-old Darya's lap. After the murder of her husband, the children's mother, who was addicted to drugs and alcohol, took up with a "bad Mafia guy" who raped and abused all three of the children. Eventually, the children were removed from the home during a gun battle with police, who came to take them away. They were sent to a triage orphanage, where they were supposed to stay until they were physically healthy enough to be placed in a regular orphanage to await adoption six to twelve months later. Instead, they moved the children through the triage orphanage quickly and put them up for adoption after only a few weeks. When Juliana and Jake visited the orphanage the first time, the children were on their best behavior. They ran into their new parents' arms and squeezed them with hugs. They had been well rehearsed and had been told that if they wanted to have a family and move to America, they would have to be perfectly behaved; they would have to be irresistible. Later, Juliana and Jake would learn that the orphanage desperately wanted to get rid of the three siblings, that they were finding it impossible to keep the other orphans in the facility safe. "Viktor was six and he was sexually assaulting the other children in the orphanage . . . all three of them were psychologically explosive and violent, hitting and hurting the other kids . . . there was bedwetting, biting, self-mutilation."

When Juliana and Jake arrived at the agency to meet Darya, Viktor, and Lev on a sweltering hot summer day, the children were the only ones dressed in long-sleeved shirts and pants; all the other kids were in shorts. And it was only after all of the legal work had been completed and they brought the children back to the apartment where they were staying that they discovered what the clothes cover up was about. "We stripped them down before putting them in the bathtub to soak, and we saw the horrible scars and cuts and bruises all over their bodies." But the physical scars were nowhere near as frightening as the behaviors that got unleashed as soon as they were safely in the arms of their new parents. "They exploded with horrific behavior . . . hitting and biting, ranting and screaming . . . hurling themselves into the walls, having major dissociative meltdowns." Juliana and Jake were terrified as they tried to put out one metaphoric fire after another; as they dealt with the rage and pain they felt at being lied to and duped; as they tried to figure out how they would possibly survive as a family.

As soon as they arrived back in the United States, they made appointments with doctors, experts, therapists, and specialists in every hospital and facility where there were clinicians trained in treating severe trauma in children. Before leaving to pick up the children in Russia, they had hired a Russian-speaking nanny, who could translate for them and teach the children English. As soon as the children were safely on this side of the ocean, they were "more than open" in telling—with the help of the nanny's translation— of the atrocities that they had suffered at the hands of their abusive parents. The tales were almost too terrible to believe, but the level of detail that the children were able to provide and the vividness of their memories, repeated over and over to the doctors and therapists who were trying to help them, made Juliana and Jake know that they were not fabrications, even though some of their stories might have been slightly exaggerated.

The first few months were utter hell, as the parents tried to keep their children safe, protect themselves, and minimize the damage to their property. Outbursts of violence happened several times a day. "They punched holes in the walls, broke windows, climbed to the roof and jumped off . . . they lit fires, tried committing suicide by self-strangulation . . . they chased after us with knives and cleavers. Viktor was the strongest and angriest, perfectly capable of murdering us . . . but all three of them were violent. They were so damaged, so harmed and traumatized." Childproofing the house did not mean "covering the electric sockets or putting gates up on the stairs" as it does in most homes with small children. It meant "making sure that there were no matches lying around and locking up all of the tools and knives.

Juliana tells me that in their early years of parenting their children—when life felt impossibly difficult, frightening, and unsustainable—her husband Jake kept a journal in which he recorded the gory details of everyday life, the daily battles for survival, and the unbearable cycles of hope and hopelessness. Jake often referred to the glimmers of progress against the steady backdrop of despair: "Life's disturbing setbacks and steady victories, its tragedy and teamwork, its unforgettable losses and unexpected blessings." Even as he recorded the unrelenting struggle to keep his family safe, he knew that he would one day want to share their experiences with other parents who are raising severely traumatized children;

and he wanted the stories to have an immediacy and authenticity that would not lie, that would not mute the pain or obscure the suffering. But he also must have believed that there might be some release or catharsis in describing the details unfiltered by retrospection or nostalgia, that writing might be slightly curative, one tiny step toward recovery and healing. He might even uncover some of the hidden strengths that have allowed them to survive.

In one journal entry just months after the children arrived, Jake recounts the brutal bedtime ritual of trying to put the household to sleep . . . the physical takedown of six-year-old Viktor who is screaming at the top of his lungs, flailing around in a rage, knocking down and breaking everything in his path, destroying the living room. Jake holds him down as Viktor uses all of his might and muscle to squirm free, biting and kicking and thrashing. As he holds onto his child prey, Jake feels blood coursing through his mouth. In his fierce effort to subdue his son, he had bitten his lip, and blood is exploding out of his mouth and onto his shirt. When his son finally stops the shrill screaming and falls silent, no longer fighting back or trying to escape, Jake cradles him in his arms and caresses him, rhythmically repeating, in Russian, then English, "Haroshe malchick" (good boy) over and over again until both of their bodies relax and curve into each other, and Viktor, exhausted and spent, falls into a deep sleep. Jake puts a diaper on his limp, sleeping body and carries him to bed. The pitched battle between Jake and Viktor has lasted almost an hour. One down and two to go!

"We began patterning physical touch," says Juliana about those early days when she and Jake tried to contain and soothe the children. They spent endless hours touching and caressing the children's bodies, massaging their backs, swimming and playing with them in the water. They did many of the same things they had done with some of the dogs that they had rescued over the years. "We had fostered abused dogs . . . being with the children was like taming an abused animal. Our role is to repattern their behavior. You wrestle the dog to the ground, keep patting it slowly, you keep saying, you are safe," Juliana says more than once that she is "not exaggerating" when she tells me that she can remember only a couple of times when she or Jake actually yelled at the kids and they never hit them, even though they were often targets of their children's physical and emotional abuse. "All the years, you are trying to model caring and love and respect. You are trying to convey that what happened in the past was not their fault but now they must begin to hold themselves accountable. They must learn to put boundaries around their behavior."

As Juliana describes the brutality and the danger, I begin to picture three small but lethal monsters capable of unspeakable violence. I am, therefore, somewhat surprised when she tells me that when they arrived they were tiny and scrawny looking: "skinny little runts." Although they were seven, six, and three, they actually looked more like they were five, four, and two, and they were physically underdeveloped and unsteady. "They couldn't walk up and down the stairs, couldn't hold a crayon, had never seen a book, and they didn't know how to swing. Darya's vocabulary in Russian was that of a three-year-old, and she was seven!" They were "wildly hungry" all the time. They ate enormous amounts of food. They would each drink a half a gallon of milk every day, and between them they would consume over a dozen eggs. They put away five or six apples each and the same number of bananas every day, and they grew very fast. "The signs of resilience were stunning," remembers Juliana, "but the resilience was all physical; their emotional lives were stunted, lagging far behind their growth spurts."

"It felt like we were raising someone else's children," says Juliana, for the first time visibly tearing up. "Their attachment to us was tenuous . . . it still is tenuous." At almost six feet, Juliana is a lean, handsome, and fit woman dressed in soft colors of tangerine, peach, and gray, her hair a halo of red-orange ringlets, her eyes covered with stylish turquoise glasses. She is energetic, talks easily, and is open and self-reflective, often revealing feelings that are raw and painful. Juliana, whose background is in engineering, has a master's degree in city planning and works as an organizational consultant in start-up companies working on urban design. And even though she presents as a well-organized, energetic, consummately focused professional, her eyes belie her suffering and exhaustion. They seem to convey years of being worn down, violated, and disappointed. In fact, she says that one of the lessons that she is continually learning is how to "sit with and live with the disappointments . . . and how to experience the rejections from her children and not have that become our whole life story."

Over the years, all three of the children have been expelled and thrown out of numerous schools and spent time in residential facilities for severely troubled and traumatized students. They have run away from home and been in jail and on probation numerous times. They have been arrested for using and dealing drugs, driving while intoxicated, for felony and theft, for carrying weapons. Without provocation, they have tortured and injured their parents, punching and pummeling them, pushing and pinning them up against the furniture, chasing them around the house with hammers, knives, and baseball bats. Even though Juliana is strong and knows how to defend herself—she is a black belt in judo—she has often not been able to protect herself against the onslaughts, particularly those inflicted by Viktor, who is the strongest and most aggressive of the three. She tells me that she has been to the emergency room so many times that the nurses there sometimes say, "Oh no, not you again," when she walks through the door. "It is a terrible thing to be afraid of your children," she says slowly as tears spring to her eyes again.

The trouble started in school immediately. Viktor was just six when he arrived, and he started in the first grade at a small, friendly elementary school in Overbrook, where the teachers had been told about his history and had strategized with Juliana about the best ways he might be socialized into the routines of the classroom. Viktor lasted there for less than a week. "He was assaulting the other kids . . . he assaulted his teacher, scratching her face and ripping her dress . . . he even managed to punch out the principal." They decided to move Viktor into kindergarten but soon realized that he needed hospitalization: there was no way to keep him contained, no way to keep the other children safe. "He was even sexually assaulting his sister and brother," says Juliana about one of the many reasons why Viktor had to be removed from the house.

Everything seemed to fall apart for Darya when she was in sixth grade. She would come home from school each day and have two hours of terrible tantrums, going into her room, shutting the door, and screaming at the top of her lungs until she had totally exhausted herself. She had always had trouble making friends, always had provoked physical fights with her classmates, but now she was playing hooky, sneaking off from school, shoplifting, and coming home drunk. After being expelled from school, her behavior deteriorated further. "She was 'sexting' all the time, putting herself on the Internet for sale. She would sneak out at two in the morning and be picked up drunk—and drugged—by the police . . . Darya's relationship to us was essentially 'fuck you' . . . everything was hostile." Finally, it was clear that they could no longer keep her at home, and she was sent off to the first of the many residential schools that she would attend over the years.

"Lev blew apart in eighth grade and got into the same kind of violence and trouble as his older siblings." The details of his journey were slightly different from Viktor and Darya, but the terrifying behavioral cycle was deeply familiar to his parents, and he, too, ended up going to a residential school. "They are all deeply troubled people," says Juliana in summary and with understatement. "And we are exhausted and burnt out . . . they are very violent and we remain frightened."

When I ask Juliana how she and Jake were able to bear the constant violence and violation over the years, she surprises me by saying that they learned a lot about themselves, their values, and their commitment to building a family through the adoption process. In the ten years that they were married before children, Juliana had had five miscarriages. They had spent years going to fertility specialists. Juliana had endured abdominal surgeries and all manner of invasive procedures, until they finally got worn down and decided to try to adopt children. Juliana says longingly, "I was desperate to have children that I would love and adore, but they did not have to be my biological heirs." By the time they proceeded with the adoption, they were in their early forties, and Juliana had been briefly married before her union with Jake. They were advised that if they were willing to adopt internationally and if they were open to raising older children, they would have the best chance of becoming parents.

Although the adoption process—with its long and detailed questionnaires, essay writing, social worker interviews, and home visits—at first felt overwhelming to them, they turned what might have been an intrusive ordeal into an opportunity for self-exploration. "The home study for the adoption raised up questions for us like . . . why do you want to raise children? We had to do a lot of reflection and explication. We had to think really long and hard, past the rose-colored glasses and idealism. Jake and I learned a lot about each other in the process, and our commitment to making a family was cemented." In the years since they completed that grueling adoption process, they have often found themselves referring back to the conversations that got sparked between them and to the promises they made to each other that they would "always take the high road," "that they would always try to be the best human beings that they could be."

But even those commitments to "taking the high road" were hard to sustain when they were faced with their children's violations on the night after Christmas three years ago. All three children—then twenty-two, twenty-one, and eighteen—were home with them for a few days. Juliana's sister and her grown daughters were also there for the holiday. The kids had been smoking dope and drinking earlier in the evening, and when Viktor walked in the door, he began screaming at Juliana and then hauled off and hit her in the face. Before Lev could pile on, Jake grabbed him and pinned him to the wall. Juliana managed to pull away from Viktor's pummeling and ran outside and called 911. The police arrived a few minutes later and found Viktor and Lev in a struggle with Jake. When the officers asked what was going on, the boys claimed that their father had assaulted them. Jake was arrested and taken away in the back of the police car. "It was horrible. Really unbelievable!" says Juliana angrily. "Later the kids recanted but it was too little, too late. . . . We had to hire a lawyer who finally got Jake acquitted, but the whole thing derailed Jake's career for at least a year."

The holiday havoc was the breaking point. "We stepped back. We were out of ideas. We didn't know what else we could do. We were really at a point of failure. We had completely run out of money. We had spent $1.7 million trying to take care of the children . . . the residential schools that they attended, and were thrown out of, cost $100,000 a year, and there were doctors' bills and therapy. We were completely broke and in debt. We had to sell our house and move into a small apartment just big enough for the two of us. We were ruined." Juliana seems to be looking through me — her voice hoarse and weepy — as she relives this painful time of loss and defeat.

"Stepping back," meant that they would try and take themselves out of harm's way; that they would not let the kids know where they lived; and that they would not respond to their children's cries for help. Viktor was by then back in jail, and they refused to pay the bail. Darya was living in a car with her drug dealer boyfriend. Within months, however, Viktor was out of jail, and all three kids were on probation, which required that they do random drug testing and live under tight constraints. "For the first time, all three kids had to get clean and sober. Without us there to rescue them, they somehow had to do it on their own."

Juliana stops abruptly and slams her fists down on the table, a gesture that seems to say, "Enough is enough." After a few moments, her face brightens slightly as she says, "Fast forward three years." "All three — if they are telling the truth — claim that they are now finished with their probation and that they are clean and sober." She repeats, "*If* they are telling the truth"; doubt and suspicion are written all over her face. But the behaviors she sees in her children are, she has to admit, promising. "They all have gotten jobs. They all have stable relationships. The boys have bought cars and gotten drivers licenses, and they seem to be in touch with one another. When I send them a birthday card or small gift for their birthdays, they do not send it back. Slowly they are reaching out to us . . . every few months, they might call and ask us to get together for dinner. A few weeks ago we met them at a Chinese restaurant in West Philadelphia."

Even though all three children seem to be in a better place —

more stable, more responsible and responsive—Juliana and Jake keep a wary distance. They still feel the need to protect themselves. "You still cannot know where I live," she says to me with great force as if she is lecturing her children, "We don't trust you. You are still hanging out with the wrong kind of people." When I ask her whether she loves her children after all of this terror and trauma, her voice softens to almost a whisper. "I don't feel love for them. I feel responsible for them. Love is not always something you feel. But love is something you do. It is my job to be relentlessly kind and interact in a way that makes me feel good about myself."

I now understand why the Labor Day move was such a momentous occasion; why what might have appeared to be a fairly ordinary family collaboration was actually a huge breakthrough; why the children's reaching out to them—offering to help—was a "stunning departure" from all that had gone before; and why the big lesson that Juliana learned from that weekend was that "you can't write the script in advance." Certainly, there is reason for Juliana and Jake to remain wary and self-protective, but this is also a moment when they can—perhaps for the first time—let themselves "see change, maybe even hope." Recently Viktor said something that Juliana never expected to hear. He confessed to his mother as she was climbing into the car after their Chinese dinner, "I was really a jerk, wasn't I? We were really hard on you." Says Juliana with great certainty, as she redraws the boundaries, "I believe that there is no such thing as a person who can't be saved. But it is not about loving them through it. It is about keeping them safe."

The experience, says Juliana over and over again, has taught them humility. "Being a parent of severely traumatized children is a humbling experience. It teaches you how little you can truly command what you want and how little control you actually have. It is not—nor can it ever be—the same thing as a growing, fully developed relationship with one's children, where there is trust and communication. We have learned lessons about powerlessness and helplessness in our role as parents, how little power we have to make others do something that they do not want to do. It is truly humbling."

Juliana is quiet for a long time before she turns to a final reflection on love and loss and comments on the ways in which we all have to absorb disappointments in our lives. "I wanted to have kids that I adored. I wanted to like my kids. We did not get that. We got something else. They are emotionally dangerous people and we have to be very careful. But I can live with that loss. Everyone does. After all, just in the process of aging, there is loss. Doing the active work of being alive involves being disappointed, delighted, loving, and grieving."

Juliana truly believes that what she and Jake have gone through with their children—however tumultuous and horrendous, however dangerous and painful—is just a "louder, bigger version" of what other families endure. She mentions the daughter of her husband's twin brother, who went through "lots of horrible acting out" during her adolescence, and her own sister's daughter who has a mood disorder that has finally been helped by drugs and therapy. Everyone has something. "It is a matter of degrees. No one has a perfect life," says Juliana. "We actually have more in common with other parents and other families. We are actually more compassionate because of this."

As she and Jake face the future, there is another reason to "believe and have faith." As long as there is still time, there is reason for hope. As long as the story is unfinished, there is a chance for redemption. "This is a long way from being over," says Juliana with a voice that is at once weary and determined. She tells me that Jake attends a twelve-step program for parents of children with drug and alcohol addictions and that just last month one of the children of a mother in the program overdosed and died. "But we, at least, have more chapters to go. Our children may turn out to be remarkable people with boring, unremarkable lives . . . or they may be back in jail tomorrow."

By surviving, Juliana Jordan traveled the closest possible road to her children's lives. She did not give birth to them, but she gave them her body. Although dispirited and exhausted, she gave them all her strength. Although she yearned to have children that she could love and adore, Juliana had to grow into a love redefined as responsibility, perseverance, and relentless kindness for her children. In a way, it is a triumph that the children are alive, that there is a glimpse — however fleeting — of them being different. Survival can seem like a very small or insignificant accomplishment, especially when the children's improvement is so tenuous and cannot be trusted to continue. But, at the same time, survival is everything. It is life itself. It is to exist, to *be* in the world. As Juliana says, survival is "doing the active work of being alive."

* 3 *

Intimacy

All morning as we talk inside the room
round the table, our bodies are as warm
with light and shade, our voices are like a web
hung in the air between us, stitching and
unstitching in the telling and the hearing,
the taking issue with, concord and discord,
every one of us around the table

"THE CONVERSATION," ALAN SHAPIRO[1]

IN THIS VERSE, poet Alan Shapiro captures the feeling of a growing intimacy among the people around the table, the light and the
shadows, the voices and the silences, the efforts to speak and be
heard, the movement through musings and misunderstandings. We
feel the familiarity of the kitchen scene on any ordinary day, and
we see the bodies bent forward, searching for the words, wanting
to connect and know one another deeply, getting ever closer to discovering their essential, innermost beings. Shapiro captures the ongoing work of intimacy—to know and to be known—and the way
it deepens through the "stitching and unstitching" of the voices.

In the narratives that follow we hear parents talk about how their
relationships with their almost-grown children taught them lessons
on intimacy; lessons on the tenderness and treacherousness—the
"concord and the discord"—that must be endured and enjoyed as
parent and child draw closer; lessons about the ever-changing, dynamic process of calculating closeness and distance; lessons about
balancing connection and restraint. The contours and depth of
intimacy change as children grow, as they move towards indepen-

dence, and as they become their own persons. Paradoxically, the distance creates the space for a deeper intimacy to develop.

It seems to me that intimacy always rests on a growing trust and respect; it is the opposite of control over the other person. The skin-to-skin attachment that mothers have with their babies, the mother's primal protectiveness that controls and limits, and the ways in which mothers see their own reflection in their babies' eyes and smiles all give way, over time, to an intimacy that is partly defined by distance and detachment, by an autonomy that gives the growing child the space to be different, to know herself. As children emerge into young adults and beg for—even demand—their parents' respect, they are, I believe, seeking to be separate enough to make way for a new, revised closeness. The image of intimacy shifts from the skin-to-skin attachment of mothers with their babies to one where the mother and child sit face-to-face, a posture where each is confronted with the other's distinct perspective and individuality. In my book *Respect: An Exploration* (1999), I focus on respect as an essential ingredient in any growing and deepening relationship, and I shape a new view of respect that makes room for intimacy and distance to grow between parents and their children.[2]

Usually respect is seen as involving some sort of debt due people because of their attained or inherent position, their age, gender, class, race, professional status, or accomplishments. Whether defined by the rules of law or the habits of culture, respect often implies required expressions of esteem, approbation, or submission. By contrast, I focus on the ways that respect creates symmetry, trust, and connection in all kinds of relationships, even those, such as parent and child, teacher and student, doctor and patient, which are commonly seen as unequal. Rather than looking for respect as a given in certain relationships, I am interested in watching it develop over time. I see it not only as an expression of circumstance, history, temperament, and culture, rooted in rituals and habits, but also arising from efforts to break with routine and imagine other ways of giving and receiving trust and, in so doing, creating relationships among equals. I am, therefore, interested in how people work to challenge and dismantle hierarchies, rather than with how they reinforce and reify them. Rather than the old-fashioned language usually attached to respect—inhibition, constraint, and dutiful compliance—I listen for the voices of challenge, desire, and commitment that carve out spaces for intimacy to grow.

In this chapter, we see young adult daughters teaching the lessons of intimacy, demanding respect, claiming space, and making themselves visible; and we see their mothers—often with great difficulty—learning to let go of their control, learning to see their children with greater clarity and subtlety, and learning to follow their lead. Two of the stories are about first-generation immigrant parents who strive to build an environment at home that will protect their children from what they see as the contaminating, materialistic influences of their children's existence in middle-class America. Their efforts to contain, rein in, and control distort the intimacy and connection that they want with their children. They are challenged to see their children as separate people navigating their own journeys. A third story describes the contestations over intimacy of a second-generation immigrant mother who wants to raise her daughter very differently from the ways in which she was raised. She is intentional in erasing the inheritance of authoritarianism and dominance that characterized her Polish mother's parenting, and she is determined to forge a new kind of relationship with her daughter that opens the way for intimacy and love.

It is not surprising that the narratives of immigrant parents seeking authority over, and closeness to, their children are ripe with struggle. After all, when immigrant families arrive, it is the children who acclimate to the new environment most quickly, who tend to take the lead in helping to acculturate their parents, who become their parents' teachers and guides. The relatively more rapid insertion of immigrant children into their new society—via school and peer groups—allows for a role reversal, where the parents rely on their children for translation of both language and culture. The children engage in the daily transactional tasks of life as well as the more nuanced work of cultural negotiation for the sake of their parents, leading the way in their families' lives. For example the term "language broker" has been coined to describe the role children play as interpreters of their parents.[3] A recent study by Corona, Stevens, and Halfond indicated that parents have both positive and negative feelings about this. On the one hand, their children interpreting for them was seen as a "team effort" for the family, while on the other hand, parents also reported feeling "uncomfortable, ashamed, and embarrassed that their children had to translate for them and these feelings were often associated with their desire to do things on their own."[4]

Children, however, are not limited to the role of translator, or literal interpreter, for their parents. In the act of translation, immigrant children can also support their parents as learners and help them develop a different view of themselves. This was the finding of a study about one adult immigrant woman's English-language acquisition. The author found that "it was not a surprise that Maria's 14-year-old daughter Rosa's role was important, given her native/native-like proficiency and her mother's limited English proficiency, but what was particularly illuminating was the exact nature of that role. Rather than being relegated to a simple translator or language tutor, Rosa helped her mother transform her identity from one who sees her limited proficiency as a disability and cause for marginalization to one who sees herself as a dignified learner worthy of admiration."[5]

In the realm of immigrant memoirs and novels, it is perhaps inevitable that the perspective of the writer is usually that of the child—the child born to immigrant parents or who has migrated at a young age and grown up in the new country. These memoirs typically trace the story of a child growing up in two cultures, living up to and shattering parents' expectations, searching for home, and developing an identity that is both dual and whole. The relationships these authors have with their parents are loving, contentious, and fierce—perhaps symbolic of the meeting of different values, cultures, and identities that is the experience of migration, settling, assimilation, and acculturation.

Paule Marshall's classic *Brown Girl Brownstones*—a novel that barely masks the autobiography of its author—is the fiercely told story of Barbadian immigrants striving to surmount poverty and racism in Brooklyn during the Depression and World War II and to make their new country home.[6] At the narrative's center is a searing and powerful account of the caustic and passionate relationship, and clash of temperaments, generations, and cultures, between Selina Boyce, the novel's heroine, and her domineering, hard-driving mother Silla, a relationship filled with noxious rage and unrelenting guilt as well as profound connection. So complex are Selina's feelings for Silla that she constantly vacillates between loving awe and a violent angry distrust. The story captures Selina's fight for survival, her brave efforts to break away from the powerful orbit of "the mother" and find herself and her way in the world. All the while, Silla resists her daughter's teachings, refusing to overturn the old-country parent-child authority and hierarchy, refusing to make way for the equality and trust that might lead to intimacy. Other immigrant memoirs echo these struggles of separation and individuation. They tell of the child's strained efforts to escape the entanglements of the mother source; of the child begging for space and the chance to be heard; of the child trying to carve out a more equal relationship with the mother that will allow for intimacy between them.

While the focus of these memoirs and novels is mainly on the interior life of the immigrant child—inseparable as it is from the contexts of family, community, and the larger society—we do begin to recognize how immigrant children also see their parents as individuals with experiences of their own, as people who they want to understand. It seems that this effort, in emerging adulthood, stems from the intergenerational conflicts and pressures experienced in childhood, when the gap between immigrant parents and their quickly assimilating children expanded. For example, in his memoir *Little Failure*, Gary Shteyngart portrays his parents' frustration with his inability to fulfill their dream of an "ideal" American life, their naïveté and their tight, fearful controlling ways.[7] After publishing two novels that draw heavily on his childhood, Shteyngart comes to see his parents as people, not just as embodiments of repression and control. His parents' experience finds expression in his voice: "And now I've published a book that mocks gently, but sometimes not so gently, a set of parents that are not entirely dissimilar to my own. What does that feel like for them? What does it feel like to be unable to respond in the language with which that mockery is issued? My father's favorite saying to me. 'Maybe after I die, you will come pee on my grave.' It is supposed to be sarcastic, but what he's really saying is 'Don't let me go.' How can I not hear the pain in that?"[8] Junot Díaz also writes about the pain that travels between immigrant parents and their children, even as the children begin to understand—or at least recognize—their parents as individuals in the world, as people navigating their own journeys. From the perspective of an adolescent girl in his novel, *The Brief Wondrous Life of Oscar Wao*, Díaz writes:

> The last time she tried to whale on me it was because of my hair, but instead of cringing and running, I punched her hand. It was a reflex more than anything, but once it happened I knew I couldn't take it back, not ever, and so I kept my hand clenched, waiting for whatever came next. Things had been bad between us all year. How could they not have been? She was my Old World Dominican mother and I was her only daughter, the one she had raised up herself with the help of nobody, which meant it was her duty to keep me crushed under her heel.[9]

The interior landscapes of immigrant parents' lives are written with deep intimacy by their children, who inherit a special and complex mixture of responsibilities; the children are charged with acculturating their reluctant and ambivalent elders, reaching across generational divides, seeking to empathize with—and understand—the old world ways even as they discover their voices and strike out on their own. The intimacy and closeness that parents and children seek will only come when the children fight for, and the parents yield, the spaces in between. In this chapter, the mothers' voices speak about the delicate—and not so delicate—calculations they make as they give distance and seek closeness with their children, as they weather the "concord and discord" and learn new ways of being intimate.

Expanding Horizons

Eva Galanis, a first-generation immigrant from Greece, works hard to protect her twin daughters from what she regards as the distractions, threats, and dangers of their American lives. She wants to shield them from the vacuous materialism, the superficiality and consumerism of fast foods and shopping malls, television and sleepovers. She wants to guard their bodies and minds from the cultural trivia and garbage that might seep in. By the time her girls reach adolescence, they are chafing at her anxious overprotectiveness; they are resisting her efforts to control them. Eva recognizes in their resistance feelings that she once had as a girl when her own parents wanted to control her life by shutting out the world around them. But the generational echoes—of her resenting her own parents' dominance and inhibitions—don't seem to be strong enough to change her pattern of rigidity and control with her twins. Her daughters—taking turns and acting strategically—push back against their mother to create a bigger space for themselves; and as they do, they expand the horizons of Eva's mothering and make room for a real intimacy.

Even her home—at first glance—feels like another country; Eva Galanis has intentionally and successfully captured the texture and tones, the passion and music, and the light and culture of her native Greece. The house has walls of glass that let the afternoon sun shine through; there are outside decks everywhere that lead to lovely gardens and sculptures; and artifacts, paintings, and weavings echo with Mediterranean colors and vistas. But it is in the huge kitchen—the heart of her home—where you feel completely transported to Greece. "Everything here," Eva says spreading her arms wide, "comes from Greece": the stone counters, the wood of the cabinetry, the large sinks, the long kitchen table covered with Greek tiles, placemats, and pottery, the surfaces everywhere strewn with flat blue stones from the sea, and the shelves filled with family photos from their summers spent on the island of Symi. Everything is Greek, that is, except the handsome cobalt blue eight-burner stove that comes from Italy. Food is a constant reference in Eva's stories—food that stands for culture and communion, gatherings and conversation, tastes and textures, family history, maternal love, and emotional nourishment. And this is the place where she creates her edible masterpieces, where she most powerfully clings to and celebrates her Greek roots.

Eva is warm and captivating, large and lovely in her long black jumper, mane of black hair, big dangling earrings and clanging silver bracelets from India. She greets me at the door with a big hug and kisses me on both cheeks. With a degree in city planning from the University of California, Berkeley, she is the president of a community development company that designs public spaces for museums, town squares, city neighborhoods, universities, and parks. Her work includes hiring and managing a team—of architects, contractors, traffic specialists, environmentalists, landscapers—for each project but also requires that she spend a good deal of time meeting with city officials and politicians and convening focus groups from the communities who come together to let the designers know their neighborhood needs, concerns, and desires. Clearly, Eva enjoys her work—the creative, technical, and design dimensions—but she seems to really relish the storytelling that is at the core of her outreach to communities. When she gathers focus groups together to hear their voices, it is "all about listening to their life stories," about weaving together a "tapestry of their yearnings." Sometimes, people will come back a second or third time, bringing their photographs of their parents, grandparents, and children, wanting to put a personal—and often cultural—face on their urban landscapes, wanting to imagine a neighborhood that feels more like home.

We sit across the table in Eva's kitchen sipping our coffee, as she eagerly and hungrily leans into the conversation. She closes her eyes in full concentration, as she listens to my opening words about the work, and responds immediately, "I have a flurry of thoughts as you speak . . . like a swarm of butterflies landing." And we are off!

Eva's twin daughters—Athene and Isidora—at twenty-two are both graduating from college this spring, Athene from the University of Chicago and Isidora from the California Institute of Technology. Eva shows me a photo of the girls at about five years old, standing in the bright sun, on either side of a huge Greek urn in frilly cotton dresses. As I comment on their differences, Eva says that the twins are "very fraternal." Athene is shorter with Eva's darker features, and Isidora is taller with the lighter complexion of her father Dimitris. "But inside they are a mixture of both parents," says Eva with a laugh.

"I have had a repetitive dream all my life." says Eva as a way of "grounding" herself and letting the "butterflies land." In the dream, which has been returning since childhood, Eva would visit her grandmother's attic, and each time she spotted an object stored there, she would ask her grandmother to tell its story. She would listen intently, learning, with each story, something more about herself, feeling more at home. There the dream ends, and it is far from the reality that Eva has experienced. In fact, her parents, survivors of World War II, both lost their own parents during the war. She never knew either of her grandmothers, never actually searched out precious objects in their attics. Instead, she had parents—both Greek—who lived all over the world, making their home in Egypt, Greece, Algeria, and the United States, traveling light, caring little for the accumulation of objects like the ones Eva saw in her dreams. "As a reaction," says Eva, again spreading her arms expansively, "I have always lived in this house with lots of objects."

Eva and her husband Dimitris—a theoretical physics professor at the California Institute of Technology who grew up in Greece and came to the United Sates for graduate school—moved to their house filled with beautiful objects just after their twin babies were born. They had been living as graduate students in a small apartment in Berkeley and wanted a place with more space, light, and privacy, with doors that would lead out to sunny gardens, and with a good school system for when the girls got older. Every summer they would leave California and travel home to Greece, a pilgrimage that became a necessary routine for their "immigrant survival." And at summer's end, they would bring back more objects with stories of Greece attached to them.

When the girls were about six, Eva and Dimitris took sabbaticals from their work, and they all moved for nine months to the large rocky island of Crete, where they stayed in a small village by the sea. Says Eva in a typical reference to the topology, "The village had tumbled down to the sea . . . agriculture had been abandoned as tourism took hold by the seaside." Each morning the girls would make the steep trek up to the top of the mountain to the one-room schoolhouse on the island, the only place that had not tumbled down to the sea. After their time in Crete, they decided that they would look for a second home in Greece, where they would be able to spend three months each summer with the girls. After a few years of searching, they found a small, charming place on the island of Symi, amazingly right across the path from Eva's mother-in-law. "That way," she laughs, "I could send her home anytime . . . not have to drive her clear across the island when I wanted her to leave. It all works out beautifully."

Symi is a tiny remote island where the "festivals are not for the tourists but for the locals." "It reminds us of our childhoods," says Eva tearing up. There are no cars there except on the roads circling the periphery. Otherwise there are medieval paths you walk in the interior of the island. If you want a loaf of bread, you put on your sneakers and walk the couple of miles to the bakery that might be closed when you get there, or maybe all out of the bread that you want. "What is hard here is easy there and vice versa," says Eva about the welcome change and counterpoint that Symi offers to their lives. "I put my heart into our home in Symi. I always seem to forget that I am going to leave, and it comes as a harsh shock at the end of every summer."

But Eva wants me to know, most of all, that their decision to make a home there was mostly driven by their wish, as parents, to give their girls a rural Greek "simple village experience." "We wanted so much to share with the girls this precious reality, and we ended up making choices that enriched *our* lives." She expresses a theme that continues to come up during the interview: in seeking to broaden and enrich the experiences of their children, she and Dimitris have learned what they value and in turn stretched their own horizons. And these lessons are often related to navigating the cultural boundaries and contrasts between their Greek and American realities, hanging onto their Greek roots and rituals at the same time as they accommodate to—and thrive in the midst of—the realities of their life in the United States. Eva repeats what is probably an ongoing litany that appreciates the balance of these two realities. "What is hard there is easy here, and vice versa."

Language is an important barometer of their Greek-American realities. Since the girls learned to talk, the language at home—in both homes—has always been Greek. There have been short phases—during their early adolescence—when the girls insisted upon speaking English; but Eva always responded "in Greek to their English." "Communication is my priority," she says about not spending "a bunch of energy" trying to get them to only use Greek at home. Of course, when they are all in Symi it is different. "Now during the summer, the girls speak Greek with each other, but after they return, by October or November they are back to speaking English to each other."

Eva can count the stone steps—768—that she descends when they walk down to the beach at noon each day from their small house in Symi. Despite her sense of being truly at home on the island, the summer routine always makes her aware of how different she is from the local folks, particularly in the way she mothers her children. She immediately thinks of the hard-working local woman who runs the boat taxi and has twins the same age as Athene and Isidora. When they were small, Eva would bring the girls down to the boat all decked out in their life jackets. As they got close to the water, she would insist that they hold her hands and walk slowly and carefully. "With each step the girls were picking up my anxiety," Eva recalls with a smile. The boat lady's twins would ride along with their mother for the whole day, often napping on the floor of the small craft in the hot sun, rarely eating a snack, and never protected by life jackets.

One day Eva invited the boat lady's twins to join them on the beach for the afternoon. She actually felt sorry for the girls who had nothing to do on the boat all day long. The boat lady immediately accepted her offer, glad to be rid of her girls for a few hours, but seemingly unconcerned about where they would be going, what they would be doing, or when they would return. When Eva asked her where she should return the girls, the boat lady said simply, "Just leave them here," "What do you mean here?" asked Eva, not trusting a plan that was so vague, unclear about whether their mother would be there to collect them. "Just here," said the boat lady impatiently in response to Eva's persistent questioning. When Eva brought the girls back, their mother and the boat were nowhere in sight. She waited a while, but no one appeared. Reluctantly—at her own twins' urging—she left the children alone by the boat dock. But before she and her girls mounted the steps up the steep hill, she looked back to see the island girls walking along a path away from the water, and she decided to follow them home, the whole time clinging to her own daughters' hands. She did not want to be responsible for their losing their way; so she and her daughters tracked the island girls until they saw them disappear into a tiny stone house.

This is one of many stories that Eva tells to underscore the contrasts between life on Symi and life in suburban California. The former always feels less cautious, scripted, and protected; the latter feels circumscribed by anxiety, hovering, and overprotectiveness. But she is not only drawing the cultural contrasts—she is also referring to the "almost-exaggerated" way that she has mothered her girls, wanting to make sure that her girls were protected from all things dangerous or toxic. In fact, when they were born, Eva immediately put a hold on her big career, closing down her office and staying home with the young infants. "I wanted to be there to screen all inputs . . . to control all of the orifices, everything coming into their mouths, ears, and eyes . . . to guard against anything that might harm or injure them or distort their experience of the world." She knows she sounds "crazily overprotective." She read every book to them in Greek "no matter what the language was that it was written in." She cooked everything they ate from scratch and gave them foods from home that were tasty and healthy, that simmered with the textures and aromas of the Mediterranean. The overprotective efforts that began during her children's infancy have over the years been resisted and challenged by her daughters and have been the source of much of her "stretching and learning."

She reaches for a "tiny example" of the ways in which Athene and Isidora have taught her about the realities of life in Symi and in the United States; they have been closer to the "edges of both cultures," and they have challenged Eva to give up some of her controlling ways. A few years ago, the boat lady had another set of twins, and Eva wanted to bring small gifts from the United States to the older girls when they arrived that summer. She went to T.J.Maxx and found what she thought were the perfect trinkets: pretty bath soaps placed in pretend plastic ice cream cones. She remembers, "My daughters scolded me . . . they said these were absurd gifts for a poor island family where there were five children and only one small bathroom. This would feel like a kind of mockery of their lives where no one had time to luxuriate in a bathtub . . . where there were no bathtubs, only one outside shower." Athene and Isidora were reading the local culture, seeing what their mother couldn't see, begging her not to make an offering that would seem disrespectful.

By contrast, Eva was "getting the opposite at home." At home, in their sprawling suburban house, Eva and Dimitris had insisted that the girls share a bedroom. When she was growing up, Eva and her younger sister had always shared a room for sleeping, and her parents never allowed them to close the door. She had always felt as if the sleeping arrangement had made them much closer as sisters: joined at the hip, finishing each other's sentences. But despite their parents' insistence, Isidora and Athene kept pushing for separate rooms like their friends had and kept closing their doors for privacy. This, they said, was the way you were supposed to live in the United States. Finally, Eva and Dimitris relented, and their daughters moved into separate bedrooms and filled them with all their stuff. Eva explains, "So the girls brought me closer into the cultural realities of both places. I was constantly being put in my place . . . those were big moments of struggle and learning for me."

As she listened and learned from her children, Eva was being

forced to reckon with the generational echoes from her own upbringing where — when they lived briefly in the United States — her
parents practiced a kind of separateness from their cultural surrounds, where her parents tried their best to "control the orifices"
of Eva and her sister. "When my family was here in the U.S.," Eva
recalls with what seems like a mixture of sadness and gratefulness,
"we lived in a very separate, protected reality." "My father, a Greek
Jew, was a psychiatrist and my mother, a dentist, was from a Greek
Orthodox leftist family. They both had to flee the country after the
war. My father was very nostalgic for Greece; my mother was more
ambivalent about being either here or there. . . . My father, in particular, never wanted to spend money on material things. He was
an emotionally sophisticated man who loved the simple, grounded
pleasures of watching a beautiful sunset or hearing a bird's song . . .
he was attuned to the textures and senses of his environment and
so much of U.S. culture felt like an abomination. My parents were
both adamant about having no TV and protecting us from the con-
taminations of pop culture. We would sing Greek political songs
together, and after dinner we would dance to Greek music . . . they
did not want us to experience a dilution of that world they were
creating."

Eva remembers, for example, her parents refusing all of her requests to have friends come to their home for sleepovers. "Why
would anyone want strangers sleeping in their beds? Going to
someone else's house overnight was strictly forbidden. How could
they trust people they didn't know? How could they know that
other families would protect their girls, and what about the fathers
and the brothers, what might they do?" Eva remembers all the
ways that she tried to hide her knowledge of the "outside world"
from her parents, surreptitiously doing things — "nothing serious
or earth shaking" — that were forbidden at home. And she sees how
her efforts to shield her own girls from the parts of the American
culture that she finds shallow or vulgar, are a "slight dilution" of the
cloistered life she lived with her own parents. "Through my children I have learned much more about what is happening in the
mainstream," she says. "They have brought me closer to the world

around me, and seeing their world has made me reevaluate what my parents were trying to protect me from."

It was Athene, at fourteen, who fought hardest to get her parents to buy a television, and then fought harder to be allowed to watch it. And it was Isidora who fought to get her parents to allow sleepovers. "My daughters were much tougher fighters than I was with my parents, who were much more authoritarian and immovable than I was." Eva finally gave in to Athene's aggressive pushing by applying strict conditions for the television's use. It could not be placed in the living room, because "that is where the family gathers to be with one another"; and the girls were only allowed to watch it for three hours a week. "We made a matrix and schedule which Athene had to fill out and sign at the end of every week," recalls Eva of the elaborate negotiations. "She could earn more hours if she did certain things, like helping me cook or reading something to me in Greek."

But even with permission granted, Eva could not help questioning her daughter about why she was so into TV. She remembers asking Athene, "Why do you want to watch people doing things you can do yourself?" Her daughter responded with her own question. "What if what they are doing is something I can't do?" For the first time, Eva sat down and watched the rest of the show with her and discovered that the people in the sitcom were ordering takeout, and the food was being delivered to their house — something that was never an option at Eva's house where every meal was home cooked and served around the dining room table. "Here was this guy named Seth Cohen," says Eva laughing about the fact that she still remembers this character's name from The O.C., "who always ordered Chinese takeout."

A few days later, Eva had the idea of giving Athene a "special, surprise treat" — a small effort to show that she "had been heard" — and she did something she had never done before. She ordered Chinese takeout for dinner, and when it arrived she dumped out the cardboard containers and put the food on large ceramic Greek platters. When Athene came to the table, she announced her disapproval. "You are supposed to put the containers on the table.

That is how you do takeout!" But even as she chastised her mother, Athene knew that Eva would never in a million years put cardboard containers on the table. Eva had—just this once—given in to her daughter's request that they order out like Seth Cohen, that they dine like the other American families she knew, but it was taking it "much too far to even think of something as obscene as eating out of containers."

"Food is a stand-in for culture," says Eva about the artistry, memories, and communal act of cooking and serving her friends and family. She draws the daily scene. You cook, enjoying the aroma, texture, and taste of the food; you sit around the table and talk; you do the dishes and scrub the counter clean. This is the "most delicious and meaningful invisible work." It reminds Eva of an old Greek saying about embroidery that refers to both the preparation of food and the raising of children. "Children are like embroidery . . . the top side you could have two that look the same . . . but you turn it over, and you see all the amazing, complex work that goes into it, every pattern unique." More than anything else food—and the artistic and soulful preparation of it—keeps them "rooted in Greek traditions." Sometimes Isidora says what everyone in the family feels. "We don't even know how to talk about so much of the food we eat and love in English."

There is one story that Eva lingers on longer than any others, a story so ordinary in its contours and yet so memorable in revealing how she has learned so much—through the teachings of her children—in the "bicultural spaces" in her life. She remembers one weekend when the girls were sixteen, during a stretch of several weeks when she had been very consumed by her work, and when Dimitris had been off traveling, when she decided that the three of them would have a "special Sunday" together. A few days before the special day, Eva began to concoct a plan that included many of the things she loved doing with her daughters. They would go to a museum, have lunch at a wonderful place by the water, maybe look for dresses at one of their favorite funky shops in town. Afterwards, they would return home and cook a delicious dinner altogether.

She had even found a new crafts museum that had a handbag exhibit that she knew the girls would enjoy.

Even as Eva tells about imagining and anticipating the special day in her mind, she recognizes, "of course, this was my ideal day, not theirs." When the Sunday morning rolled around, the girls immediately asked whether they could drop by the mall first before proceeding on with the rest of the day. "I don't want to take them to the mall," says Eva switching to the present tense, with an intensity that she still feels years later. "I feel hurt by their request. . . . I feel angry and inadequate as their mother." She lingers on the word "inadequate" and I ask her why that is the primary feeling she had. "I ask myself, how come I have not been able to give them the strength to overcome this peer pressure to go to the mall? What could I have done to be a better mother who would support them in making a better, healthier choice?" Even with all of those strong feelings rumbling underneath, Eva delivered them to the mall and pretended that she was fine with it. She knew in her heart that the "mall was their town square," a place to gather and hang out with their friends. They rarely shopped there. They only went there to see and be seen, to meet and greet, "to waste time."

When Eva went to pick them up several hours later, she was "acutely feeling the pain" of having been deprived of her special day with her daughters. After delivering their friends back to their homes, the three of them drove along in silence, the girls aware of their mother's disappointment and barely masked rage. Athene, who was sitting in the front next to Eva, turned on the radio, and the loud hip-hop beats cut through the silence—more evidence of the ways in which the girls were getting completely swept up in the American "materialism and superficiality." "I tell her turn the radio off. Now I am screaming at the top of my lungs. I've completely lost it. . . . I tell them okay, from now on, you can watch TV every day and go to the mall every weekend, and eat junk food if you like." Her screaming out of control suddenly makes her feel "like a child in this encounter," especially when Athene shoots back with a "more mature" question. "Well then, why did you say that it was fine that we go to the mall? If you felt that strongly, you should have told us." Eva is aware of her daughter "holding her ground and sounding more grown up" than she herself feels as she responds, "You must have known that I was upset, and it is up to you to apologize." During this heated exchange between Athene and Eva, Isidora says nothing. When they arrive home, everyone silently retreats to the bedrooms. Doors slam as Eva tries to get in the last word of high-pitched screaming. "I give up," she howls, "Do whatever you want to do with your lives." She feels depleted and done.

The next morning, Eva finds a message from Isidora on her desk. She has put out *Chicken Soup for the Teenage Soul*, a book that they have over the years read together, and she has drawn an arrow and written "read this." The book tells the story of a foster child who moves from family to family because at each home she provokes trouble, and they decide she cannot live with them anymore. They throw her out. It is a story of multiple abandonments by parents who refuse to go the distance. Finally the girl gets to a foster home where the mother responds to her trouble making by asking her what she can do to help her; how she might make it better for her. "She didn't give up" is the book's punch line. "This was a teachable moment," says Eva recalling how desperate she felt and how the girls each took the high road, the more mature stance. "I was feeling immature in their shadows," she says poignantly.

In retrospect, even in this retelling, she recognizes that her out-of-control rage was an expression of her feelings of "inadequacy." "I was in struggle . . . trying my best to keep the orifices under control. I was working to keep the girls close to me, wanting to make them strong so that they would not be swept away by the commercial cover of American culture. . . . At the same time, I was working to understand how much they wanted to belong and being reminded that as a girl I also wanted to belong when my parents kept me from being engaged in the world around me. I also knew in my heart that I wanted the girls to be able to straddle both worlds. I wanted them to be adult in making wise choices, but there was also a big part of me that wanted them to make my choices." Her face seems to show the lines from all of the strained layers of conflict and struggle she has felt as a mother; all the reverberations that linger from her own childhood of straddling cultures; all the echoes from her sustained attempt to protect her girls from the bad influences that surround them; all the ways in which she knows that they need to feel as if they belong to their world. A long silence surrounds us as Eva seems exhausted by offering up these competing interpretations, as she searches for the origins of her pain and rage on that special Sunday when the plans went awry. Finally she sums up her "hard-won" learning. "If things change, then I have to change. I must learn to be flexible and resourceful, not dogged and resistant. I am learning how to adapt in order to meet my kids where they are and in order to engage the world around them."

The summer before the twins went off to college, Eva cried every day. They were all in Symi together, and the beauty and familiarity of the scene made the pain of their departure feel even more intense. "Why," I ask, "were you weeping all the time?" First she says that she knew that things would never be the same again after the girls left. "I had envisioned all my life being married and having two daughters, being a mother with children around me. I was extremely involved as a mother. I loved it and couldn't imagine finding anything more meaningful or important. Mothering brought me a daily infusion of meaning." She remembers the "homeschooling" she did each day after school when she would pick up her daughters and their friends and teach them all a poem, or ask them a hard question, or get them interested in discovering something about the landscape outside the window. It was always an intentional effort to give them something more than the school served up each day; something that would extend their horizons and deepen their thinking; something that did not "conform to the ethnocentric, narrow curriculum that they were learning" in their classrooms. Sometimes the girls would resist her efforts at "homeschooling after school," and they would claim that they were too tired. But when their friends joined them in the carpool, and obviously were getting great pleasure from "participating in this weird moment," then Athene and Isidora would happily—often proudly—join in. They liked having a "weird" mother who did things differently.

But the weeping that summer before the girls went off to college was more than just a response to losing her "daily infusion of meaning." She also was crying because she was filled with regret. She felt a deep sadness about those parts of her mothering that she might have done better and more wisely. "I was crying because I thought I had not done my best; it is such a difficult concept, weighed down by so many of the wrong expectations and impossible standards." She was crying for all the things she would "not be able to redo." She was crying for the disappointing Sundays when her husband would go off to work and not spend time with the family.

It was Isidora who one day towards the end of the summer asked her mother why she was crying. When Eva began to list her regrets, her guilt at not doing better by her girls, Isidora grabbed her by the shoulders and looked straight into her eyes. Her voice was "mature and maternal." "Look, you did everything you could and more. When could you have done more, when you were sleeping? You never stopped doing for us. I know other parents who are selfish and harm their kids. You never did that. You're talking about details that don't matter. They are just part of the flow of life." At that moment, Eva felt very much like "the child" who was being given the greatest gift of appreciation and reassurance from her daughter. She stayed very still in the grip of her daughter's sturdy embrace, trying to take in and absorb the beautiful words Isidora was speaking, trying to resist the waves of inadequacy that she always felt when she made the mistake of taking stock of her mothering. Isidora was teaching her mother about acceptance, about how she needed to accept all those things that were good and generous in her parenting. And she was helping Eva learn to forgive herself for the "details," all those moments of vulnerability, confusion, and failure that are embroidered into all good mothering, which is by definition imperfect.

Moving back and forth from Greece to the United States—collecting and surrounding herself with the precious objects from Greece in her California home, adapting to the simple village life in Greece, speaking both languages, eating both kinds of foods—

makes a life in motion for Eva Galanis. But motion does not always mean distance or space, and it is her twin daughters who have expanded Eva's world and her understanding of who she is. Eva's mothering was marked by anxiety and overprotectiveness, the very opposite of space and freedom, and the location of Eva's learning. Her daughters' resistance was for themselves, and for their mother's worldview, but their resistance opened Eva's eyes and mind to the meanings of control and constriction, to what is lost by holding onto boundaries. In struggling with her daughters over TV, Chinese food, and trips to the mall, Eva learns what it was she wanted and needed as a child: the chance for belonging and engagement in the world—the present world, not the world her parents chose for her. As Eva's daughters push against their mother to create a bigger space for themselves, so Eva has to expand and stretch. Her biggest stretch, perhaps, is in expanding her understanding of being a "good mother." That space of mothering is huge and includes "vulnerability, confusion, and failure" within its borders; it includes the "details" and the essentials. Motherhood is bigger than controlling orifices and retaining culture; its horizons are as big as the world her children live in, always expanding.

Intimacy

In learning to love, and be loved, by her daughter Zoe, Simone Ray lives with the haunts of her authoritarian immigrant parents who saw "love as ownership" and were often "mean spirited" and arbitrary in the rules that they insisted that she follow, the clothes they made her wear, the choices they refused to give her, and the tough punishments they meted out. But unlike Eva Galanis, whose twin daughters had to push hard against their mother's "crazy protectiveness"—a "scar and a trait" inherited from her own parents' old world ways—Simone Ray knew from the moment she brought Zoe into the world that she wanted to create a life that was different for her daughter. Simone wants her relationship with Zoe to be freer, more reciprocal, respectful, and embracing, and she knows that in forging their mother-daughter bond, they will have to recognize and honor the large differences between them, the differences in their temperaments and the differences in their "kinds of intelligence." As they do their approach-avoidance dance, Simone learns — and continually has to relearn and practice — the paradoxical lesson that intimacy is, in fact, sustained by boundaries, restraint, and distance. In letting her daughter be herself, in honoring who she is, Simone experiences a love she never felt before, an intimacy possible only when she realizes that the space between them will draw them close.

In her late sixties, Simone Ray moves quickly and energetically. I have heard her referred to by those who know her well as "a force of nature," colorful, passionate, creative, impatient. She wears flowing garments in purples and black, large ornate earrings, and funky designer sneakers. Her home is an eclectic blend of folk art, draped fabrics, constructed sculptures from found objects, mosaics she has fashioned into altars, and beautiful photographs taken by her late mother. A large dining room table is the gathering place where people come for dinner and stay late into the night, eating vegetables and fruit from her city garden, joining in vociferous conversation, and listening and dancing to Stevie Wonder and Marvin Gaye. Over the years, she has had many overlapping jobs . . . filmmaker, restaurant server, union leader, community organizer, arts and festival promoter — all of which are guided by a progressive political agenda, a commitment to social justice and community building.

She was thirty and married when Zoe was born, and it was a dream come true. The one thing that she always knew she wanted out of life was to raise a daughter. Several years later she and Eliot divorced "amicably but very sadly," and he moved close by so that he could continue to be in Zoe's life. Soon Eliot remarried and had other children with his second wife. But Simone has been on her own for the last twenty-five years, and her stories of parenting often refer to the power and centrality, intimacy and intensity of her mother-daughter relationship with Zoe, where she has had to learn — particularly now that Zoe is an adult — the hard lessons of restraint, how to draw the boundaries that will allow her daughter the space, privacy, and autonomy that she "needs and deserves." This dance of distance and intimacy has been part of the hidden—and occasionally manifest—curriculum of their family of two ever since Simone can remember, a never-ending balancing act.

The stories and memories tumble out of Simone's mouth, in a rush, as if there is some urgency to tell them. She has just returned from spending six days in the Arizona desert on a road trip with Zoe who is now thirty-five and an executive in a large arts-based non-profit in Chicago. The trip has produced so much "fresh material" and too many converging memories and images, it seems, to figure out the story line she is searching for. In her work particularly as a filmmaker, Simone relishes stories: the details, the twists and turns, the surprising detours, the suspense and resolution. So instead of harvesting the "new stuff," she begins with the still vivid moments and vignettes from Zoe's childhood, and the declaration that there are two ways that she has learned from her daughter over the years: learning that grows out of "opposition, conflict, and struggle" between them and learning that happens "side by side."

Simone begins with a side-by-side example from when Zoe was about twelve and they went to a furniture store to look for a sofa. As soon as they got to the store, Zoe charged across the showroom to a large, white, leather L-shaped sofa and said that it was perfect for their living room. It was unlike any other piece of furniture they had at home, not at all their taste—a choice that seemed to Simone "lacking in style." But there was something about Zoe's certainty and clarity, and her insistence that the top priority should be "comfort," not "style," that quickly convinced her mother—who always thinks about aesthetics first—that they should go with the sofa. They did not even measure the sofa before making the purchase and setting up the delivery date. Three big strong delivery guys had a terrible time getting the sofa through the front door and up the narrow stairs, and the sofa—"definitely a white elephant"—barely fit into the space. But it ended up being "perfect"—a perfectly comfortable place to land after an exhausting day, a perfect place to cuddle and watch television, a perfect purchase. I ask Simone just what she learned from the buying spree, and she says that her daughter, the two of them standing side by side, taught her to think about the choices before them differently. She also learned that she could allow herself to be open to Zoe's guidance and priorities, even her hunches and appetites. Zoe could take the lead from time to time.

Opening with the couch story, Simone turns to the ways in which the differences between them have always been a good source of learning for her. As a matter of fact, the differences stand out most vividly because there are also many ways in which they are uncommonly close and very similar. Simone begins by drawing the contrasts in the ways they think and learn, their qualities of mind and their relationship to knowledge. "Zoe loved learning everything, and she had the capacity to consume information so quickly. I remember when she was ten months old, showing her the way to get off the bed so she wouldn't tumble onto the floor. I demonstrated the move once, then I had her do it, and that was that. The same was true of her potty training. I just had to show her once."

Simone believes that Zoe's capacity to take in information and directions with such precision and speed also has to do with her "love of learning," her desire to "do the right thing," and her "wanting to be good." She marvels at the ways in which there "never seem to be any impediments" to Zoe's learning, the way she takes it all in with no resistance, sifts through it, and integrates it in her own way. It is a splendid, just-right intelligence for school learning, where she has always excelled, "never receiving a grade of lower than A in her whole career from elementary school through two graduate school degrees." By contrast, Simone calls herself a skeptical learner, someone whose first impulse is to challenge the legitimacy and usefulness of knowledge. "I always ask, how do they know that? I question authority compulsively. I resist the cocky certainty of expertise." This learning stance, of course, has not made Simone particularly "school worthy." She has never liked school, nor felt that the structures, routines, and rituals of school were compatible with her learning style.

The last remark about their different ways of taking in, and resisting authority, is clearly related to the ways they engage the world more generally, the kinds of settings or situations where they each thrive and feel comfortable. Zoe is "fiercely private"; she was incredibly shy and watchful when she was a young child and still—at thirty-five—she seems to find social occasions somewhat awkward and taxing. Even now, although she has learned how to appear smooth and comfortable in her social and professional encounters, her mother can see the shadows of shyness underneath. By sixth grade, remembers Simone, Zoe had "figured out how to put that fake smile on" and enter the fray, but it is not her "natural way of being." When Zoe was an adolescent, Simone had always expected—and wished—that their house would be a place where folks would gather, where Zoe's friends would come and hang out. But Zoe rarely had her friends over at the house. Instead, she would go out, and when she returned she rarely talked very much about where she had been or what she was doing. By contrast, Simone thinks of herself as very social; she enjoys being in the midst of the action: organizing events, throwing parties, and building community. She is "extroverted to the max." Zoe's shyness is connected to her need for privacy, for quiet places where she can be alone and separate.

Later on, Simone asks me whether I know about "shy bladders," a term Zoe introduced her to on their recent road trip to the desert. It refers to people who are so shy and private that they can't go to the bathroom if someone else is in the room. "Zoe admits to having a shy bladder and that is just one sign of—actually a metaphor for—her need for privacy," says Simone remembering how they had joked about it on their trip when they were sharing a hotel room. Zoe had taken out her smartphone and asked whether she could take a video of her mother—who has a "bold bladder"—peeing on the toilet. Zoe wanted to create a piece of family footage, a graphic way to mark their differences. Staying in character, and without hesitation, Simone sat demurely on the toilet, the doors wide open to her daughter's prying camera.

Zoe's shyness and need for privacy also seem to be related to her gentle nature; her style is both nonconfrontational and nonjudgmental. Simone learned very early on that "confronting her is not a good thing." When you do, she completely clams up and closes down. Her preference is to "avoid conflict by going around it," whereas her mother is likely to head into the center of the conflict, naming it, claiming it, and taking it on. Simone remembers the two of them sitting together on the big white couch several years ago, watching the Tavis Smiley show, and she recalls lobbing criticisms at the host, putting down his politics, his chauvinism, his superficiality. Finally Zoe spoke up—as she often does when her mother spews criticism—asking Simone why she was always being so judgmental and inquiring about what pleasure she got in being that way anyway. "I realized," says Simone a little meekly, "that is how I approach the world. My first impulse is to observe, judge, and criticize and it sometimes bleeds into a steady cynicism . . . Zoe was calling me on it." "Were you transformed in that moment?" I ask skeptically. "Of course not," Simone shoots back. "It begins with a heightened consciousness; the behavior changes much more slowly. You just can't stop being critical on a dime if that is the way you have functioned your whole life."

Recently Simone has tried very hard to bring that consciousness and behavior to her encounters with Zoe. She has explicitly worked on self-imposed rules of restraint, "dampening down her power" and muting her critical voice. Before the trip to Arizona, she made herself a new rule: "I will not offer a comment unless I am explicitly asked." And for the most part, she managed to keep her mouth shut. But it was hard. "Very challenging," says Simone with understatement and a smile. She gives me an example. One morning in Phoenix, Zoe was getting ready to go off to a business meeting with some economists at Arizona State, and she began to get dressed. They had been traveling across country in jeans and sweatshirts, and Simone watched quietly as her daughter put together a "really crazy costume." "I looked at what she was putting on and I said she must be out of her fucking mind!" She had long black pants that dragged on the floor with white stripes down the side. On her feet she had moccasins with fur inside making them look like slippers. Over her shirt, she had a vest crossed in front with its tails hanging down, and then a jacket over the vest that was white on top with stripes on the bottom. "It was horrible," exclaims Simone about her daughter who is naturally tall, graceful, and elegant and typically wears clothes that are somewhat understated. "And her hair looked strange, too. But I did not say anything. I was so proud of myself." Zoe went off to her meeting and returned after a couple of hours saying they had had a productive session and that the economists were thrilled to be talking about arts-related environmental projects, about things other than their usual diet of models, tables, and graphs.

Later that afternoon, the two of them combed through several of the consignment stores in downtown Phoenix and found some nice clothes for Zoe. With each item that she tried on, Zoe asked her mother for her opinion, and Simone—sticking to her rule—remained silent. At one point, Zoe put on a long woven sweater over clingy silvery pants. "Actually this looks better than what I had on this morning," she confessed. And Simone could not help saying softly, "You're right about that." To which Zoe responded, "Well, why didn't you tell me that this morning?" She reminded Zoe of her new rule and then proceeded to break it as she described in detail the "layers of mess" her daughter had worn to the morning meeting. By then they were both laughing at themselves and reminding each other of one of their good friends, a mother who has a daughter about Zoe's age, who always makes a point of signing off at the end of their cross-country phone conversations by saying, "Oh, by the way, I like your hair." Thus insuring that she has complemented her daughter on something, even something that she can't see. "Try it," says Simone to me, the mother of a thirty-year-old. "Even though it's a big joke every time, it works . . . it spreads good will."

Before the desert trip, Simone and Zoe had survived a difficult and painful negotiation. Initially, Zoe had invited her mother to spend a week with her in Austin, Texas, just the two of them, a chance to play around the edges of Zoe's work. They have taken many trips together—to London, Hawaii, Brazil, Costa Rica—and have always enjoyed the pace and rhythm of hanging out together. But as the time drew nearer, Zoe had called to say that she actually wanted to spend some of the time in Austin with her longtime partner—a woman who Simone likes and admires—and that they would only be able to count on being together for a couple of afternoons. The change of plans made Simone feel sad and rejected, "pushed to the margins." After brooding on it for a while, she picked up the phone and told her daughter that she had decided not to come, that she felt squeezed out and was not going to travel all the way to Austin if they only had a few hours to spend together. The conversation was hard and edgy, filled with silences and awkwardness. Zoe clammed up and closed down. After she hung up, Simone felt "relieved and righteous" but also "down and devastated." About a week later—seven days that felt like forever to Simone—Zoe called back, her voice upbeat. She had another plan to propose: a weeklong train trip to the desert where she had some work to do but also a lot of open time for adventuring—a time for just the two of them.

As Simone and her daughter navigate this terrain of distance and restraint, she is aware of wanting to be a very different kind of mother than the one she had growing up. "We are," she says soberly, "always acting out of where we came from . . . and unless you break that pattern, each generation does the same thing over and over." Her voice is forgiving when she says that her immigrant parents had "a disadvantage coming where they came from." Her mother was born in Warsaw, her father in Zurich, and just after they married in their early twenties, they immigrated to America. "They always thought they had the divine right," says Simone as her voice sharpens with accusation. "My mother would insist that I do something . . . she would walk into the room and just turn off the TV before issuing her next directive . . . she decided what we ate . . . we had no choices. She was always carrying disrespectful power over me."

Simone can recall only one time when her parents gave her a choice, and it was an odd one. When she was in fourth grade, her friend Julie asked her whether she wanted to come and swim at the country club where her parents were members. It was a club that excluded Jews, and Simone's parents—who were Jewish—knew all about the club's discriminatory policies. Surprisingly, they presented Simone with a choice. "They said, 'you'll have to decide whether you want to go' . . . and I went!" says their daughter who, at nine, did not struggle over her decision. "I have always wanted to give Zoe more choices," says Simone, remembering a visit from her own mother when Zoe was about five. One morning, she asked her daughter whether she wanted fried or scrambled eggs for breakfast, and her mother exclaimed with disapproval, "You're giving the child a choice!"

This kind of restricted life—where you had to fight for months before your parents would finally let you stop wearing those "little white anklet socks" to school, or "where they would not let you go out with certain outfits on, so you had to sneak clothes out of the house and change them later in someone's bathroom"—always made Simone question their love. "My mother was not loving," she says bluntly. I wonder out loud whether it might be that her mother just had a strange way of showing her love. But Simone shoots back that it was a love that felt "more like ownership." She tells me that when she was an adolescent, she used to look up the meaning of love in the dictionary, or she would read love poems and try to extract the essence of its meaning, always on a search for that feeling of connection to her parents, particularly her mother. Yes, she admits that her parent's fierce determination that she get the "best education possible" was surely a sign of their love. But it never felt that way as she endured their dominating presence and overprotectiveness.

Now, when she and Zoe are together—talking over a meal, traveling across the desert, taking an art class—Simone feels the love moving back and forth between them. It is carried in the way Zoe welcomes her mother to her apartment, creating a small "altar" in the extra bedroom where Simone sleeps—a gorgeously set table with a selection of things she knows her mother appreciates: a bottle of tequila, flowers, candles, and a bit of marijuana. It is carried in the way in which Zoe makes plans to introduce her mother to new adventures and experiences. "You know I don't like the desert," admits Simone, "but Zoe took me there and I found it stunning and strange. She showed me a new way of experiencing it . . . the silence, the delicious smelling air. It was lovely and powerful."

About a year ago, when Simone was visiting Zoe in Chicago, they were sitting in the sun out in the tiny garden behind her apartment, and Zoe asked out of the blue, "Mom, you want to try a quick meditation?" (Zoe had been practicing meditation for a few years.) They sat down on the little patch of grass, surrounded by "nasty old broken-down chairs, a collection of pots with half-dead cacti, and odd plastic figurines," as Zoe set the timer on her phone for five minutes. She began to demonstrate to her mother the slow rhythmic breathing, repeating the mantra "Receive and Send" with each breath in and out. "I was immediately struck that the words sounded as if they came from the computer," says Simone smiling, "and I translated it into, 'receive the love and send it out' . . . the same with pain . . . 'feel the pain, take it in, and transform it.'" Each morning for the rest of the visit, mother and daughter found their way to the funky backyard for their daily short meditation. Zoe also gave Simone a gift of Norman Fischer's book *Taking Our Places: The Buddhist Path to Truly Growing Up* to take home with her, and she took to it immediately. In fact, she found herself reading some passages over and over again when she was "feeling rejected by Zoe" and the words and images helped her. "I am just going to let Zoe go so that she can move more freely."

Through all of these experiences—most of which Zoe designs ahead of time with so much care—the love is expressed and affirmed in her eagerness and pleasure in just being with her mother. Tears shoot to Simone's eyes and her voice is almost a whisper. "You know I was so mixed about loving my mother. But Zoe really loves me. She actually wants to spend time with me."

Space, freedom, privacy, autonomy—preserved and sustained by boundaries, restraint, and distance—somehow make a stronger and deeper intimacy. This is the central paradox, dilemma, and lesson of Simone Ray's relationship with her daughter, in which she experiences the gift of love that she had never known as her mother's daughter. As I listen to Simone, I hear the choreography of the "dance" they are composing, the sense of mutuality and completeness, a sort of complementarity and give-and-take in their relationship. The dance metaphor is apt, as Simone allows her daughter's tastes and hunches to take the lead sometimes, to open and enlarge her world. And there is a kind of mirroring too, as in dance moves, one partner steps forward and the other steps back, as one leans in and the other leads out. Maybe this is how "differences" fit together to create intimacy.

Joy

Like Eva Galanis, Zarina Nielson wants to protect her two adolescent children from what she believes is the materialism, superficiality, and crassness of American culture; and like Simone Ray, she has inherited the "wounds of pain and sadness" from parents who were emotionally unresponsive, dismissive of her dreams, and stingy with their love. A first-generation Danish immigrant and college professor, living with a debilitating chronic disease, Zarina equates "good mothering" with maintaining a restrictive, protected household, free of the contaminating influences that might put her children at risk on any ordinary day when they walk out the door. No sugar is allowed in their diet, no plastic toys, no video games or television. Her high standards, she discovers, are maintained at great cost, undermining the spontaneity and closeness, the play and the laughter, that she yearns for in her relationship with the children. It is only after Zarina lets go of the "impossible standards," and begins to accept her daughter Christina's choices rather than being driven by her own, that she is able to take pleasure in the joy that is part of her daughter's being, a radiant joy that admits the moments of sadness cloaked underneath, a joy that becomes the bedrock of their developing intimacy.

When I ask Zarina Nielson her age, I am not surprised when she tells me she is forty-seven, but that she has always felt—since adolescence—like she was about seventy. There is something ageless about her; at moments, she seems like an old soul, tired, weary, and wise; and at other moments she morphs into someone who seems young, reticent, and uncertain, even naive. At over six feet,

she walks purposefully and swiftly, carrying her stoutness gracefully but seeming, as she admits to me later, "not at home" in her
body. There is some awkwardness, even a sadness, about her that
she believes has both temperamental and cultural roots. Raised in
Denmark, the oldest child of very "restrictive and domineering"
parents, she says that there was "an absence of joy" in her family
growing up and she admits that Danes have a well-deserved reputation for being "joyless." Just look at the fairy tales of Hans Chris-
tian Anderson—the stories that Danish kids are raised on—they
are all, she reminds me, morbid, scary, and dark. Although she has
been in this country for twenty years, her huge English vocabulary
is delivered with a lilting Danish accent; and she often apologizes
for missed cues or missteps that reflect her incomplete "acculturation to American modes and idioms." As she walks into my home,
for instance, Zarina says tentatively, "I do not know whether this is
appropriate for me to say, but in Denmark we always comment on
a beautiful house."

As an undergraduate in Denmark, Zarina majored in business
and economics, "cold disciplines" that left her feeling empty and
unsatisfied. One day, she had a "mystical experience" that "opened
up a path" to her decision to study theology. But over the course of
the next few semesters, she also found herself struggling with the
language and frameworks of theology, where the "words seemed
to be used as props," where real feelings and "imagination were
masked in dogma." Zarina decided to "travel to the source" and
spent her final two years of college in Israel studying Hebrew and
training as a biblical scholar. In Jerusalem, she met her husband,
David, who is Jewish and was on a path to becoming a rabbi. When
they married, neither of their families was happy with the interreli-
gious, intercultural union, and many of their friends thought they
were an "extremely odd couple."

Despite their many differences, they shared a deep love of learning, an exciting and energetic intellectual engagement, and a hard-
driving ambition. "We will do the impossible," was their mantra,
she says wearily. "I think we wore each other out." Soon after their
marriage, Zarina became pregnant, and they both decided to come

to the United States to earn their doctoral degrees at the University of North Carolina. (By then, both of them had decided not to take the pastoral route of becoming a rabbi and a minister, respectively.) After arriving in North Carolina, Zarina made another disciplinary transition, shifting from theology to the PhD program in the philosophy of religion. The move to the United States was very hard for Zarina. "I was hugely pregnant. There were too many big changes for me all at once. I wanted to go home, but that was before I realized that you can never really go home . . . and by then I wasn't even sure where home was for me."

As soon as she arrived in Durham, she was overcome with weariness and depression. At first, she thought that her blues were just the result of the move, a feeling of being overwhelmed by feeling so displaced and homesick. But when it lingered on for months, and after a parade of doctors' visits, she was finally diagnosed with chronic fatigue syndrome (CFS). The illness has stubbornly and painfully held on; for the last twenty years, Zarina has suffered the debilitating effects of the disease — severe pain, exhaustion, allergies, depression — and she has often been bedridden or in a wheelchair. The CFS mysteriously disappeared a year ago, the morning after David moved his stuff out of the house following their divorce. Zarina awoke all alone in her bed and experienced the strange and unfamiliar sensation of feeling rested. "A true story," she says to me as she sees the surprise on my face. Over the last several months, she has slowly gotten better and better, although the tiredness still lingers, and the painful memories of being incapacitated are daily haunts.

As a matter of fact, most of Zarina's stories about mothering and learning from her two children (Christina, now eighteen, and Niels, who is twelve) begin with her illness: the ways in which she was compromised physically and emotionally by the pain from CFS, the way that she was never able to do the normal caretaking and nurturing things that healthy parents are able to do. Although Zarina has "learned a hell of a lot" from both of her children, her stories are mostly centered on her "powerful" relationship with her daughter Christina, whose arrival in the world "defined the family script." "It is amazing how much you can do from bed," she says remembering her daily attempts to be physically engaged with her children. Zarina has memories of nursing her infant daughter, wincing at the pain of just cradling her in her arms, reading Sartre for one of her graduate courses as she held her baby, multitasking in order to dull the pain, "finding refuge from the pain in the intellectual engagement."

Several times during our interview Zarina tells me that she has always thought of herself as an "incompetent mother." "As a family, we had created a story that my husband was the perfect parent and I was not. Because of my illness, he was very much with our daughter physically. They would play and nestle together and go off on adventures. My friends would sometimes comment that when Christina was a little child and needed something, she would yell out 'Mommy! Mommy!' and then she would run over to my husband." Sometimes Zarina would feel pangs of sadness and jealousy as her daughter would gleefully run into David's arms; but she also felt enormously grateful that her husband was so capable of giving the kind of maternal attention that she was unable to give. Over time, Zarina also learned to find pleasure—rather than resentment—in other people's pleasure. She says adamantly, "I learned a lot from being in pain for twenty years. You can find joy in other people's joy." And in the year since her divorce, she has discovered that the family script that contrasted her husband's good parenting with her bad was itself a distortion, a source of inhibition and defeatism that limited her relationships with her children.

It is not that Zarina didn't try mightily to be a good mother. In fact, she set standards that would be very hard for any parent to meet and sustain. When Christina was little, "We did not own a TV, no plastic toys were allowed, and she did not have sugar for the first two years of her life . . . and this was during the time when I had to have sugar all the time just to try and stay awake." Zarina shakes her head at the strict and uncompromising standards that she and David completely agreed upon and implemented together. "We were involved in a very nontraditional raising of our children: refusing to give into the media, refusing to break what we saw as the sacred code of our home." But when Christina began to "encounter mainstream society," she started to gently resist her parents' "sacred code," asking—then begging—them for things that she saw and played with at her friends' houses.

The Christmas when Christina was eleven years old has been etched into the family lore, an emblematic story that marked when their "clash of desires' became too visible to ignore. Zarina had decided to give Christina a handmade wooden barn. "It was what I would have loved to get at Christmas at her age," she admits. One of the traditions in their house, carried over from Zarina's Danish childhood, was that the children would write wish lists to the Christmas fairies and elves and leave them under the tree the night before. When Zarina was putting the carefully wrapped wooden barn under the tree, she discovered Christina's note addressed to the fairies. In the nicest way, she was asking them to bring her a "Runway Barbie" for Christmas. Zarina's heart sank. She immediately knew that she had made a "glaring mistake." "I had given her something I wanted her to want, and I knew my daughter would be crushed if she got the barn." Her head was pounding and her "anxiety was sky high" as she rushed off to the mall (a place she hated to go) on Christmas Eve to find a "Runway Barbie"; and of course, since it was the hot gift that year, there were none left on the shelves. She chose one of the few leftover Barbie dolls languishing on the near-empty shelf—a brown "Calypso Barbie"—but she knew in her heart that the substitute doll would not make her daughter happy. In fact, she knew that Christina's request was one that she had pondered for a long time; she knew that her parents were opposed to Barbie dolls, that they would not be happy with her for asking for one. She knew that she was risking their disapproval, risking her role as the good, accommodating child. Looking back on that Christmas, Zarina sees the lesson that "keeps on appearing" and catching her off guard. "This taught me that my daughter had to be allowed her own choices. I had to learn to give into her culturally engineered desires."

Even though Zarina describes how hard it was to break the sacred code of their home, and contaminate it with Barbies and other "materialistic artifacts" that deeply offended her, she feels as if she has been much more open and liberal than most American parents when it has come to responding to the "rites and rituals" of her daughter's adolescence. "American parents worry so much about drinking and drugs. That was never such a big deal for me. Coming from a culture where everyone served beer to kids at parties, and where sex and sexuality were accepted and expected by the parents of teenagers, I have been comfortable and liberal about all of these things with Christina." Zarina also notices a "bit of a hypocritical stance" from American parents who use "code words" when speaking about their kids' involvement in drugs and sex and who "refuse to see and speak the truth to each other about their concerns and worries." By contrast, Zarina has had a candid and honest relationship with her daughter; they speak openly about everything that goes on, even those moments of "poor judgment or things going wrong." Mostly she trusts Christina to do the right thing. "She has shown good discernment," says Zarina about how she believes their openness and candor have yielded a rare maturity in her daughter.

Recently, Christina asked her mother if she could have a party at the house for a dozen of her friends, knowing there would be a lot of drinking and drugs. Zarina agreed, but said that if they were going to be doing drugs and drinking, her friends would have to stay overnight. She did not want them drinking and driving. She thought she would try to make herself scarce that evening, but Zarina actually found that she enjoyed hanging out on the edges of the party, absorbing the youthful energy, playfulness, and conversation. At one point, one of the boys got sick and began throwing up all over the place; and Zarina watched the way everyone took care of him, and how throughout the night "they all seemed to moderate each other." Their enthusiasm felt infectious. "I don't drink or smoke. Even when I tried to smoke pot to help me with my CFS, it had no impact. I was not able to let it take hold," says Zarina "When I was young, I was a Goody Two-shoes. I did everything that was prescribed by a family that was exceedingly restrictive, which I now understand, was not so great for me and is still a source of my inhibitions. So it felt good to allow these things in my home and to

see how much more fun these kids were having than I ever had . . .
I love the energy that they bring."

Feeling the energy of these young people reminds her of the
ways in which she and Christina are so different—a difference that
has helped her to remember that her daughter is on her own path.
"It is easier for me to let her be who she is because we are so different," Zarina says more than once. "I can't control her. It would
be ridiculous for me to even try." She has, for instance, always mar-
veled at how grounded and content her daughter is, how, even as
a toddler, she seemed to know how to make her life satisfying and
good. Zarina recalls one summer when her father was visiting from
Denmark and he fell asleep one afternoon in the chair. Christina,
who was playing with colorful silk scarves at the feet of her grandfather, began to drape them over his body. When he awoke, he was
decorated from head to toe with scarves. "She takes what is there,"
says Zarina in awe, "and makes it as beautiful as she can. Her contentment is mind boggling." And she remembers, Christina sitting
on the floor when she was about three years old, happily playing
with her dollhouse, her tiny hands quietly opening and closing the
shutters, and the way she got such simple joy from doing it. "In that
moment, I recall being happy that she was happy, but I also remember feeling guilty at not being able to experience the equivalent joy."

Zarina's lack of contentment and the guilt that flows from not
being able to fully share in her daughter's "deep reservoirs of well-
being," she traces back to her childhood in a "joyless family." As a
very young child, she remembers withdrawing from "being present" with parents, who always made her feel "remote, lonely, and
other." She learned how to move away from seeking "emotional
responsiveness" and retreat into "intellectual contemplation." "I
always would go to the mind first, hyperconscious of repressing
any happiness." Even though Zarina sees the contrast between her
joyless childhood and her daughter's deep contentment, and even
though she occasionally feels guilty for not being able to experience
Christina's love of life, she has learned to "mostly enjoy her joy." She
is aware of the great effort it takes to resist the generational echoes
and cultural haunts, to pull herself out of a lifelong silence; and she

recognizes the insight and discipline it has taken to "break the dysfunctional patterns" so that she will not inflict them on her children.

After the divorce, and after her CFS had, miraculously, almost disappeared, Christina was able to finally reveal some of the sadness that had been lurking underneath her calm and content exterior. She was able to tell her mother—in a family therapy session that they attended together—how much she had missed her during her long illness, how much she longed for more "good mothering" from her. "The therapy allowed her to open up to the sadness," recalls Zarina. "Even though I think Christina romanticized the notion of my absence, holding onto the old family script, it was still so hard to listen to what she was saying . . . hard for me to admit that my happy child had places of sadness in her."

Her daughter's revelations of pain allowed Zarina to see the ways in which she has throughout her life—but particularly in her mothering—set impossible standards for herself, standards that were only reinforced in her marriage. She recalls the way she and David had colluded in their ambitious pursuits. "My husband would always want to do the impossible—the perfect day, the pursuit of high academic standards, the expectation of wonderful relationships with our children—and we pursued the impossible to our detriment. It was a setup." Every day, they would take on some challenge to do the impossible. Zarina remembers buying furniture for their living room that they knew would not fit and taking it home determined to squeeze it into the space. After much maneuvering, sweating, and pushing the pieces around, they managed to defy the objective measurements—doing the impossible. The furniture got squeezed into the space, but the room looked ridiculous and overstuffed. Zarina looks exhausted just thinking about what a fiasco it was and how her marriage was full of these challenges to do the impossible. She lets out a huge sigh. "Now that I am divorced, I just want to do the possible." She wants to turn the tables, to set different "standards for joy." She wants to learn how to accept the sadness in her happy daughter and see the goodness in her imperfect and "fragile mothering."

She describes the ways in which in the last year she is beginning to learn how to moderate her standards and learn lessons from her children about caring for herself and them. "I have always had high standards for how the house looks," she explains. "I want the floors to be nice and clean, the kitchen to be spotless. I now realize that these things are completely irrelevant . . . that clean floors are just a metaphor, a cover for something else. I should not be putting my energy into making things seem perfect." Instead, she has opened herself up to new learning, to mastering things that have always been hard for her, even out of her reach. Recently, for instance, she bought a power lawnmower, one that she carefully selected, after spending weeks consulting the *Consumer Reports'* ratings online. Buying the lawnmower felt like a major move towards mastery and independence for her, a move towards doing the possible.

However, after she got the mower home, she was unable to figure out how to assemble the pieces, and so she—as usual—turned to her daughter for help. "I am a non-commonsense person. Christina has always been the super competent one in the family. She is better at parallel parking than I am and she has always been very good at putting things together . . . so she assembled the lawnmower for me, and then she was fearless in pulling the chord and starting up the motor." It all felt "impossible and scary" to Zarina—the big Honda motor, the rush of the loud engine noise—but this time, rather than backing off, she grabbed the big handle from her daughter and began pushing the mower across the lawn. "I don't want her anymore to be the mother," says Zarina, with tears in her eyes. "Each time I achieve one more thing, my children cheer me on. We celebrate those things that I am learning to do." Liberation rings in her voice. She is beginning to free herself from setting impossible standards of joy; free herself from cleaning floors as a cover for other things she can't control; and free herself to learn those things her children can teach her that will help her be a more common-sense mother.

Zarina throws her head back laughing as she describes one of the things that her daughter has tried to teach her without success. "Christina has tried and tried to get me to dress better, to have some sense of fashion in the way I put myself together, but I am a

hapless student." Ironically, when Zarina was an adolescent she remembers wanting to become a fashion designer, even though she
neither possessed "the imagination nor the aesthetic." "It is like the
artistic gift and sense of my body completely skipped my generation, and now my daughter has it in abundance." Every time Zarina
goes shopping—which is not often: she hates shopping—she takes
Christina along to guide and supervise her—and save her from
some disaster. "She will tell me that something really does not look
good and then give me the reasons. I completely trust her opinion
on clothes." She smiles, admitting that Christina never takes her
along on shopping sprees. "I would not have anything to say that
would be helpful."

Something about our conversation about bodies and clothes
prompts Zarina to tell me, almost casually, that a couple of years
ago Christina announced to her that she was bisexual. Zarina remembers that she was neither surprised nor disturbed by the news,
although she felt some concern for how her daughter's discovery
of her sexuality might "limit her in some way." Her concern was
short-lived. "After she told us, I had twenty-four hours of worrying about how she would be judged. Then I snapped out of it . . . I
thought, 'That is who she is and I am not going to worry about it.'
She needs my support." She speaks about all of this with a lightness and humor that she was not able to duplicate when Christina
came to her a couple of months ago with another announcement.
She rehearses the moment with a hearty laugh. "I thought to myself
there is nothing more she can bring to me. We've survived tattoos,
piercings, loving boys and girls . . ." her voice trails off. But when
Christina told her that she wanted to drive a motorcycle, Zarina's
response was immediate. "No way! That's way too dangerous!" As
soon as the words escaped her lips, however, she was thrown back
to a time in her early twenties when she wanted nothing more than
to put on a black leather jacket and ride off on a motorcycle. But it
was a dream she kept to herself, not one that she dared announce
to her parents. So here was Christina ready to live out her mother's
"squashed dream," and the thought made her change her mind.

"Can I ride with you?" she asked her daughter. "Only if you lose weight," teased Christina mischievously.

When Zarina thinks of coming into her own as a competent mother and considers all the things — "and ways of being" — she has learned from her children, she says that none of her growth and development would have been possible without the support of a circle of friends. "It has always been an incredible strength to have community," she says with great emotion. "There were lots of aspects of the mother archetype that I did not embody, and we were lucky to find pieces of mothering that other folks could play." Ever since Christina was a small child, there have always been women in their lives who shared some of the maternal duties and brought a "different kind of energy in the house." When I ask Zarina about how these folks arrived in their lives, she claims that "they found us," and she says "they never felt like nannies." They were more like "grandmothers or godmothers"; "they were friends who mothered and who loved the children for a few hours every day.

Florence, Christina's kindergarten teacher at the Waldorf School, was such a person. Even at five, Christina sometimes said that Florence felt more like a mother than her real mom. "Christina saw her as more fun, more energetic, more physically connected . . . and she was right," recalls Zarina. "Florence always brought a kind of open exuberance into the house, but mostly it was the way that she would really see the children . . . see who they were and what they needed." Zarina admits that she would sometimes feel jealous of the relationships that these mother surrogates established with her children and jealous of their temperaments and personalities, which allowed them to be so emotionally expressive and upbeat. But Zarina's gratefulness always outweighed the occasional flashes of jealousy. And since Florence, there have been a string of extraordinary women who have become a part of the household, bringing their "exuberance, not just their contentment." Interestingly, their presence has always made Zarina more able to hear the lessons her children are trying to teach her. "It is almost as if they have been generous and insightful translators of my children's lives, offering me another way of knowing them," says Zarina thoughtfully. "Over time, the experiences have taught me that we needed them in our lives if we were going to be more whole. It has been a humbling but not a humiliating lesson."

There were many moments of insight and recognition that allowed Zarina Nielson to chip away at her sadness and discover joy and intimacy with her children. She was able to rewrite the old family script that had characterized her as the "incompetent mother" and David, her husband, as the "good one, a caricature that had kept her feeling inadequate and emotionally remote from her children, kept her defined as helpless and hapless. She admitted to not being the mother archetype and was able to reach out to a circle of generous "godmothers" who brought exuberance into their home and helped her see her children more deeply and fully. The now iconic Christmas family fable—when she raced to the mall to replace the handmade wooden barn with the plastic Barbie—helped her realize that she did not have to inflict her choices on her daughter, that Christina was a separate person whose contentment and joy she could appreciate and emulate—a joy that she could learn to take inside, a joy that could blunt the long family legacy of darkness and sadness. Ironically, it was the realization that her daughter had "places of sadness in her" that helped Zarina understand the importance of letting go of the "impossible standards" and letting in pleasure and lightness into her life. There is joy, as well, in her daughter's recovery of her mother's childhood "squashed dream," riding off on a big motorcycle dressed in black leather. I hope they do ride, Christina in the front, Zarina seated right behind her, together and close.

* 4 *

Acceptance

Those who believe their suffering has been valuable love more readily than those who see no meaning in their pain. Suffering does not necessarily imply love, but love implies suffering, and what changes with these children and their extraordinary situations is the shape of suffering—and in consequence, the shape of love, forced into a more difficult form. It doesn't really matter whether the meaning is there; it matters only whether it is perceived.

FAR FROM THE TREE, ANDREW SOLOMON[1]

IN HIS 2012 BOOK, *Far from the Tree,* Andrew Solomon writes about the experiences of families in which children are very different from their parents, about how the parents—who through the entanglements of their love and suffering—find ways to change how they assess the value and accept the personhood of the individuals who are their children. Solomon begins by stating the obvious but profound truth: children are not their parents, even as the subconscious desire behind "reproduction" is to see ourselves live forever, not to produce an "other." He distinguishes between two kinds of identity: vertical and horizontal. Vertical identities are passed from parent to child across generations genetically and culturally. Ethnicity and language, for example, are vertical identities. Horizontal identities can also be genetic and cultural in origin, but they refer to traits and characteristics that a child does not share with his parents. Horizontal identities might include being gay, having a physical or mental disability, genius, or psychopathy.[2]

The degree of otherness—how far the children's identity is from the parents', how far the apple falls from the tree—can test a parent's love, endurance, imagination, and sense of self. In *Far from the Tree*, Solomon writes about families who "tolerate, accept, and finally celebrate" their children's profound differences from themselves, embodied in the identities of deafness, dwarfism, autism, Down syndrome, schizophrenia, crime, rape, being a prodigy, and being transgender. In raising and caring for children with conditions alien to their own, parents undergo a myriad of material, social, emotional, and spiritual transformations.

Solomon's interest in this relationship of difference between parents and their children is rooted in his own experience of being dyslexic and gay. "How is any parent to know whether to erase or celebrate a given characteristic?" he asks, reflecting on how these two conditions shaped his relationship with his parents.[3] With dyslexia, his parents "trounced a neurological abnormality" by providing him with enormous amounts of extra support with reading and writing so that he could succeed in school and ultimately become a writer. But gayness—his other "abnormality"—was different; it was an identity, not an illness. This dichotomy between disparaging a way of being by naming it "illness" and validating the same way of being by naming it "identity" is something that Solomon wishes us all to examine. In dealing with the distinctions and fusions of identity and illness, parents begin to reshape their views of difference and transform their relationships with their children. Often, they come to reassess their own personhood and identity as parents as well, becoming different because of having a child with a difference.

Solomon writes with great sensitivity and empathy for these parents. He writes about the stigmatization of parental ambivalence, how hard it is to admit and speak about feeling burdened and hopeless without fearing that one's love for the child is diminished. He writes about managing the social perceptions that the child's "deficit" is the parents' "fault," and the challenge of attending to a severely disabled child through his adult years, never quite shedding the role of caretaker. And he writes about the sense of aloneness and chronic stress that the parents experience, along with the exhausting, ever-present decision making: "How urgent is the problem and how dire is the solution? That is the proportion that must be entertained. It is always both essential and impossible to tease apart the difference between the parents wanting to spare the child's suffering and the parents wanting to spare themselves suffering. It is not pleasant to be suspended between two ways of being."[4]

Suspended between these two ways of being, the parent has the difficult task of deciding who their child is, and whether the child's difference—perceived as an illness or identity, a mark of difference or deviance—obscures the child's true self or is integral to it. Being a parent of a child so different from oneself is a constant experience of paradox, chaos, and complexity.

Solomon acknowledges that parents are both "worn down and strengthened" by the experience of having a child who is profoundly different from them and that many parents actually speak of transformation or enlightenment in their lives. While the "anger and tedium of parenting can be crushing," Solomon writes that parents' positive transformation and growth is possible; achieved when the "initial disequilibrium, which is traumatic and brief, gives way to psychic reorganization which is gradual and enduring."[5] He cites studies that parents of children with intellectual disabilities reported more personal growth and maturity and hypothesizes that parents can find new worth in their lives because of the knowledge and strength they have gained parenting a child with difference.

Solomon's suggestion that the generative power of the initial disequilibrium—which initiates a change in the parent's "psychic reorganization" and leads finally to acceptance, even celebration of the child—is perhaps not so different from the disequilibrium that propels growth and development for parents raising "normal" children. The difference in experience may be more a matter of degree than kind. In critiquing the narrow frame of many of the stage theories of parental development, for example, Demick claims that many of the processes that Solomon sees in parents' adaptation to, and acceptance of, their profoundly different children are evident with parents who rear children much like themselves in a cultural and social environment that is rapidly changing around them.[6] Demick suggests that developmental processes—for parents and children—occur in response to the frequency and complexity of everyday life in a swiftly transforming cultural context and that the central task of parenting is attaining "equilibrium" within this changing and demanding environment.

Like Solomon, Demick sees the initial disorientation and trauma of disequilibrium experienced by parents as provocative; in seeking equilibrium, in searching for ways to bring balance back into their lives, parents grow and change. The process of restoring equilibrium helps to propel parental development, even if the equanimity turns out to be ephemeral and short-lived. Demick writes about the "dialectical process" that parents experience when they are faced with a stimulus from their children that is unfamiliar, unanticipated, maybe even disturbing, and the ways in which there is growth and learning in their striving to achieve a new stability, however tenuous.

Even though the search for equilibrium may be a universal developmental experience for both parents with "normal" children and those rearing children with profound differences, it is clear that the latter face more trauma and suffering, more severe and terrifying bouts of "disequilibrium," and a much more difficult road to acceptance. Importantly, in seeing the entanglements of love and suffering for parents with profoundly different children — "suffering does not necessarily imply love, but love implies suffering" — Solomon is careful to say that, while there is an opportunity for growth, it is not a guarantee. Rather, a parent's growth is an "act of will."

Above all, Solomon views the parents of children profoundly different from them as "choice-makers," even as they are locked up with their children's madness or genius or deformity and trapped by their own personality, history, and fallible humanity. The choice they make in loving their children — despite and because of their difference — opens up a precious enriched life: "These parents have, by and large, chosen to love their children, and many of them have chosen to value their own lives, even though they carry what much of the world considers an intolerable burden. Children with horizontal identities alter your self painfully; they also illuminate it. They are receptacles for rage and joy — even for salvation. When we love them, we achieve above all else the rapture of privileging what exists over what we have merely imagined."[7]

The enriched life and greater understanding of self is vividly illustrated in this chapter's narratives of parents raising children with "horizontal identities": children who are profoundly different from themselves. They, too, struggle with the contrasting and converging labels and interpretations of difference and deviance, the fusions and confusions they face in seeing identity or illness in their child. They, too, speak about the trauma and pain, the disquiet and disequilibrium, and the weariness and exhaustion they experience as they cope with the unexpected and disorienting otherness of their child. And they tell of those moments when they became "choice-makers," seeing their acceptance, even their love—and the growth that flowed from it—as an "act of will."

The fact that in some sense every child is an "other," a separate being endowed with his or her own will, thoughts, and desires, is the truth parents all face as they encounter difference—large and small, visible and invisible—with their children. Throughout this book, we have heard almost-grown children teaching their parents to give them space, honor their individuality, and see them as "other"; and we have seen the parents practicing restraint, recalibrating the distance in their relationships, and learning to see their children more deeply and fully. The differences may be small—differences that appear to be inconsequential and largely invisible to others looking in from the outside, such as differences in temperament, appetites, body shape, habits of mind, and political persuasion. Or the differences may be larger, even life-changing, like the stories of the four parents in this chapter who are raising their visibly different children: a mother struggling to support and accept her transgender son; a mother learning to see the gifts and strengths in her autistic son; a mostly closeted father whose adopted straight son helps him find acceptance and publically declare his homosexuality; a father who moves through the stages of denial, tolerance, reluctance, and finally celebration as he deepens his relationship with this lesbian daughter.

As the parents begin to navigate these differences, they look to their children as their greatest teachers, as the best translators of their worldview, and often as the most reliable and helpful sources of strength—a strength born out of their mutual struggles and suffering. Mostly the children are patient and generous pedagogues, well aware that their difference is disorienting and painful to their parents, that it is difficult for their parents to hear their pleas for understanding and honor their choices. The children know they must lead the way, insisting upon the rightness and truth of their different identities but empathizing with their parents' struggle to come to terms with who they are and who they are becoming.

Understanding

Naomi Sawyer understands the parents of the special needs students she teaches in a way that no one else can, no one else except a parent of a child with a disability. Mothering Jonah, her autistic son, she is "able to hear both sides of the conversation," identifying with the parents' fears and frustrations, their disappointments and their denial, and empathizing with their long journey towards respect and acceptance, as they learn to see and honor the strengths in their children. It is, of course, somewhat easier to be a professional on the other side of the desk, patiently and strategically dispensing wisdom and guidance, than it is to be a mother living through the despair and disequilibrium, the suffering and loving, and working to recognize and appreciate Jonah's extraordinary gifts and unusual traits, which often appear opaque and mysterious. Naomi fights to understand and appreciate her son's capacity for unselfishness and kindness, for "loving without judgment," even as she watches him get hurt and bullied in school. And she begins to understand her own limitations and inhibitions as an artist as she witnesses the spontaneity, freedom, and boldness she sees in her son's amazing paintings. Part of gaining understanding and acceptance is releasing the need to control or worry about others' negative perceptions of Jonah, not needing to prove how bright and talented he is, not needing to "fix" him.

Naomi Sawyer remembers an old photograph of her son Jonah reading at thirteen months, sitting in a basket of books. Weeks earlier,
Naomi and her husband Walter had discovered that he could read
the word "stop" on the television screen when he watched Sesame
Street, and the name of Mickey Mouse on the cover of one of his
favorite books. He was, Naomi explains to me, "hypolexic." But
even though he was an extremely precocious reader, he was not
able to use language to communicate. When he uttered words — in
short staccato spurts — he always seemed to "be talking into the
air," never looking at, or relating to, the people around him. Naomi
and Walter knew very early that something was wrong, and they
worked hard to discover the things that might help Jonah to relate
to them and better connect to the world around him. Walter, an
engineer, designed various templates that he would hold up in front
of Jonah's face, pointing to the missing blank spaces that might help
his son put his random words into full sentences. And he wrote
a software computer program that tracked Jonah's utterances and
progress. Naomi, originally trained as a graphic artist, used design
and color to help focus his attention and played with games, flip
cards, and talking puppets, rituals practiced for hours each day to
bring Jonah out of himself. "Jonah was very verbal, but he used
idiosyncratic language. Each day, even now at twenty-six years old,
he shows us how hard it is for him to use spontaneous language,"
Naomi says about the detective work that she often has to do to uncover what he is thinking and feeling.

Naomi remembers one day when Jonah was about four, when
he kept on repeating the words "Bonk. Bonk. Bonk," each time
with more urgency and frustration as if he wanted to communicate
something about how he was feeling. She remembers struggling to
find a connection, a link to something he might have read, an association with something visual. Finally, she recalled one of his favorite books, *Ten in the Bed*, where the characters hit their heads as they
are pushed out of the bed and land on the floor. Jonah, it turned
out, was trying to tell her that something was hurting in his head.

When their son was about three, they received the official diagnosis — of pervasive developmental disorder — from the leading ex-

pert in autism at the children's hospital. As Jonah walked into her office, he spotted a dictionary on the shelf and read the cover. But when the doctor called his name, he showed no response. By then, Naomi had given up her graphic arts business and had their second son, a healthy boy, eighteen months Jonah's junior, named Wade. "It was just too hard and demanding trying to balance my business and raise the baby boys, especially after Jonah's diagnosis made it clear that he would need a great deal of extra attention" says Naomi.

But it wasn't just the difficult balancing act that made Naomi want to leave graphic arts; it was also that she found that in working with Jonah, she discovered a gift in herself and a deep curiosity about learning disabilities and differences. She found that she was drawn to the patient teaching, listening, observing, and problem solving that were part of her daily interactions with her son; and she wanted to know more about the origins and ontology of his behaviors and learn more strategies to help him along. So Naomi decided to go back to school to become a special education teacher, a decision that she has never regretted.

Her graduate courses and training always seemed deeply connected to the demands and responsibilities of her mothering—a satisfying convergence that helped her forge the connections between theory and practice. Jonah was as much her teacher as her professors at the university; and she hungrily drew lessons from both. More important than her training in any particular strategies, intervention, or diagnostic language, Naomi learned—from both her son and her schooling—to develop a "focused curiosity," a "way of listening and watching and problem solving," and "a determination to understand what Jonah was trying to say, and how he was seeing the world."

Naomi offers an example of the "focused curiosity" that she uses with a high school student that she is currently working with who has severe cerebral palsy and is unable to speak or communicate with anyone but his mother, with whom he has developed a private and primitive sign language that only the two of them can decode. "He is in his twenties and he has never gone through stages of language or reading development," explains Naomi, her voice full of energy and optimism. "So I am always searching for clues, asking what can I use, trying to find out what can I do to facilitate his language and communication skills. I try to find a way to put myself in his place. How can I empower him, motivate him, get him to work harder? How can I open up his world and find the things that interest him, the things he wants to know?"

All of these questions and observations have now become woven into Naomi's practice with special needs high school students, but she always tests her repertoire and her progress against the high standard of what she would want from any one working with her son. And she always finds a way to identify with the parents who come to her with a heavy heart, usually anxious and afraid, often resisting the diagnosis that they can't bear to hear. As a parent and practitioner, she is able to hear both sides of the difficult conversation: the child's need for respect and validation and the parents' need for comfort and hope; the child's need for autonomy and the parents' wish for control. If it were not for Jonah, Naomi believes that her work with special needs adolescents and young adults would "probably not be as determined and unflinching." By now, with seventeen years of teaching experience under her belt, she has developed enough craft to be improvisational in her work; she has learned to balance restraint and truth telling, intimacy and distance—another kind of balancing act that draws its courage and contours from mothering and learning from Jonah.

Although Jonah has made great strides in communicating with words, he still, at twenty-six, struggles mightily with facing "discord or conflict"—struggles that often find their expression in a jumble of perseverating words. He hates it when people get angry with one another or when someone is made to feel disappointed, diminished, or disrespected. He perseverates over even the smallest slight or gesture that is hurtful and it fills his mind with "negative feelings" that are hard to let go of. His antennae are always raised in response to injustice. Naomi offers an example of Jonah's despair at an event that should have brought him pride and joy. A couple of months ago, he won the first prize in a walking race at the Special Olympics. But instead of glowing, or even gloating, over his victory, he immediately expressed sadness for those who did not win the race. "Jonah hates competition and avoids winning," says Naomi. "He doesn't want to see a loser. He is the most unselfish person I know and he has taught me a great deal about humility."

Sometimes his efforts to avoid conflict leave him vulnerable to the assaults of others. He seems mystified and disbelieving in the face of meanness and often "goes the extra mile" or "turns the other cheek too many times" in an effort to seek reconciliation. In high school, he was often harassed by classmates, most of whom were also having difficulty fitting in, and being successful at, school—classmates who "may have seen some of their own shortcomings in Jonah" and did not like the reflections that they saw. In his senior year, for instance, there was Timothy, a very aggressive boy with Asperger's syndrome in Jonah's special education class, who was "more laser beam and rigid than Jonah" and who was constantly "snapping at him verbally." Each day, Jonah tried to reach out to Timothy, "to build a bridge, and find a way to make peace." And each afternoon, he would come home and talk to Naomi about feeling defeated in his efforts to change Timothy's mean behavior. "He just wanted everything to be copacetic, and when it wasn't, he felt very down and defeated," says Naomi sadly. Jonah did not seem to have the protective instincts that might allow him to withdraw from the fray or even decide to himself that it "was the other guy's problem," not one that he had to take on or one for which he had to feel responsible.

Naomi often faced tough choices in trying to guide her son through the thicket of emotions he was feeling and she was witnessing. How could she help him learn to protect himself? How could she lessen his anguish and help him understand that some things could not be solved by gestures of patience and goodwill? How could she teach him those things without destroying his deeply loving instincts? More than once, Naomi tells me that Jonah is extraordinary in the way he "loves everyone unconditionally." Her eyes overflow with tears as she describes his most tender qualities. "He sees the essence of people. He never judges. It is deep in his spirit, this capacity to love." In this way, despite the vulnerability and unease it may cause him, and the negative feelings that get awakened, Naomi sees her son as a "more evolved human being" than most of the rest of us, as conquering a way of being with others that "we all have a problem being and doing." It is from Jonah that she learns "lessons of love" all the time and from him that she learns that sometimes love comes at great risk and cost.

This impulse to love also expresses itself in the way he tries to guide and protect others who are more impaired than he is. For the last several months, for instance, he has been working with a twenty-three-year-old man who he met in an art class, who also suffers from autism, but who is completely nonverbal. Jonah goes to his house each week, and they stand side by side and paint together, mostly in silence, their time occasionally punctuated by Jonah's support, guidance, and praise. "He tends to seek out people who have disabilities greater than his," explains Naomi, who has a few times witnessed the two artists together and found their inter- actions "profound and amazing." And once a year, Jonah goes over to a graduate seminar in special education at the community col- lege, taught by an old mentor he had in high school. Jonah talks to the teachers in training about his life, his daily routines, his art, his hopes and dreams, "and whatever comes to his mind." He is incredibly open and honest and seems to know that he has some- thing important that they need to know and learn, and he relishes being the teacher. Jonah has told his mother that his goal is to one day become an art teacher of special needs children. Naomi shakes her head wistfully. She loves his motivation and purposefulness, but she also knows his limits and worries about the frustrations and challenges that he will face in trying to reach his goal. "This is both comforting and extremely difficult for me to hear," she says about her son's ambitions.

Even though Jonah's goal to become an art teacher of special needs kids may seem unrealistic given the difficulties he has with using spontaneous language, he is an extraordinary, gifted artist from whom Naomi has learned a great deal. "Do you want to see some of his paintings?" Naomi asks me hopefully. We look at sev- eral of his pieces, large abstracts with bright and intense colors, graffiti like, full of boldness and spontaneity. The first one, called *A Child's Imagination*, is full of symbolism with odd-shaped hybrid animals, protecting, caressing, and running wild with their young. Another painting depicts religions coming together, animals and humans throwing down their swords and bridging their differences. Naomi tells me that Jonah has always been fascinated by religion, Judaism in particular. "He has great empathy for the people who have been persecuted and he often paints stories of their journey to freedom." I sit there mesmerized by the canvasses, which seem so mature and spontaneous in their artistry, both sophisticated and primitive in their symbolism.

Naomi and I are sitting on the back sunporch, the place where Jonah has produced most of his paintings. "He is amazing to watch when he is painting . . . I began a few years ago, just setting up the easels and paints on the porch, and he would stand here for hours at a time in intense concentration, seeming free and absorbed." Naomi would often stand right next to him, quietly watching and sometimes suggesting that he fill in this or that space. "He seemed to be more prolific when I was standing by him," she says about how her presence close by seemed to be motivating to him. But she learned quickly not to interfere with his aesthetic choices. Early on, Naomi remembers looking at the unlikely colors that Jonah put together on the canvas; from her point of view, they seemed to clash. But when she restrained herself from making a suggestion or correction and let Jonah finish the piece, she would discover every time that the colors worked. "Oh my God," she would say to herself, "he just made that work."

But it was not the way that Jonah used color so creatively or even the symbolism that he evocatively captured in his paintings that impressed Naomi the most. What really fascinated her was the way he worked, the spontaneity and freedom he showed when he approached the canvas, the way he never seemed inhibited or harnessed, the way he did not judge the pieces he produced. He seemed to do it all without thinking about it and yet his paintings seemed to be the best clue for figuring out how Jonah was seeing and making sense of his world. Naomi, who had majored in graphic arts in college, watched and learned from her son's exuberance and engagement. "Jonah taught me to be free in my painting," she exclaims proudly. "He taught me to be more spontaneous and expressive. I learned from him that I needed to stop controlling it and overthinking it, but to get it down on the page, fast and fresh . . . and I learned that it was important to just enjoy it!"

About a year ago, when Jonah left home and moved into a "semi-independent living situation" in the city, Naomi put up an easel for herself on the porch. After years of watching her son—his engagement, his movements, his productivity, his freedom—Naomi could feel his imprint even as she produced her first painting, a still life of peonies in a vase. This was the very first time she had stood at an easel and used a brush, the first time she had tried being a fine artist (not a commercial graphic designer), and she was surprised and amazed by what came out of her. We walk together around her home and see the paintings Naomi has produced in the last several months, many framed and hanging on the wall next to her son's masterpieces.

Naomi has now become completely absorbed in her art making, coming home from school each day and working at her easel late into the night and taking painting classes a few times a week. Her paintings do not look like her son's. Neither do they seem like the work of a beginner. They are figurative pieces, more traditional compositions, confidently composed, attractive, and colorful. And like Jonah, she is prolific; she works fast. Not with the abandon and ease that she observed in her son, but with a freedom she has never known before. She is learning how to suspend the judgment that inhibits her progress; she is learning to get it down on the page and move on. For all of this she is thankful to Jonah for his inspiration and example, for his consummate teaching.

It has been a long journey getting to this place of acceptance; of feeling comfortable—and proud of—who her son is and is becoming. For so much of Jonah's early life Naomi struggled with feelings of sadness, fear and disappointment, focused on those things that Jonah could not do, and was preoccupied with his challenges, deficits, and difficulties. Admiring his extraordinary artwork and focusing on his gifts and "specialness" sometimes brings up the opposite feelings — those moments when she longed for him to be "normal" like everyone else. Naomi can still recall in detail the "triggers" that would make her feel angry and sad. Twenty years later, Jonah's kindergarten class picture still sends a dagger through her. "Jonah could not stand still and look straight at the camera like his peers, so his teacher gave him a book to look at. When I opened the class picture, it was like a knife in my heart. There he was standing out like a sore thumb." Naomi remembers how she wanted to yell and scream and throw the photo across the room, so fierce was her rage. She wanted to shout at the teachers who were probably "doing the best they could under the circumstances." "Instead," she recalls with a sadness that still feels fresh, "I masked my very strong feelings. I was not proud of the way I felt." Looking back, she knows that she was "still in denial" and that the rage erupted out of her refusal to accept who Jonah was. And she also knows that acceptance is hard-won; denial dies hard.

By the time Jonah was in the fourth or fifth grade, Naomi began to say to herself "Jonah is who he is . . . we will continue to work with him . . . we will continue to find accommodations." There were fewer triggers that would set her off, and she began to appreciate the progress that she saw. But, she admits, "It was still hard when the choir did not want him in the performance or when he was the only one not invited to a birthday party." By this time, Naomi had completed her training as a special education teacher and she remembers experiencing two shifts in her view, and expectations, of her son. First she learned to recognize his gifts and see strength in those capacities he had that were different from his peers. "I began," she says, "to embrace his differences." And second, now that she was a teacher herself, she began to empathize with Jonah's teachers. She began to see how hard it was for them to be truly inclusive and "make it work for every child." She began to accept "the limitations of educators."

Looking back, she also realizes that her acceptance of Jonah's differences was reinforced by his capacity to make and sustain relationships with the people around him. "He is not your stereotype of the self-absorbed, autistic person who cannot relate to the people around him. In fact, he loves people, and people love him. Every tutor, teacher, or counselor who has worked with him responds to how unique and special he is. They all stay in touch with him." Seeing her son through other people's eyes, seeing how he was loved, accepted, and appreciated, how he brought out the love in everyone else, helped Naomi embrace him for "who he is."

One of Jonah's large paintings is of Dr. Howard, the psychologist who has worked with him weekly for several years. Jonah titled the painting *The Wizard of Wisdom*. It is a beautiful, exuberant, colorful painting that not only captures the doctor's huge likeness, it also conveys his large spirit and, I believe, his love for Jonah. When Jonah finished the painting, they had it framed and presented it to Dr. Howard who immediately recognized himself and hung it on the wall behind his desk. Every time Jonah walks in, I suspect that he feels seen by his doctor, but I also have a hunch that the doctor feels known by his patient.

Naomi's life experiences with Jonah have been the best teacher in helping her work with, and support, other parents of special needs children. "I see parents and I get it," she says. She gets that parents suffer mightily from the triggers when a part of them is still in denial and that the severity of the disability is not the measure of their anger or their sadness. "Even if they have a child who has a very mild form of dyslexia, it is as real to them as if their child had nonverbal autism. There is no metric to measure their pain. It hurts just as much." I ask Naomi how she helps parents become more accepting, and she is crystal clear in describing the steps she takes. "First I validate what they are feeling . . . second, I try to explain to them where those feelings might be coming from . . . and third, I try to explain that if they felt a different way, it might benefit their child . . . if they were more sensitive and nonjudgmental, things would be better for them and their child . . . I try to be honest in a respectful way." Over the years, Naomi has discovered that parents, despite their efforts at denial, really want to know the truth about their child. "They do not want you to sweep things under the rug." As she navigates the treacherous territories of truth telling, Naomi feels the raw and strong emotions that are always just below the surface: "The pain of not seeing your child included . . . the diffi-culty in trusting the people who work with your children . . . and the anguish in seeing how your child measures up to other children."

Since mothering Jonah has given her the inside track with parents and has allowed her to stand in their shoes, I ask Naomi whether she tells them that she has an autistic son and whether that gives her some legitimacy in their eyes. "I hold that card close," she ex-plains carefully. "I do not generally disclose that . . . I do not want to appear to know it all . . . I want to show that I understand. At the very least, I want them to work with me before they know, and feel my empathy for their story, for the particular things that they are struggling with." She also tells me that "pulling out the ace card" can sometimes backfire. "If it turns out that my child has a signifi-cant disability and theirs has a mild disability, the parents become defensive and feel as if I am one upping them. I get that."

Like so many moments in our interview, Naomi moves back and forth between identifying with the parents of her special needs students and reflecting on her own struggles, and continuing chal-lenges, with her own child. There is no way, it seems, to make it through this journey without some regrets, without wishing that you had done some things differently. Naomi's face is sorrowful as she reflects on how hard it was to decide that—at twenty-five— Jonah needed to move out of his parents' home. "The situation here was not sustainable. We are not going to live forever, and Jonah needed to learn how to be more independent." Walter was clearer and less ambivalent about the need for Jonah to move on with his life than Naomi, who found the whole process wrenching. "My hus-band is an engineer: the practical one. I am the emotional one," she says drawing the contrast that has defined their different ap-proaches—his tougher and hers softer—to their son throughout his life.

Like this past weekend when Jonah was home, they were all sit-ting on the sun porch and Jonah was working on his computer. Wal-ter reminded him not to unplug his computer, an instruction he had given several times that day. But when Jonah finished what he was doing, he closed the computer and pulled the plug. His father scolded him for being irresponsible, and Jonah immediately grew anxious and despairing. "I'm always such a disappointment to you," he said to his father. Seeing her son's despair over something so seemingly trivial, Naomi tried to deflect her husband's stern reprimand. "It could have been an accident, Walter. Don't be so hard on him," she said defensively. "He needs to learn these things," responded Walter impatiently.

When Naomi thinks of that one small, very typical example of the different ways in which she and Walter relate to Jonah, she admits that she has "played an enabling role" with her son. She has been the one who has "encouraged a kind of dependency." She looks back and sees the pattern of enabling and wishes that she had, for example, done much more in teaching Jonah the life skills that he would need when he set out on his own, "in order for him to be able to open more doors." "I really wish," Naomi says earnestly, "that he had learned much earlier how to cross the street on his own (he still has trouble with that) . . . how to send an e-mail, make a phone call, make his own lunch . . . I enabled a lot by doing those things for him." This admission seems like Naomi's biggest regret, as she searches for the reasons why she might have discouraged the kind of independence that Jonah is surely capable of. She looks off into the distance and seems to be talking to herself. "Parents hold onto the dream too long. All along, I wanted people to know how bright Jonah really was, even though he was different. Even though he presents as an autistic person, I wanted them to see and acknowledge his intelligence. I wanted to show the world that he makes sense. By his appearance you might see only a cognitive deficit, but there is so much more that is amazing."

Underneath all of this anxiety about how her son might be negatively perceived by others, Naomi recognizes another quality in her that has encouraged her enabling of Jonah. "I always wanted to control everything. I was always worried that he might act inappropriately . . . that he might make strange noises in a restaurant, or suddenly get up and dash out the door and we would have to chase him." She credits her younger son, Wade, with teaching his parents that they were not doing themselves or Jonah a favor by worrying about his behavior. "Wade always took his brother everywhere. I would sometimes be surprised at how he would just bring him along to a rock concert or to a bar to meet up with friends. Wade loved his brother unconditionally and he was never embarrassed by him, never."

Slowly, over the years, Naomi has learned how to "let go of the dream," give up some of her need to "control everything," and she has learned to care much less about how other people see Jonah. She reflects, "I have had to take a hard look at myself . . . and it is still an ongoing process . . . but Jonah and Wade have led the way . . . they have been our teachers." She continues, her voice almost a whisper, "I wanted to fix Jonah and then I realized that I couldn't fix him . . . and that let me see his gifts and his contributions to the world." But even as she occasionally mourns the lost opportunities and laments the ways in which she might have moved more quickly in abandoning her need to control things, Naomi weighs the extraordinary benefits of being Jonah's mother. In some ways, she admits, he has made her an endlessly curious, a deeply questioning "lifelong learner." In trying to see the world from Jonah's perspective, she has had to expand the frames and lenses through which she regards her reality. "He has opened my mind to every angle," she says proudly. "My perspective taking has expanded because he has had to expand."

"You see Jonah's world through his art . . . and it is poignant and beautiful."

Naomi Sawyer has come to understand her son as a "more evolved human being" because of his capacity for nonjudgmental, unconditional love. She has become a lifelong learner, endlessly curious about the world around her as she searches for clues that might unlock the tangles and mysteries in Jonah's mind. She has come to recognize her own limitations and inhibitions as an artist because of her son's spontaneity and freedom in his painting. She has had to "take a hard look" at herself and open her mind to "every angle," recognizing always that there is "no metric to measure" the suffering, no way to live without regrets. Maybe this understanding is a deeper consciousness, a keener and wider perspective, grounded in her son's "limits."

Acceptance

Like Naomi Sawyer, Andrea Hunter discovers that the path to knowing and accepting her transgender son is "letting go of the dream." And like Naomi, right from the beginning Andrea noticed something with Travis that caused her worry and frustration. Even as an infant, he was "difficult to read," to feed, soothe, and get to sleep, a challenge to her hopes and expectations that things would go "normally." Ironically, as Andrea had to learn to navigate each experience of "disequilibrium," as she faced each bump in the road, she would admonish her child to accept "what is"; "you must learn to love your body." But Andrea, over time, discovered that it was she who had to learn to accept "what is" about Travis. Acceptance came through the pleas and insistence of her son, through other people's stories of their similar experiences, through the counsel and guidance of doctors and therapists, through the empathy and support of friends. But acceptance is an ongoing, disquieting question—it is deciding what is real and what is not, what should be allowed to grow and what should be tightly controlled, what is permanent and what can change.

It has just been two weeks since Travis, Andrea Hunter's fifteen-year-old son, was hospitalized after threatening suicide, and I expect that she will arrive looking worn and weary, exhausted and sleep deprived. Instead, she comes to my door—a pretty, petite woman with curly, cropped black hair and bright eyes that look through modern designer glasses—looking energetic and eager. We sit down over our strong French roast coffee—both of us are caffeine addicts—and she listens patiently through my introductory welcome and comments and then leaps right in. "This is all I have been talking about for weeks, so I am in the groove," she says only half joking. Hard and painful conversations—with psychiatrists, counselors, and social workers, close friends and family members, teachers and rabbis, and her transgender support group—have filled her days and evenings, as she has sought support and guidance; as she has tried to figure out how to keep her son safe; as she has looked for moments of respite and release.

Andrea is clearly a person who is strategic in seeking out resources, adept in getting the help that she and her family need, and skilled in forming the deep relationships with friends that she can count on during ordinary times and times of crisis. She also seems immensely likable, and I suspect that she is someone who people enjoy helping. Even though she has been talking about her son Travis nonstop, Andrea's talk does not sound the least bit scripted; she does not seem reluctant to go over the same ground. Rather, she seems to welcome the opportunity to talk and feel deeply; maybe she will unearth an important insight that will help her move forward as a better, stronger parent.

"I guess I have to start at the very beginning when Emma was born fifteen years ago," says Andrea as she tries to find an opening to our conversation. She immediately warns me that she may flip between the names Emma and Travis and the pronouns "her" and "him" as she talks to me. But only once do I hear her refer to her transgender son, who was born in a girl's body, as "she." Andrea has worked—and continues to work—extremely hard to be consistent in calling her son Travis: a discipline and respectfulness that has consumed an enormous amount of her psychic energy. But even as she spins out the birth story, she calls the newborn "Travis" and says that, right from the beginning, he was a "difficult" child. The labor was long—about twenty-four hours—and very intense. They expected it to be a natural childbirth but is turned out that Andrea was "wimpy about the pain," so she was given an epidural, which caused further complications, including "threatening him with a vacuum cleaner to get him to come out." Breast-feeding was difficult and painful, but mother and son persevered, even though it would have been much better for both if she had just fed the baby with a bottle. Andrea is laughing at the pressure she felt—"as a progressive, deeply maternal, feminist" — to breast-feed her child. Feeding your baby with a bottle felt like "a major failure."

Then, when Travis was six months old, he began having breath-holding spells — several episodes each day when he would stop breathing, pass out, and then start breathing again. The first time it happened was when Andrea and her husband Daniel were having their first "real date" after Travis was born. They had hired a baby-sitter for the evening and received the call at the restaurant just as they were sitting down for dinner. ("There were no cell phones back then," Andrea reminds me.) They rushed home and discovered that Travis's breathing had already stopped four times earlier that evening, only to resume after he had fully passed out. It was horrifying to watch, "made your heart stop in panic." The pediatrician told them that this was a behavior that could not be abated or controlled and that it was likely to go away within a year's time. "This was one of my first fundamental lessons as a parent," says Andrea, "that you cannot control everything no matter how diligent and protective you are." So they endured the scary breath-holding spells, and as the doctor promised, the episodes magically stopped when Travis turned eighteen months.

As Andrea looks back on the first year and a half of Travis being a difficult baby, she says "you know we assign these characteristics to our kids, and then we proceed to reinforce them." Travis's sister Lilly, five years younger, was the "easy baby." Born after only fifty minutes of labor, she popped out rosy and healthy and attached easily to her mother's breast when she was nursing. Andrea has always tried to actively resist the assigned roles and family scripts because she knows that as long as she even "thinks" about Travis as a "difficult" child, he will know that is the way she feels. "You know children have special antennae for knowing what their parents are feeling even if we try very hard not to reveal that in our behavior," says Andrea wearily.

In sixth grade, when Travis was eleven, he got his period and, in the next year, began to develop a curvaceous female body. By the time he was in eighth grade, he had large breasts (Andrea's good

friend commented to her that he had an "enormous rack") that required a size DD bra. In school, kids teased him all the time about
the breasts, "not mean teasing, often a kind of noticing and admiring of his breasts." But Travis hated it; and "around that time, he
began to say that he hated being a girl and wanted to be a boy." Several times during the telling of this story, Andrea points to a painful irony: that, despite being a transgender boy, Travis continues to
look extremely feminine, endowed with feminine curves, moves,
and features, and lovely curly hair.

At first, Andrea and Daniel did not take Travis seriously. "We
were closed off from listening. We were both wearing earplugs,"
remembers Andrea. "His pleading annoyed us." They were also
annoyed by some of his new adolescent habits and preoccupations, which they considered creepy and unhealthy. He got deep
into looking at Japanese cartoons and would sit for hours watching
videos that became increasingly weird and pornographic; like gay
men in various physical relationships and sexual poses. Andrea and
Daniel were in constant arguments with him about the inappropriateness of this material. "We did not want him to feel like he was
a bad person, but we also wanted to convey to him that this was
inappropriate," she says about a message that even to her ears felt
mixed and confusing.

But the real battle lines were drawn around Travis's constant requests that his mother get him a "binder" for his breasts. He was
relentless; it was "the constant conversation." Andrea resisted. "I
kept saying that I would never agree to a nose job, and this was
very much the same kind of thing. I told him over and over again,
'this is your body and you must learn to love your body.'" She mim-
ics shaking her finger in his face like an old schoolmarm. Andrea
was just as fiercely certain in her denial of Travis's request as he
was insistent in making it. She admits again, "We were closed off
and not listening." It was at the grocery store one day where the
logjam finally broke. (It turns out that the grocery store is the site
of many difficult and revelatory moments between them.) Once
again, he was "bugging and harassing" her about the binder, and

Andrea finally lost it. "Can you, for once, stop talking about it?" she screamed in his face. He stared directly back at her, his eyes flashing. "There is a reason why I talk about nothing else." "It was at that moment," remembers Andrea, "when the bell went off in my head." Her next words were a mixture of "caving in" and admitting to a "new understanding" of her son's urgent and insistent begging. "Okay," she told Travis, "you do the research, you find it, you pay for it, and you can have it." Strangely, although Travis had won that round, he never followed through on finding and purchasing the binder. Perhaps the months of harassment were as much about getting his mom to listen as they were about purchasing a binder.

Several weeks later, when the binder negotiation was still tugging at Andrea, she was talking to two of her friends at work—this was before she was using the term "transgendered"—about her son's request for a binder. Both of these women—who were big breasted themselves told stories about how in high school they were mortified and embarrassed by their breasts. One said that she had dressed like a boy in order to mask her "big boobs," and the other told how her mother helped her wrap ace bandages around her chest so that she would be more comfortable. Another bell went off for Andrea. When she got home that evening, she told Travis that she did not want him to be uncomfortable any longer and that she would buy him the binder. They went online that night and purchased it.

Travis was determined to begin his first year of high school as a boy; he wanted a fresh start. He had been at a small K–8 public school with about thirty-five kids in his class, and by the time they graduated, they knew each other very well—in fact, they were all "sick of each other." If there was ever a moment to change his public identity, it was at this moment of transition to a big high school where he was unknown. But in the weeks before high school, Travis seemed agitated and confused about how he would enter, how he would look, what he would call himself. Just months before, in the midst of adamantly declaring himself a boy, he had had his bat mitzvah and had chosen to wear a strapless dress that he picked out himself. His aunt had bought him a corset to go under the dress, a kind of all body binder for his curvaceous body. These gender fluid signals were a source of confusion for everybody.

In an effort to help Travis move forward into his freshman year, and perhaps wishing to have some measure of control over the transition, his parents grabbed the reins. "We are going to tell you what to do," they said with more certainty than either of them felt. Everyone was making it up as they went along. Daniel and Andrea decided that he would be "Courtney," a new "gender neutral name that no one really liked," as Travis kept saying definitively that he wanted everyone to refer to him as "he." "This is a kid," says Andrea, "who is always persistent and stubborn. When he was a little baby girl we always thought those would be wonderful qualities for her to have as a grown women . . . but at the same time he has never been that great at standing up for himself." It was almost a year later when they settled on the clearly masculine name of Travis, which it turned out was the name that Daniel and Andrea were planning to have named Emma if she had been a boy.

In early November, after Courtney had been in high school for a couple of months, Rachel, a young woman from their synagogue who is in rabbinical training, called Andrea up. The family goes to a very liberal synagogue, and Rachel is "gender queer," "part of that generation for whom this is all much easier." Rachel told Andrea that she was very concerned about Courtney, that she thought he was deeply depressed, and that she told him to talk about how he was feeling with his parents. She also said that she had told Courtney that she would be calling his parents to urge them to "really listen" to him. That very evening Courtney told them things that they had never heard before, things that really frightened them. He said that he was feeling so bad that he wanted to step in front of a car, walk into the ocean, or take an overdose of pills. He was clearly, seriously depressed. "At that moment," recalls Andrea with tears in her eyes, "I said I'm done fighting about it . . . even though I'm scared for him, even though I don't want this to be true, I'm done fighting."

The timing was actually perfect. In about a week, they were

having a large group of family and close friends over for Thanks-giving dinner, and Andrea decided to let them know in advance that Emma was now Courtney and that he was a boy. It was the first of many announcements—usually tied to ritual family gatherings—that served to advance the cause of Travis's masculinity. Making it clear and public to loved ones seemed to solidify Andrea's mind-set. But the process of taking it public was always deeply exhaust-ing for her. Finding the right words, the right tone, the right mes-sage, which did not smack of defensiveness or embarrassment, was always hard. But it turned out that the Thanksgiving guests were uniformly accepting. Andrea says, her voice full of gratitude, "I am amazed by other people's tolerance for him. The guests were not fazed at all; they were all supportive. A few of my close women friends worried along with me about what his life would be like, but that was their empathy for me shining through."

As a matter of fact, in all of the years since Travis's seventh-grade announcement that he was a boy, Andrea has only had one slightly upsetting exchange with someone about his sexuality. One of the dads, named Doug, who is part of their carpool that takes the kids back and forth from synagogue, approached Andrea one day with a comment that struck her as deeply offensive. He is a guy who is not very socially adept, and even though his comment stung, it was apparent that he was not trying to be hurtful. He said to Andrea, "Your older daughter seems like a nice, although disturbed, young lady. She tried to talk to my five-year-old about being transgen-dered." Andrea was stunned by his comment and said something vague about talking to her son about the inappropriateness of his engaging a five-year-old on this subject. "He kept saying 'she' about Travis, and I kept saying 'he.'" By the time she got home, the ex-change with Doug had begun to fester and settle in her belly as pain. She decided not to let it slide or hold it inside and sat down immediately at her computer to shoot him an "unfiltered e-mail." She smiles when she reports to me that it was "respectful . . . well not completely respectful." "You might be disturbed." She wrote in a rush, "My child is fine." Doug wrote back immediately with a genuine apology, and it was over: like a flash in the pan.

But even as Andrea declares that Travis is fine, and even as she works to protect him from those who might diminish him, she is often scared by what is to come of him. "He looks feminine and he likes boys . . . he is transgendered and gay." She notices the cultural and generational shifts that should cause her to be less frightened, but the worry persists. "The kids are all fine with this. This partly has to do with what has happened in our society, and partly has to do with the hugely progressive culture of Park Slope. But in general, no one cares anymore about gays and lesbians. I do believe that transgendered may be the next horizon, when people begin to appreciate and understand . . . and eventually, not notice."

In fact, Andrea can remember her first contact, about eighteen years ago, with a transgender person who was a coworker at her job. "I am not proud of it, but I was very judgmental." She remembers how she greatly disapproved of his decision to become transgender, "as if it was his choice." She had thought of him as "selfish, choosing to do this to his kids . . . walking his dog and taking his kids to school dressed like a woman." She had "thought it was his responsibility to squelch any urges he had to be a female for the sake of his children." Looking back she "knows how he couldn't help it" and she truly believes that if he had not become transgender, he would "have been dead by now." "Why do you say that?" I ask. "Because he would have committed suicide," she responds with a certainty that now identifies with, and feels deeply connected to, his struggle and his pain. The world has changed, but so has Andrea's understanding and empathy, now informed by a maternal heart that feels protective and admiring of the courage it takes for another human being to walk that path.

The day of Travis's hospitalization was an ordinary day. Travis was at home playing on his computer, and Andrea was on her way to pick up Daniel and Lilly at the Natural History Museum when she got the call on her cell phone. It was her son sobbing into the phone, inconsolable and desperate, saying he was going to cut himself. Before she could even try to console him, he abruptly hung up the phone and then would not pick it up when she tried calling back. Andrea turned the car around, gathered up her son at home, and took him to the emergency room, where he was hospitalized immediately. When the doctors told her that Travis would be there for at least two weeks, she second-guessed herself, thinking that maybe she should not have told them about the cutting and worrying that Travis might be further depressed by being in an inpatient psychiatric ward. In fact, the two weeks he was there went by very quickly and provided the family with some much-needed relief. Besides, it was "nice to have him someplace that was safe." Andrea admits letting out a huge sigh.

Although the family visited each day, the visits were short and nonintrusive. It turned out that Travis did not want to see them too much. "It was not that he didn't want us," says Andrea making the distinction, "it was that his demons would appear in association with home." Most of Andrea and Daniel's time at the hospital was spent with the various psychiatrists, counselors, nurses, and social workers who were part of Travis's treatment team. For the most part, the therapeutic sessions felt confusing and "destabilizing" to Andrea, as the doctors probed for the "foundational issues" that were haunting Travis, as they searched for a way to reframe and understand Travis's pain. "In fact," recalls Andrea, "I found that the conversations were a disservice to me; they disturbed my hard-won, fragile mindset." The doctors said, for example, that it was "not so much that Travis feels like a boy; it is more that he hated developing into a girl"—a message that confused and agitated Andrea.

By the time Travis returned home, Andrea was anticipating another coming-out event. For more than a hundred years, her large, extended family, now including sixty-five cousins, has gathered for Passover; and Andrea began to feel her anxiety rise as she realized that this year "it was going to be a totally different experience." This year she would have to find a way to tell the family—who are all Jewish but from a range of very different backgrounds, including different classes, educational levels, work experiences, and political persuasions—that Travis, not Emma, would be coming to the Passover celebration. Her voice is wistful as she admits her first—"easy way out"—impulse. "If it was up to me, I might have said let's just go with 'she' for Passover. But I've come to see that what is best for the kid is what I should do, even if that means putting him in an uncomfortable and vulnerable place." She looks straight at me and delivers the lesson she has learned from her struggles with coming to terms with her transgender son. Her voice underscores each word as if every utterance is heavy with the gravity of love and suffering. "I've learned to respect what my kid wants. I've learned to lighten up and follow his lead."

About a week ago, Andrea began to compose the letter to the extended family, laboring over each sentence, writing and rewriting it until it was just the way she wanted, trying to get rid of the defensiveness and anxiety that kept weighing down her message. She decided to write a real, hard-copy letter and not risk putting it on e-mail. "I thought that they would take the letter more seriously, and I did not want them to begin shooting e-mails to each other about this." By the time she was almost ready to send it off, she had pared it down considerably and it was almost devoid of explanation. "I figured that they didn't deserve all of these elaborate and cautious explanations . . . it was none of their business." She even put "stuff in the letter that would lighten it up," like the fact that even though Travis is a boy and should be referred to as "he," he still sometimes wears bright magenta bows in his long green hair. And at the end she wrote provocatively, "If anyone else among you has any other announcements to make to the family, this would be a good time to make it." Andrea throws her head back in laughter as she says to me in a stage whisper, "I can't believe that with sixty-five cousins, there is no one who is gay!"

As she worked on the Passover letter, Andrea felt the heavy weight of responsibility landing on her shoulders, and she began resenting the fact that she always seems to be the one to have to offer explanations and make announcements. It is endlessly exhausting. "I've been carrying this entire load," she said to herself. But as she thought about it she realized that she was not the only one bearing the load. Travis was definitely doing his share. After all, he was the one who had gone to school and told his friends; he was the one who had individually approached each of his teachers and sought out the rabbis at the synagogue. Everyone had been extremely supportive, but it took an enormous amount of courage to do it, and Travis had initiated each of those "coming-out" conversations. Recognizing what he had already done so honestly and gracefully, Andrea decided to ask Travis whether he might want to add anything to her Passover letter to the cousins. "What would you like me to say?" he asked. "Anything that you would like to say," she said, hoping not to sound pushy or directive. In short order, Travis sat down and wrote the note, the first and only draft.

Dear Cousins,

I would like you to know that I am transgendered. When I look in the mirror, I no longer see Emma, I see Travis. I can't explain why or how this happened, I just know that is the way it is. When you see me you don't have to treat me like Clint Eastwood, please just acknowledge my masculinity and use the male pronoun.
Thank you.

Love, Travis

When Andrea read Travis's note, she pared down her own letter even more and included both in the envelope that was mailed off three weeks in advance of Passover. The part of his note that moved her the most was the line about Travis acknowledging his inability to explain why he had become transgender. "I have a logical and very organized way of approaching things, probably inherited from my father who is a chemist," says Andrea, "and the fact that Travis couldn't explain it always bothered me. I was touched by his admission of not knowing, and his ability to live with that."

Something makes me ask Andrea whether she ever misses Emma, and her eyes fill with tears again. "I miss Emma terribly," she moans. "Last night Travis was having a hard time, and seemed very sad. I said to him, 'why don't you come and snuggle in bed with me?' And it all felt so cozy, so lovely and warm, and I could not help feeling in my heart, that's my girl." The tender, poignant moment, makes Andrea think of her own mother who died when Andrea was just thirteen years old. It makes her miss all the mothering that she did not have, all the ways in which her mother was not around to help her grow up to be a woman. "I never learned to be a girl," she says softly. "And I see my own shortcomings in my not knowing about girly things . . . like being clueless about the minimizing bra." Her voice trails off.

We both seem to be searching for a little levity—some lightness and laughter—when Andrea brightens and tells me how much Lilly adores, and looks up to, her big brother, how close they are, and how she defends his boyhood to anyone who asks. It makes Andrea's heart sing to see their devotion to one another through all of these stressful times. Then she finds the funny underbelly that makes us both laugh. The other day Lilly asked Andrea, "What does bisexual mean, mama?" "It means someone who loves both men and women," she explained. "I think I am bisexual," Lilly retorted. "I have a crush on Carolyn." Andrea was up in her daughter's face. "You are ten years old. You are not sexual anything!" Case closed. Lilly casually walked away, seeming satisfied with the exchange.

And then there are the moments when the struggles with Travis seem less about his being transgender and more about the "hard stuff of adolescence." Andrea can usually hear the difference in the tone of Travis's voice and in her own impatient response. Like the other day in the grocery store—over the meat counter at Whole Foods—Travis held up a big long sausage and said to Andrea, his voice too loud, "Maybe I'll have this surgically attached." Andrea got very annoyed, really "pissed off." "I'm not a prude, but I was sick and tired of his pushing me to the edge." Undaunted, Travis continued the taunting: pretending to lick the sausage. "This tastes so good, just delicious. Yum-yum." Andrea turned on her heels and walked away. "But even in that very moment, I knew this was a typical adolescent shtick."

Both Daniel and Andrea are clear that there will be no physical interventions at this point, when confusion and uncertainty about Travis's transgender status still hover over them. "He can do what he wants when he is eighteen. That will be up to him," says Andrea with certainty. She has decided, however, that she will allow him to have breast reduction surgery, a decision that she made when Travis was in the hospital—a decision that his doctors wholeheartedly supported. "Somehow during Travis's hospitalization, things got broken free," she says, about the way in which she was able to get some distance and relief when her son was away from home, the way she was able to lighten up a little. Andrea recognizes that there are some possible side effects with breast reduction surgery—the possibility of no breast-feeding later on or some difficulties if he grows more—but she thinks the advantages far outweigh the potential disadvantages. "It will be more physically comfortable for him . . . and it will be easier for him to bind." She feels so clear about the decision to do breast reduction surgery that she even admits, "I think I may be more excited about it than Travis is."

In a way, breast reduction surgery "leaves the options open" for Travis. It also underscores a central contradiction that Andrea lives with all the time. On the one hand, she has been told by all who counsel her—her rabbi, the doctors and social workers, the other parents of transgender children—that she must develop a mindset that sees Travis's male gender as "permanent," that this is the only way that she can find peace of mind, the only way she can get rid of the hovering hopes for his reversal. On the other hand, Andrea also has learned that in order to survive the tumult, she must "live in the moment"; she must learn to adapt to things being uncertain and unclear. "I have to learn to not have a clear idea of what is happening . . . the biggest is that I do not know if I have a boy or a girl . . . who knows what is going to happen," she says with weariness and frustration. I ask her bluntly how she is doing with these contradictory messages of "permanence" and "instability." I'm not managing it well," she admits. I push further. "Between the two, which is the more comforting mindset for you?" "The most comforting is impermanence," she responds. "That he will grow up to be a girl, then a mother who will breast-feed his baby." She stops herself in the midst of her reverie. "But I have to be very careful because if Travis senses that I am feeling that way, he will feel horrible, and his antennae for my feelings are very acute . . . I need to recommit myself to the idea of permanence and not hope for change."

Small moments and community support help her recommit to seeing Travis as permanently boy. Sometimes, she is even able to feel "blasé" when she introduces Travis as transgender. Recently, Andrea wrote a short e-mail to a few close friends—who they do not see regularly and with whom they would be attending a bar mitzvah in a few days—telling them, "BTW, looking forward to our getting together . . . Emma is now Travis." Full stop, short and sweet. It was such a relief for her to just dash off the note and not labor over the feelings and the sentences forever. And the e-mail— without fanfare or explanation—was enough for everybody at the bar mitzvah. To a person, everyone was very welcoming and sweet to Travis. At one point, when all the guests were up dancing the hora—the women in one circle and the men in the other—one of their good friends reached out his hand to Travis and drew him into the male circle. It was the "sweetest moment . . . that gesture meant everything," says Andrea smiling about the memory.

Over the last few years, Andrea has learned some "big and difficult lessons" as she has gotten better and better at letting Travis lead the way, as she has tried to lighten up and live in the moment. At the end of our time together, she is eager to sum up what she has learned.

The first big lesson feels like a litany; discovered many times over during the last five years. "People are much better than I thought they were. There are good human beings all around us. I am still scared for Travis's future, but it helps to know that we are surrounded by genuine goodness most of the time."

The second big lesson: "Live with uncertainty and do not look into the future. . . . Focus on what is happening now." Andrea tells me that coincidentally she has for the last few years studied "mindfulness," which has helped her to develop and sustain this perspective. I ask her how she interprets mindfulness as a philosophy and strategy. "Most importantly, it is being able to step back and observe your behavior and emotions . . . and it is about not making a whole story out of one thing . . . not letting one incident or moment cascade into a whole bunch of other things that end up scaring you . . . the discipline of seeing things only for what they are at the moment." Andrea's search for peace of mind through mindfulness training was certainly provoked by her struggles with Travis;

but the training has also helped her develop the discipline to be a better mother to her son.

The third big lesson: "I have learned that even if you don't feel love all the time, there is something stronger—an urge, a drive—that allows you to carry on and persevere through the struggle. It is a more primal instinct, than love: the drive to protect your kids at any cost." Andrea's voice is as strong as I have ever heard it as she recites this lesson, this capacity for endurance that she now knows she has.

The fourth and final lesson is one sentence long: "Your kids are not you."

Acceptance is personal, private; and it is public. Acceptance stumbles as it finds expression, fluid as it boomerangs between "seeing and appreciating" and "understanding and not noticing." Acceptance is admiration of another person's strength in walking a path that is so hard and so difficult to understand. Acceptance is acknowledging "not knowing" and "not having an explanation," an admission that there are things beyond explanation, beyond one's measure. Acceptance is endurance. Acceptance is also loss: it is Andrea missing the girl her child could have been, missing the mothering she could have done, missing her own mother who died when she was young, missing the reverie of her child becoming a mother. Acceptance is "lightening up" and living in the moment, of being mindful that the present is everything at the same time as it is fleeting. Andrea says, "It is not about making a whole story out of one thing," so maybe acceptance is also a kind of faith that, in the multitude of stories, a happiness can prevail.

Trust

Andrea believes that sometimes a mother's love is actually expressed through a "primal drive to protect"; it is fierce, it is active, it is unrelenting, it's what lets you endure the struggle and the suffering, the disappointment and the losses. It is very different from the way that Steve Saltzman takes the journey towards acceptance of his daughter's lesbian sexuality and his younger son's mental illness. He waits, he trusts, he is patient. His trust that, "however terrible things are, one day they will resolve and work out" is a trust he believes he inherited from his father, who always trusted him. But he also sees trust as an intentional choice—"an act of will"—in his parenting. Steve chooses to trust—he "decides to exercise restraint and a measured faith"—as he endures his daughter's turbulent adolescence, and as he watches his son struggle with "chronic discomfort and unhappiness." As Steve waits patiently, always hoping for the best, he is comforted by the way he was loved by his paternal grandfather—another powerful inheritance—who loved him beyond measure, loved him just the way he was. He hopes to achieve the same kind of love with his own children.

Even before he takes off his winter coat and hat on this frigid day in January, Steve Saltzman is taking out his smartphone in order to show me the photos, and he is crowing about the upcoming wedding of his daughter Julie, who will be married this spring. "I completely adore the woman she is marrying. I'm mad over her. She's the real deal." He grins proudly, finding a photo of his daughter's fiancée, Tina, with her mother and aunts, sitting outside their home in rural Washington State. "Isn't she beautiful?" he asks, without letting me answer, as I try to make the photo larger so I can actually see her face. And yes, she is lovely, a quiet, natural beauty that shines through her rugged garb of jeans and work shirt. The photos were taken at the occasion of Steve's first meeting with Tina and her family, people who have deep roots in the Northwest, who live in a simple house that only twenty years ago had no electricity—hardy, strong people with an openness in their faces and an obvious connection to the lush green land in the background. One photo shows Steve, a short, compact, seventy-year-old Jewish man, squeezed between the tall, strapping women on either side. They are all obviously enjoying their first encounter as the parents of the soon-to-be betrothed.

This opening flourish—of joy and anticipation—does not feel forced or inauthentic. Steve is bubbling over, tripping over his words, almost giggling with pleasure. He is thrilled that Julie has found such a wonderful life partner: kind, successful, substantial. He tells me that Tina is a high-level executive who left Microsoft about a year ago and has landed in an even more senior spot at Apple. He is puffing out his chest in fatherly pride. Later on, as he tells me about his daughter coming out to him after her sophomore year at college, I begin to see that his pleasure in anticipating this wedding has a great deal to do with his own long evolution, with his own struggles to come to terms with his daughter being gay. After a long journey, he has arrived at this place of pride and acceptance; he is being, at least in part, self-congratulatory.

Julie's mother, and Steve's first wife, Marion, died when Julie was twelve years old, a loss that she and her two older brothers—who were then nineteen and seventeen—took very hard, but one that seemed to land most painfully on the shoulders of the youngest. Although Steve does not describe Julie's adolescence in detail—almost as if he doesn't want to relive the pain—he does admit it was extremely difficult, that she was hanging out with the wrong crowd; that she was hugely provocative and stirred up trouble at home; and that, perhaps, some of her rebellion might have had to do with her having to hide her true sexuality. "Half the time I wanted to shoot her," says Steve intensely, his voice laced with exasperation and weariness. The chronic worry she caused him seemed to "trump the rage." "It was the worrying that was driving me crazy, almost making me sick." As he recalls it, one day, in an effort to save himself, Steve finally decided that the only thing he could do was "to trust her."

Learning to trust is a huge theme in Steve's parenting stories. Trust, he admits, was as much about self-preservation as anything else, about trying to survive tortuous times with his three offspring. Rather than make himself sick with worry, he chose the path of trust, a discipline, as alluded earlier, that he says he inherited from his father who always trusted him. He recalls, for example, a request he made of his own father when he was sixteen years old. He and his friends wanted to drive to Newport, Rhode Island, for the jazz festival. They planned to be away for four days, and Steve had only gotten his license three months before. He warms to the memory. "My father was old enough to be my grandfather. He was forty-eight when I was born. We never did stuff like playing catch together. . . . He had no education, left school in the eighth grade. . . . He came from the poorest immigrant family in a poor town in rural New Hampshire." When Steve asked to borrow the family car, his father—with no hesitation or fanfare, without skipping a beat—said yes. "In that moment," remembers Steve, "I learned that my father trusted me." Interestingly, it was not the kind of paternal trust that saved his father from worry. Steve recalls his mother telling him that, when he went out on dates in high school, she would go off to sleep and it was his father who would sit up in the living room waiting for his safe return. The trust came with his father's belief in the goodness and worthiness of his son; but it also held a heaviness, a weighty wait for all to be well in the end.

Steve felt the echoes of his father's trust when he decided to exercise the same restraint and measured faith in his own daughter during her treacherous adolescence. Through the tumult of her teenage years, he says that he must have at least suspected that Julie was a lesbian. She never had boyfriends or dates in high school; she was seeing slightly older women. But "you never ask and she doesn't tell." "You know," he says, underscoring a line he uses several times, "denial is a powerful force in parenting." So Steve was not surprised—nor was he pleased or ready—when after her sophomore year at college, Julie staged an announcement over dinner at one of their favorite Chinese restaurants. Steve remembers her looking straight into his eyes; "insisting that" he see her. "I am gay," she said without any preliminaries or embellishment.

Drawing the extremes, Steve says, "You know some parents might say immediately, 'that's fine, I accept you' . . . whereas others would disapprove and be horrified . . . but I was somewhere in the middle. I was not surprised, but neither was I thrilled." And he makes a clear distinction between "knowing deep down somewhere" that Julie was lesbian and being "confronted with the reality." Following her announcement, there was an awkward silence as they both tried to avoid "the elephant in the room" and find other things to talk about. "I no longer have any problem with it," he says, in understatement as he looks back over almost two decades of accommodation and growth. In fact now—as he boldly announces his daughter's approaching wedding—he feels proud, proud of his wonderful daughter and her lovely spouse and of himself for now feeling this way.

Now, in fact, he exclaims with a big smile, "I have coined a phrase. I say that I've come out of the parent's closet." I ask him how he has come so far after his initial reaction of denial and ambivalence, and he first points to the broad cultural and legal changes that he has witnessed and absorbed. "Society and social change helped me," Steve says, as he points to the legal cases, with opinions written by his close colleagues. A trial lawyer, who loves the logic and performance of his craft, and the elegance of discerning analyses, Steve studied every word of the legal brief—the *Goodridge* case—written by his longtime friend Margaret Marshall, the chief justice of the Massachusetts Supreme Judicial Court, which allowed same-sex unions. He read and reread the brief—of course with Julie in his heart—and felt convinced and supported by Marshall's ethical and legal stance. He also felt—in a not-so rational and litigious way—the broader shifts outside of the arena of the courts, the ways in which society was becoming more tolerant and accepting of gays. Steve's face expresses his vulnerability to the harsh appraisal of others, and he says softly, "It makes a difference when the world is not frowning on you so much . . . when you are not so worried about getting criticized or your child getting criticized."

The second step in "coming out of the parent's closet" is, Steve believes, related to his daughter's patience, her gentle but unyielding approach. "My daughter gets a lot of the credit," he admits. "She hasn't pushed me, hasn't lobbied me, hasn't rushed me." And he thinks that Julie's restraint has a lot to do with her "being comfortable in her own skin." It was almost as if she had nothing to prove; she was clear about who she was and was not waiting on her father's approval or acceptance. "It did not turn on that." Even though acceptance came slowly, with cycles of doubt and confusion, Steve remembers the moment—as if it were yesterday—when his acceptance was complete, when there was "no turning back." Julie's long-time partner at the time was very ill; suffering from the last stages of colon cancer, a virulent cancer that was attacking her body for the third time. Steve had noticed the amazing changes in Julie when she began to live with Laura, and he had always been grateful. "My daughter was domesticated by being with Laura, if I may say so. . . . She grew up . . . became neat, began to cook . . . she began living as an adult," he says reminiscing about the impact their partnership had on Julie who had always been something of a rebel, indulging her immaturity, living on the edge.

But when Laura became ill, the tables were turned, and Julie nursed her through her last months with a patience and vigilance, a devotion and love that he had never seen in his daughter. "As a result of that experience, Julie is now a nurse midwife," Steve says with tears in his eyes "and she midwifed Laura" through those last years and days. "That is the moment that I gave up caring whether Julie was a lesbian." As he flew out to Laura's funeral in California, he could only feel gratitude that Julie had experienced—even once in her life—such a deep, powerful, and reciprocal relationship.

Recently, Steve wrote a short article for a regional paper in New Hampshire—part of an autobiographical series that he contributes to monthly—that he titled "My Daughter's Disclosures and Coming to Terms," another step in his "parents' coming out of the closet" journey. It is a very spare, truncated, telling of the story, short on details and nuance. But it still manages to convey the love and admiration he feels for Julie, and the *naches* (proud enjoyment) he feels in being her father. Before sending it in to the editor, Steve showed it to Julie, who immediately understood that the piece was more about her father than it was about her "disclosures" and then announced that she thought it was "great."

The third factor that Steve identifies as important in his "coming to terms" with his daughter being gay has to do with his being raised in a small town in rural New Hampshire, in a state where "libertarianism" flourishes. "This may be a little far-fetched," he says warming to the idea that this is the first time he has seen any connection between his opening up to his daughter's sexuality and his roots in

New Hampshire. "I don't like the 'live free or die' motto," he admits, "but there is something about people being left alone to do what they want that may play into this as well." Steve reminds me of the political context: New Hampshire, in fact, enacted gay marriage under Democratic legislative law, but when the Republicans came into power, they kept the law in place.

Beyond the legal mandates of the state, however, Steve traces a connection to his father who was a "conservative Republican"—"very unusual for a Jewish man"—but who was also incredibly tolerant and open-minded. And he thinks, perhaps, that there was something about growing up in a small town that allowed for the development of this kind of tolerance. This sounds counterintuitive to me; my caricature of rural small towns sees them as parochial and prejudicial, with folks limited by local scripts that inhibit individual or societal change. Steve surprises me by saying that in small towns—at least in Piermont where he grew up—there were "no ghettos, no class-consciousness." In fact, his family was considered well-off in Piermont; his father and uncles made a very good living manufacturing textiles, and Steve and his sister attended the small public school. The separations and hierarchies—geographic and psychological—that you find in big cities did not exist. Even now, when Steve returns to the town where he grew up, he feels the comfort and familiarity of the community and loves greeting his old friends, who may be on the police force or working as clerks in the local drugstore. "They are still my friends. I know them," he says with appreciation.

So for all of these reasons—Julie's patience and solicitousness, shifting legal and cultural norms, and the live-and-let-live environment of Piermont—Steve has learned to first tolerate, then appreciate, then celebrate his daughter being a lesbian. "She was a benign teacher," he says in summary about his daughter, who "waited patiently and led the way." As the entire extended family anticipates Julie's spring wedding, there does not seem to be an ounce of ambivalence or regret left in her father, only full-throated, openhearted acceptance.

Later on, Steve closes our interview with what is perhaps the most tender and poignant story in his large repertoire. It is about his paternal grandfather, but it echoes with his growing sense of gratitude for who his children are, and who they are becoming. When Steve was in elementary school—and always a star student—his mother, "who was extremely calculating and judgmental," would give him twenty-five cents each time he got an A on his report card. Steve rarely disappointed her, as he racked up a small endowment at the close of each marking period. But Steve's grandfather, a generous, sweet man would always counter with an opposing offer. He would say, "I'll give you twenty-five cents every time you don't get an A." Even though Steve remembers not knowing for sure why his grandfather made the counterintuitive offer, his words always felt comforting and protective, like he was special and valued in his grandfather's eyes. "Actually, says Steve looking backwards and discovering an irony, "by then he was in his seventies, and he had lost his vision because of macular degeneration, but I now realize that he really saw me, in a way no one else did. In essence, he was saying, grades are not everything. They are not the measure of you." Steve's voice cracks and his eyes mist over, as he looks across the table at me. "He was saying, 'I love you the way you are.'"

When he thinks about what he learned from Julie, he hopes he is getting closer and closer to his grandfather's evolved and loving vision. "It takes a long time to get there," he says solemnly. Then he catches himself being overly sentimental and twists it around—as he often does—into a joke. Yes, that all-encompassing nonjudgmental love "comes immediately in the first week of life, and then it sort of disappears until much later." His weariness shows through his big hearty laugh, which rings out with that beautiful/ugly truth.

Even though the silence separating Julie and Steve during her adolescence still evokes some sadness and a sense of wasted and lost time, it is his son Keith, five years older than his sister, who always seemed the most different and difficult child. As a matter of fact, throughout his childhood and early adolescence, Steve and his wife Marion would often say to one another in exasperation, "Whose child is this? Where did he come from?" At birth, Keith was small and sickly. When they would take him to his pediatrician appointments, "he didn't even make it onto the growth charts." When he began to talk, he stuttered badly; and when he began to walk, his gait was strange, his movements awkward. He was a fussy eater. "Still is," says Steve. His parents worried about him constantly. When Steve would fall into despair, his wife would strike a hopeful note. "He'll catch up . . . he is on his own path." His strange ways were enlarged by his refusal to seek help to correct them. "He rejected the speech therapist, refused counseling, and would not talk to his therapist." Defiance lurked underneath every encounter as he struggled to find his way in the world. And he was, in so many ways, the opposite of his big brother Josh, whom Steve and Marion found so easy, appealing, and familiar — so much like them.

Steve remembers, "Keith was a couple of years behind Josh in school and all the teachers Josh loved, Keith detested . . . all of Josh's friends turned Keith off." Even though Keith was something of a stranger to his parents and siblings, everyone recognized his brilliance. He began writing stories when he was four, and by the time he was in middle school, he had developed a photographic memory and become a keen and discerning "observer of the world." Writing was his refuge, a way to avoid the awkward demands of friendships and the humiliations of a social life.

Steve often found himself surprised by Keith's prodigious and exacting mind and the way he held onto a vast array of dates and facts and studied whole fields of knowledge without ever letting anyone know what he was up to. He recalls driving up to New Hampshire with the family when Keith was about twelve, when somehow the casual conversation migrated into a discussion of British history. Someone referred to the reign of Henry the VIII, and Keith, who didn't even seem to be listening, made the correction. "No, Henry the VIII was not a king during those years," he said. "How do you know that stuff?" asked Steve who had never heard his son even talk about the British Empire. "I know all of the reigns of all of the monarchs of England. I know all about who they were, what they did, and how they made history," said Keith, without an ounce of boastfulness.

Steve laughs as he recalls how Keith's expansive and detailed knowledge did not just include rarified topics; he also — amazingly — knew about popular culture, too. Many years later, when Keith was in his early twenties, Steve was preparing to attend some charitable dinner, and he noticed that Gladys Knight and the Pips were performing at the event. Not wanting to embarrass himself by seeming completely out of it, he phoned Keith. "Give me a quick rundown about Gladys Knight," he said, and Keith was able to recite to him all of their records and big hits, even the names of the three Pips, her backup singers. "No one ever remembers the names of backup singers!" Steve exclaims admiringly. He remembers using these "small pearls of knowledge" as he socialized and circulated at the fundraiser. "Keith knows every movie that has been made, the details and facts about everything. He seems like an omnivore to me," says Steve with both pride and bafflement.

Keith was easily admitted to every elite college to which he applied and chose Amherst, where he thrived academically but always seemed to be hiding out, "alone and miserable and distant." It was hard for Steve to witness his son's chronic discomfort and unhappiness and the "mess he made of his life." Keith rejected every attempt Steve made to reach out and offer guidance; there was a gulf between them that rarely seemed to abate. And Marion — who died just before his freshman year — was no longer around to offer words of hope and encouragement to Steve. Without her voice, he often felt at sea, rudderless.

Steve, who had thought that Keith might choose to go into journalism, given his amazingly lucid and exacting writing and his analytic and observational skills, was completely surprised when his son announced that he was going to apply to law school — his own field. Steve knew better than to try to dissuade him, but he worried that he would never find contentment or success in a field that required strategy and relationship building, and he was completely puzzled about why his son — who was so different from him — would choose to follow him into the law. Was this his way of trying to connect with his father? Did he want to make Steve proud? These questions were never broached or answered, even as Keith survived law school, was hired at a prestigious corporate law firm, and harvested fees that allowed him to make a very good living. But through it all, "his life was lonely and miserable"; and Steve continued to worry, trying to calculate the distance between them that would maintain a thin thread of contact, but enough of a closeness to assuage his guilt for feeling the way he did. After practicing law for a few years—not surprisingly, but very painfully—Keith fell into a severe depression; and for two years he hid out in his tiny apartment, totally dysfunctional.

On Steve's mother's side of the family, people have suffered mental illness across several generations. Going back as far as Steve can trace it, there have been suicides. "It is built into the family's DNA," says Steve, shaking his head sadly. When Keith became severely depressed, Steve, of course, worried that he might succumb to the violent family legacy, but he resisted hovering, "not wanting to infantilize him or push him farther over the edge." But after two years, Keith somehow got better and emerged from the darkened room and the shadows of his ancestors. He did not feel or act perfect; there were scars and a lingering awkwardness and fragility. Keith still stutters and he still has sleep problems. But his life is reasonably good; he is back to being a lawyer. And he has found a good wife, who "married him when he was down and is very maternal in her ways. Perhaps she is the replacement for the mother he lost." "Today, he is mostly fine; it's about as good as it gets," says Steve, sounding relieved and surprised. And as Marion promised, Keith "has found his own path."

When I ask Steve what he learned during this long journey of struggle with his son, he responds without skipping a beat, "Be patient and hope for the best." And he says again that it was Keith's differentness that motivated the hard lessons. "I learned more from Keith than I did from the other kids. He was the most different from his mother and me. The other two we got . . . with Keith, I am still on a learning trajectory . . . trying to move ever closer to understanding and acceptance."

Steve admits that his patience and trust in accepting his children's "otherness" was as much about self-preservation as it was about "strategic restraint," as much about an "intuitive inheritance" from his father as it was an "act of will." Rather than being tied up in knots and worrying himself sick during the most tumultuous years with his children, he chose to take a step back and create a safe distance. He admitted that he was not, and could not be, in control; he had faith that things would turn out better. The distancing "worked" for Julie who never pushed and patiently—by example—led the way, who was "comfortable in her own skin," her self-confidence not seeming to rest on her father's approval. And the distancing worked, more or less, with Keith who needed to push his father away as he descended into his depression, keeping only the thinnest connection that could be renewed when he emerged from his darkest time. We also see in Steve's story the public side of acceptance, the powerful role of shifting cultural norms and legal precedent in helping him move from seeing identity, rather than illness, in his children. He says poignantly, "It makes a difference when the world is not frowning on you."

Anchoring

Just as Steve Saltzman's grandfather—his character and his teachings—was the anchor and inspiration for his grandson's growing acceptance of his own children, so, too, does Ryan Calabrese's father figure large in the way he leads his life. Ryan's father has always been his hero, his touchstone, the person that he has wanted to emulate, and the reason he decided early that he wanted to adopt a son so he could become a father like his own. With trepidation—actually terror—Ryan comes out to his twelve-year-old son, Zach, on the eve of his adoption, anticipating rejection. Instead, he gets open-hearted, uncomplicated acceptance. The adolescent years are full of turbulence and conflicts, huge noisy fights, as Zach seems to want to test his father's forbearance, test his promise that he will never "throw him away." Surviving the struggles and passing the test seem to pave the way for a father-son bond in which they know that they will always be there for one another, always be watching each other's back, always be each other's anchor.

"My father was my hero," says Ryan Calabrese several times during our interview. He speaks about him with reverence and admiration and tells me that it is because of his father that he always wanted to be one. "My father worked three jobs, yet he was always there for us . . . like an anchor, a touchstone." Kevin grew up in East Hartford, Connecticut, on a street where his family—his parents and four siblings—were "treated like third-class citizens." Surrounded by newly middle-class, striving families who owned their own homes, the Calabreses were the only renters on the block, the only children not allowed to swim in the neighbor's pool across the street, and the only ones who from time to time went on welfare and food stamps. His father worked fifteen hours a day at three jobs, but he always had time for his kids and their friends. He was the father who would take a bunch of kids to the park to play after he got home from work. He was the Cub Scout leader, and the president of the Parent Teacher Association.

As soon as he graduated from college, Ryan did the next best thing to being a father like his dad: he became a Big Brother to a ten-year-old boy. For two years, they built a solid and satisfying relationship, meeting every weekend, taking trips together, playing sports, collaborating on homework. "I just loved mentoring and the chance for intimacy, hanging out, and time together," says Ryan, who at forty-six is now in his twenty-fifth year of teaching high school physics. But after two years, the boy moved away, a huge loss but one that Ryan knew would be short-lived. He reapplied to the Big Brother program and, almost immediately, was matched with nine-year-old Zachary, whose twin brother Robert and two older siblings had been in foster care for the last six months. They had come from a horrible situation: a father who was in prison for life and had given up custody of his children, and a mother who was a drug addict and alcoholic and could no longer care for them. The bond with Zachary—always called Zach—was immediate and they had wonderful times together.

Ryan was devastated when he received the news that the Division of Social Services had found new foster homes for the children in Las Vegas and that they would be moving out of state within months. "I had fallen in love with this boy," says Ryan simply. "I couldn't stand for him to leave." In a chance conversation with Zach's caseworker, he expressed his sadness, actually his grief, at Zach's leaving, and she said, almost casually, "Well you know you could adopt him." Ryan was beside himself with excitement and terror. Excitement that Zach might one day be his son, terror at the possibility that it all might not work out. He immediately signed up for training as a foster parent (a state legal requirement before adoption can go forward), then he talked to his family, and they were very supportive and encouraging. They had met Zach several times when he had come over for picnics, holidays, and family events, and they were ready for him to join the big clan. Then Ryan talked to his live-in partner, Raphael, who also agreed that the adoption plan was "okay with him," although his enthusiasm was dampened by what Ryan understood to be a "level of distance and resistance that never really went away."

Having completed the foster parent training, Ryan began to talk to Zach about the possibility of adoption, and he immediately said that he wanted to be adopted by Ryan. Several times during our conversation, Ryan says that Zach "does not express his emotions openly," that he "never shows crazy happiness or deep sadness . . . he is always on an even keel." So he was not surprised when Zach said yes to his adoption offer very matter-of-factly, without fanfare, without smiles or hugs or tears of joy.

"At this point," says Ryan, "he did not know that I was gay." Ryan dreaded the conversation and was worried about Zach's response. He arranged with Zach's foster family to have a special meeting, and before they got together, Ryan told Zach that he had something very important to tell him. Ryan's anxiety was "through the roof," but he tried to keep his voice even and calm. "His life was a mess," says Ryan, "and I was the only stable person he knew and could count on . . . and here I was breaking this news." Ryan seems to be reliving the moment of panic. "I will never forget the look on Zach's face. It just lasted a half a second, but it destroyed me . . . it will always be seared into my brain. The look seemed to say, 'everything in my life is screwed up and now you are saying that you are screwed up as well.'" But it took only a few seconds before Zach's face relaxed with acceptance and his voice rang out clearly. "I don't care. When can I come live with you?" It was the summer of 2000 when the adoption became legal. Zach was twelve and his new father was thirty-four.

Ryan, Zach, and Raphael moved into a lovely carriage house right around the corner from Ryan's parents in East Hartford. A couple of Ryan's siblings were still living at home, so Zach "got everybody in one fell swoop." He grew very close to his grandparents and enjoyed his coveted status as their eldest grandchild. Often, he would walk over to their house to hang out for the afternoon or to mow their lawn or help to bring in the groceries, and they often gathered there for extended-family dinners. Ryan says his family was a source of enormous support, acceptance, and "validation." Raising a young teenage son proved to be very difficult and extremely exhausting, but the grandparents' participation made "the impossible possible"; the cross-generational relationships were a salve for the explosive conflicts between father and son.

The three of them lived in the carriage house until 2004 when Ryan and Raphael ended their twelve-year relationship. They sold the house, moved out, and split the profits. "Zach chose to live with me," says Ryan evenly. His steady voice barely masks the pain of the separation and the disappointment that he rarely allowed himself to admit about the distance that had always existed between Zach and Raphael. He reflects sadly on the "thinness" of their relationship: "They never really bonded." Ryan thinks that part of Raphael's reluctance to get deeply involved with Zach had to do with his own upbringing. He had "lousy, abusive parents, who pushed him away and never offered him any validation." But Ryan also now sees the seeds of jealousy that were always there for Raphael; he felt displaced by Zach and resented his presence. He competed with Zach for Ryan's attention. Ryan spent a good deal of energy trying to make their relationship better. "I remember one time that someone gave me two great, ringside tickets to the circus, and rather than my going with Zach, which I really wanted to do, I said you guys go ahead and enjoy. I was always trying to do things to make them feel close."

Just as he vividly recalls the many times when he tried to arrange for their closeness, Ryan remembers something that Raphael said during the adoption process that stunned him and caused him some discomfort. "He told me that with Zach as our son we would have someone to take care of us when we got old," says Ryan "I would have never thought about that . . . not in my wildest dreams." In the ten years since they split, Raphael has seen Zach only twice. "That is fine with Zach," says Ryan, about a feeling of "disinterest and distance" that he believes is mutual.

But it is also very possible that Raphael was simply worn down by how hard Zach was to raise. "He was difficult, obstinate, and sometimes very mean," says Ryan, not exaggerating and not mincing words. The conflicts and fighting were the steady diet of their lives as Ryan tried to respond to Zach's transgressions with equal force, as they went toe-to-toe in battles that could go on for days. When Zach would get angry he would slam his door and hide out in his room. Finally, after numerous warnings, Ryan just removed the door from his room; the slamming ceased. On Fridays, when Zach came home from school, Ryan would insist that he do his homework first before any weekend activities. The rule was that he could not go out until all the homework was completed for Monday. "So just for spite, Zach would go into his room and not do his homework on Friday, Saturday, or Sunday . . . just stubbornly staying in his room refusing to do it . . . only finally relenting late Sunday night." At school, he would neglect to write down his homework assignments and often found himself in after-school detention, where his work could be closely monitored. Ryan was constantly being called up to the school for special disciplinary conferences with counselors and teachers. Ryan—who says he is like his son in being an even-keeled person—sighs with exasperation and weariness at the "chronicity of these battles" and of the ways in which his son's meanness was sometimes hurtful. "He was thrown away so many times in his early life," says Ryan, trying to give explanation to Zach's constant provocations, "that he was always terrified that I would decide to get rid of him. He would do awful things to make me want to throw him away."

There are so many stories of conflict and embattlement, of Ryan's exhaustion and hurt at confronting Zach's anger, that I ask Ryan how he managed to sustain his love for his son through all of the hard years. And his answer is immediate and upbeat. "When he is not being difficult, he is an amazing kid." He tells me that their best times occur when they are doing things they want to do together; then he is a "wonderful companion." Three years ago, Ryan invented a summer ritual as a way of creating these congenial spaces where their lives would pleasurably meet. He tells Zach to pack his bag, tells him how many days they will be away, but does not reveal where they are going. The first time they went for three days to Cooperstown, New York, to the Baseball Hall of Fame—perfect for the boy who "lives, breathes, and dies for the Yankees." The second summer they flew out to Cleveland, Ohio, where Ryan's brother lives, and hung out in the city and saw the sites. It was Zach's first time on a plane. And the third time, they packed their bags for a week and traveled to Naples, Florida, where they toured the Everglades, saw the alligator swamps, went to the beach, rode on go-carts, and had terrific southern cuisine. On these trips, they are "alone together," on a big adventure, and it is always a lot of fun.

Times are wonderful and companionable on these adventures; there is no tension between them, and Zach is "so easy to love." Ryan also sees Zach as amazing in the ways in which he—even in the most difficult times—stands up for his father. "He is very protective of me," says Ryan gratefully. "He has my back." The story he tells about Zach's protective instincts puts another one of Ryan's partners at the center of the conflict. After separating from Raphael, Ryan got involved with Carl, "a really wonderful guy, really sweet and kind, but he drank too much." He was a binge drinker, had a couple of tickets for driving under the influence, eventually lost his license and then his job. By the time Carl moved in with Ryan, Zach had moved out and was on his way to Westbrook Community College. "I was determined not to have any new partner come live with me until after Zach left," says Ryan "I'm always the one who tries to protect everyone from everything. I knew Carl was a drinker and I wanted to protect Zach from his drinking."

But the first time Zach came home from college for a visit, Carl was passed out on the bed, wine was spilled all over him, and there were empty vodka bottles on the floor. The evidence of his alcoholism was everywhere, and Zach was "not surprised but he was pissed." He did not say anything to his father, but he was clearly worried about him. Soon after — as things went from bad to worse — Ryan kicked Carl out and threw away all the booze bottles that he found hidden around the house. About six months after Carl left, Ryan bought himself a bottle of vodka and put it in the freezer for his occasional evening cocktail. A couple of weeks later, Zach came home, opened the freezer for some ice, and saw the vodka bottle. "Is Carl here?" he screamed to his dad, his voice threatening. "Is that his vodka in the freezer? I will kill you if you go back with him!" His rant continued long after Ryan assured him that Carl was not there, that he had left months before, and that he was completely out of their lives. Underneath all of Zach's yelling, Ryan could hear the love, his "fierce protectiveness." "Zach knew, and could see, how rough the relationship with Carl had been on me. I could tell that his anger was coming out of his fear for me. . . . It was at that moment that I felt the relationship flip. Zach was protecting and fathering me, and I loved him for that."

There are other very tangible ways that Zach has taken the lead at home, ways he has been the "expert" and Ryan has been the "learner." Even though Ryan has an advanced degree in engineering and feels pretty competent taking care of things that need fixing at home, it is Zach who usually takes over. Recently, Ryan moved into a new house, and Zach texted him from college to say that he should just make a list of things that need doing, and he would take care of them when he came home over the weekend. One of the chores was wiring the stereo system with its elaborate surround sound. "It would have taken me at least six or seven hours to put it all together and get it going," says Ryan. "Zach did it in an hour. He is much faster and more intuitive than I am." Zach is a "tinkerer," an expert in all things electrical; and his father marvels not only at his skill and mastery but also at the confidence and ingenuity he brings to the work. "The electrical stuff is all his; that's not me," says Ryan about how "inspiring and instructive" it is to watch him do his thing, and how much his son, in these moments, seems to enjoy being in charge, being the teacher.

Remembering Ryan's description of the terror he experienced before the adoption when he first told Zach that he was gay, I ask him whether his homosexuality has ever been a source of tension or unease between them. "Zach has always been fine with it," he says evenly. Rather, it has been Ryan who has, from time to time, gone through moments of panic. He recalls a time soon after Zach came to live with him, when he and Raphael were lying up in bed watching television. Zach came in the room, and Ryan startled. "I was freaking out inside. I was worried how Zach might feel, but he just casually laid down with us on the bed, and watched the show."

Zach showed the same kind of nonchalance and acceptance when, about a year later, Ryan switched teaching jobs. He moved to Wilton High School, where he was hired to teach junior and senior physics courses. Zach followed him to Wilton and attended the middle school there. Even though Ryan was out to his family, his son, and his friends, he decided that he would not tell the folks at his new job that he was gay. "I was always very afraid of what people might think of a gay man adopting a boy," says Ryan about one of the reasons for his secrecy. Before the first day of school, he told his son that he was not going to disclose the fact that he was gay to anyone at the high school, but that Zach was free to tell whomever he wanted to tell. His father's mixed message seemed to be okay with Zach; he did not question Ryan's decision or reasoning and proceeded, over the next couple of months, to tell a half a dozen of his good friends—those who often visited them at home—that his father was gay. Zach did not swear his friends to secrecy; there just seemed to be a level of trust between them that signaled that this was not information that should be passed along at school. As

Ryan looks back on Zach's handling of these disclosures, he sees his "courage and his self-confidence" and the ways he does not get caught up in "what other people think of him."

For the entire time Zach was in school in Wilton—through middle and high school—Ryan remained "closeted." Certainly most of his close colleagues knew he was gay, and so did Zach's close circle of friends, but it was not generally known by the students and their parents. It was not until three years after Zach graduated, in fact, that Ryan came out publicly. It was October of 2009, and a gay student (a senior at the time) and his boyfriend were harassed and bullied at a school dance, and no one stood up for them. Ryan heard about the incident afterwards, as word spread around the school, and there was a groundswell in the community that something needed to be done. Ryan and some of his colleagues decided to hold a "diversity assembly"; and they asked various students to stand up, tell their stories, and speak about their experience of being outsiders, of being excluded or stereotyped: a white girl disabled by cerebral palsy, an African American boy in "a 99 percent white school," an athlete speaking about confronting the "dumb jock stereotype."

The planning group also wanted to include a faculty voice, and they asked Ryan whether he would speak about being gay. He did everything to resist, suggesting, among other deflections, that the other senior physics teacher who was "out gay" give the speech instead. "Not only did I not want to take this on, I also hate public speaking!" says Ryan, his voice still ringing with exasperation and defensiveness. But his colleagues persisted, and he finally agreed to do it. His final decision to participate, Ryan realized even then, had a lot to do with wanting to do right by his son. "In my own head, more than 50 percent had to do with Zach. If he was brave enough to tell his friends, I should be brave enough to come out to the school. It was high time. Because I wasn't out when Zach was at school, kids would be joking around about queens and fags, and Zach would overhear it and not be able to say anything. It was not safe for my own son in my own classroom."

Ryan spent huge amounts of anxious time preparing, writing

and rewriting drafts, practicing in front of the mirror, and finally standing up in front of the whole school assembly. When he looked out at his audience — full of young faces eagerly listening — the fear fell away. He decided to lead off by telling the story about coming out to his family. It was 1990, and he was at home in East Hartford watching a movie on television with his younger brother. The movie, *Doing Time on Maple Drive*, tells the story of a kid who discloses that he is gay, is rejected by his family, and in an act of final desperation, commits suicide. When the movie ended, Ryan watched his brother — who was going off to his work as a security guard — start towards the door. As he walked out, he lifted up his shirt and revealed his gun. "This," he said pointing to the gun, "is my fag killer." I am stunned by what I think I heard, and ask Ryan to repeat it. "At the time, my brother did not know that I was gay. Remember twenty-five years ago in East Hartford, it was funny to say things like that." His brother walked out of the house; Ryan said nothing.

A couple of years earlier, when Ryan was in college, he had fallen into a clinical depression. He looks back on that dark time and tries to piece together the reasons for his depression. "My grandfather had died recently, and I was very close to him . . . I was the first in my family on my father and my mother's side to go to college and I felt under a huge amount of stress. . . . I was not yet really conscious that I was gay, but I am sure that was weighing me down. I was so low that I tried to commit suicide." At the insistence of a college counselor, he spent several months in therapy with a psychiatrist who prescribed Prozac for his depression and who helped him uncover and admit that he was, in fact, gay. "During this time," says Ryan sadly, "I tried to distance myself from my family." But the next time he was home from school, it was his younger brother — the one with the gun — who would have none of it. He got up in Ryan's face and said, "You are being such as ass. If you are gay you should say it. Who gives a shit?" Ryan remembers "feeling frozen" and giving no response, his face placid and noncommittal.

It was his father who finally broke through the wall of silence. He just came in from work one afternoon, and said to Ryan, "If you are gay, that is alright with me. And if your brothers have trouble with that, then they'll have to come through me." So it was his father, the man Ryan calls his "hero," who first "received the truth" from his gay son; and then the brothers followed. There was no drama, only simple acceptance. Ryan found it hardest to tell his mother. "That was a tough one," he says grimacing. Years before, when he was in his late teens, he recalls his mother saying to him out of the blue, "Can I ask you a personal question?" To which Ryan had responded, "Don't ask me anything that you don't want to hear." His evasion was enough to keep his mother at bay for several years, until everyone else in the family had been told and there was "nowhere to run, nowhere to hide." Ryan's mother responded to his disclosure with "all the typical stages of denial," even though she must have already known the truth. "First she said to me, 'you can't be gay, you are too handsome.' Then she said, 'that can't be true, you could have any girl you want.' Then she moved on to self-blame, 'I shouldn't have let you vacuum the house.' . . . Final acceptance came slowly."

In his speech to the school assembly, Ryan told the coming-out story as a cautionary tale. He talked about what it was like growing up in East Hartford at a time and in a place where homophobia was rampant, when gays were routinely harassed and ostracized. And he talked about how important it was that he had found professional support and guidance and that he had a family who loved and accepted him. He said that everyone was responsible for creating safe spaces where no one would be marginalized, excluded, or bullied. Along with the other speakers, he wanted most of all to say, "Everyone is different. Everyone has a story to tell."

The whole time he stood up on the stage talking, he felt Zach standing beside him protectively, offering him encouragement. He felt, as well, the ways in which the long struggle he had waged to get to this point of public disclosure was so different from his son's natural acceptance of his father's homosexuality. Right from the beginning Zach had seemed so comfortable with having a gay dad; "it was always fine with him." Some of Zach's comfort (even nonchalance) comes from being raised at a time and in a place where homosexuality is more widely accepted. These days everyone seems to have a family member who is gay, and Wilton, where Zach was a middle and high school student, is "one of the most liberal towns in Connecticut." Several of his peers came from "untraditional families"; a few had two moms or two dads.

But Zach's ease and cool with his father's homosexuality seem to come from a "deeper place." Ryan shakes his head, with fatherly pride and admiration, as he describes one of his son's "most amazing qualities" and admits that he finds little of that in himself. "Zach has a strong sense of who he is and what he wants. What people think about him or say about him do not matter to him at all." Sometimes Ryan looks at his son — sturdy and confident — and says to himself, "Who is this kid? How did this strength of character grow up in him?" At those moments, they sometimes "flip places." As he has watched Zach grow up into "this assured and determined young man," Ryan has marked the contrasts between them and learned some valuable lessons about the freedom that comes with "knowing yourself so well."

Zach's self-confidence helps him as he builds and sustains the primary relationships in his life. Ryan immediately thinks of Zach and his girlfriend Maria, who have had an "awesome bonding experience." Maria, who Zach met during his freshman years in community college, is also adopted; her parents brought her back from Guatemala when she was three. After Zach and Maria were together for a couple of years, their relationship hit a rocky patch — they were fighting a lot — and Zach decided to break up with her. Ryan was devastated when he heard about the breakup. "I love her to death," says Ryan about the "light and loveliness" that Maria brought into their lives and the ways in which she made Zach glow with happiness. When he asked Zach why he had ended the relationship, he said, "I love her tremendously, but it got to the point where it was not fair to her or to me. We were both unhappy and we both deserve better. . . . It is more important that each of us find a way to be happy in our lives than it is that we carry on, but be unhappy, in this relationship together." Again, Ryan shakes his head in admiration. "Zach's insight is amazing. I'm forty-eight years old and at twenty-four, he is more insightful than I am! I find myself asking, where is this thought coming from?" Before the end of our interview, Ryan assures me, with great relief, that Zach and Maria are recently back together. Their reunion after several months apart "mirrored their breakup"; they showed the same maturity, love, and empathy towards one another.

Ryan offers another example of Zach's "strong sense of who he is," an illustration that has a surprising twist. He traces Zach's peripatetic eight-year journey in and out of a series of colleges, each leave-taking punctuated by returns home. "After Zach finished high school, he enrolled in Westbrook State College. Before the end of the first semester, he quit and came home. . . . Then he went into City Year in New Orleans for six months, quit and came home. . . . Then he went to live in an East Hartford apartment, got a job as a busboy, quit, and came home. . . . Then he went to Windsor College, stayed for a year and a half, we ran out of money, he left and came home. . . . Then he went to Camden State, stopped going to class after a semester and a half, announced to me that he was through, that he was done for now . . . that he would get a job and figure it out." As Ryan rattles off the comings and goings, the advances and the retreats, he does not sound like the overwrought, frustrated parent who is at his wit's end; nor does he seem to be describing his son's path as one of self-destruction or irresponsibility. Rather, he sounds optimistic, even certain that one day Zach will find what he is looking for, and it will be right for him. What might appear from the outside like "fragments and pieces" is, Ryan believes, a long, steady march towards "something meaningful." And over time, and at first with some difficulty, Ryan has learned to step back, keep quiet, and trust his son's "self-knowledge and resourcefulness."

The last several years of accommodation to Zach's circuitous navigations have been very different from the ongoing conflict that marked and marred their relationship before he left home at eighteen; and Ryan has calmed down and "let him do his thing." "Zach wants to be a social worker and he will be a great one," says Ryan about the clarity of his future goal, "but so far the academic track has not worked for him." This summer he is working as the assistant director at a camp that he went to as a kid, work that he loves and is good at, work that has "a lot of social work as part of it." Recently, Zach called his dad and told him that he had concocted a plan going forward. "He told me that he didn't want to jinx it by telling me what it is," says Ryan having learned that the worst thing he can do is try and insist that his son divulge his plan. "But I believe in my heart that he will get where he is going."

All the time we have been talking, I have been trying to picture Zach so I finally ask Ryan what he looks like. "We look alike," he says immediately. "All through school, his friends would never believe him when he said that he was adopted because we resemble each other completely." Ryan digs in his pocket for his cell phone and pulls up a picture of both of them on Zach's Facebook page. And there they both are, lean and handsome, angular with chiseled features, their sandy brown hair closely cropped, arms around each other, smiling into the camera. Father and son. No one would ever mistake them for anything else.

Several times Ryan says that he and his son "flipped places"; Zach became the father, expressing the maturity and self-confidence of an elder, protecting his father, taking the lead. Flipping father-son places was the surprising bounty that followed a torturous adolescence where they fought meanly and mightily, where each gave as good as he got, where Ryan had to keep on proving to his son that he would never abandon him. The unwritten covenant between them, that the warfare seemed to yield, was that they would "always be there" for one another. Zach was there for Ryan's breakups, for home repairs and electrical installations, for Ryan's public coming out at work. His devotion to, and admiration for, his son was more than 50 percent of the reason he forced himself to speak out at the school assembly. Ryan and Zach seem to be touchstones for each other, as if they both "chose" to be father and son. Their trips "alone together" are a symbol of this special place where they have each other's backs and relish each other's company. With his son, Ryan has another hero.

Cross Currents

Teaching and Learning

Ryan and Zach's handsome close-up shot of togetherness and like-ness casts a glowing light on their father-son journey together, a moment frozen in time that marks and celebrates their anchoring and intimacy, their mutual support, admiration, and protective-ness. It is not the end of the story, but it is a nice place to land after the anxious, tentative beginnings of choosing one another, after the adolescent years of testing and torturous fighting, after Ryan's long struggle to come out of the closet publicly. In their story, we hear currents that flow across all of the narratives in this volume. We hear the powerful role of "witnessing" as Ryan testifies—with awe and amazement—about who his son has become and is be-coming and wonders out loud about the origins of his extraordi-nary self-confidence, and as we recognize the ways in which Zach's self-knowledge—his temperamental ability to take his own mea-sure, to not care what other people think of him—has become em-bedded in Ryan's courageous public coming out. We hear Ryan and Zach's developing "intimacy": a closeness born out of fierce fight-ing and conflict; a testing of each other's commitment to the rela-tionship; a covenant cemented in the warmth and comfort of their father-son, alone-together adventures. And we hear the acceptance that is mutual and grows deeper over time: the father's acceptance of his son's zigzag journey in and out of school, and his certainty that Zach will find his way, and the son's acceptance of his father's long journey towards a wholesome identity as a gay man and father. In Ryan and Zach's story, then, we hear the themes of teaching and learning that thread their way across these chapters, underscoring the interconnectedness in the design and tapestry of parent-child pedagogy.

As I look back on the extraordinary experience of listening to parents tell their growing-up tales, I am struck by the ways in which the interview—the actual process of questioning and listening, of reflecting and storytelling—was itself a rare opportunity for parents to consider, and then realize, the myriad ways in which their offspring have taught, and continue to teach, them life lessons, and the ways in which their evolving and deepening relationships with their children become unique sites of learning for them. Our interviews, which invited parents to tell their stories in different ways, from different perspectives and vantage points, which encouraged them to voice the often contradictory emotions and impulses that are embraced in our parenting repertoire—the bad and the good, the suffering and the love, the painful and the redemptive—allowed them access to thoughts and feelings that they had seldom considered before. The interview, then, was itself, an opportunity for bearing witness, for instigating growth, for reframing intimacy, and for finding acceptance in their role and experiences as parents.

I was not only struck by the generative, reflective experience that got provoked for parents during the interview process, I was also surprised by those moments of learning and revelation that they chose to talk about with me, as well as by the types of teaching and learning encounters that rarely came up in our conversations. Their preoccupations and their silences were noteworthy and framed a learning map that had unanticipated contours and detours. The parents, for example, rarely spoke about their children teaching them how to use the various new and emerging technologies: how to work the apps on their smartphones, how to log onto Facebook or use Twitter, or how to conceptualize the invisible "cloud." And if parents did mention their children's instruction in technology, it tended to be a throwaway line—assumed, expected, and inconsequential—as if the directionality of the teaching and the flow of knowledge were naturally supposed to move from the young to the old.

Occasionally, parents would briefly refer to the fact that they "learned everything about computers" from their offspring, how they turned to them constantly whenever they hit a technological glitch or roadblock, and how their children would respond to their desperate calls for guidance and rescue. But parents usually referred to these skill-based technological interventions as a jumping-off point for exploring the ways in which their children's guidance and help taught them new ways of approaching learning and mastery. Just like the techie tutoring I received from my son Martin—when he would sit at my elbow, patiently watching, waiting for me to figure things out on my own, encouraging me to lighten up and play—the parents I interviewed often discovered a capacity within themselves that went far beyond mastering the bells and whistles.

So, too, parents spoke to me about how the technological teachings of their progeny gave them new insights—that had often gone unrecognized before—about their child's maturity and patience, his passion for learning, his capacity for deep and sustained focus, that they began to see new aptitudes and achievements in their child. One parent even talked about how his child's tutoring in cyberspace helped him discover the importance of "experimenting, tinkering, and multitasking" as central to "exploring the edges of new learning."

Rachel Goldstein, the dentist who saw herself as both an artist and a scientist, an "empiricist and a craftsperson," was the only parent I interviewed who claimed that she was more "in love with" and "proficient in" the world of technology than her three daughters, who are in their late teens and early twenties. But her love for technology had less to do with being enamored with its speed and its scope, its immediate access to vast amounts of information. Rachel loved technology for its "cultural resonance and significance." Facebook, she raptured, was becoming "the collective unconscious of society."

It was not only that I heard little mention of young people sharing their technological expertise, but parents also rarely mentioned that their children's pedagogy was formal, intentional, or didactic. Their stories seldom referred to their children teaching them a new skill—like the electric slide, skateboarding, or horse-

back riding, like hearing the poetry in rap music or being introduced to the regimens of a vegan diet. Again, if the teaching of
these skills or competencies was mentioned at all, the learning narratives were woven into a larger lesson. In her interview, Eva Galanis, for example, returned time and again to the significance of food
as an expression of "community and family, culture and roots," and
said that her daughters often reminded her that there are no words
in the English language sufficient to describe the tastes and textures
of the Greek food that they prepared together in their kitchen. But
even though Eva exclaimed about the deep connections between
food and Greek culture, the significant lesson she claimed she
learned from her twin daughters, as they introduced new dishes
into the family repertoire, was the way food could become the symbolic and nourishing vehicle for crossing cultural boundaries, for
balancing and merging Greek traditions with eclectic American
variations, for losing some of her fear about the threats of American materialism. Eva's daughters were teaching her that, in taking
on aspects of American culture, she did not have to relinquish her
precious Greek traditions; she could value and embrace both. Following her daughters' example, Eva was learning some of the ways
in which she might comfortably and creatively straddle and enlarge
her cultural boundaries.

If parents do not tend to tell stories about those aspects of their
children's pedagogy that focus on skill-based learning, didactically
delivered, then what kinds of teaching and learning seem to capture
their interest and claim their attention? As the narratives in this volume attest, parents are most intrigued with — and appreciative of —
the lessons that teach them something new about themselves —
about their capacities, their values, their appetites; about their fears,
anxieties, inhibitions, their gifts and their strengths; about their
own early childhoods and autobiographical journeys. And they
learn those things about themselves from someone — namely, their
child — who arguably knows them better, and more deeply, than
anyone else, from someone who serves as a mirror in their learning
(they see in their child that which is also in them), their adversary
in learning (lessons that grow out of conflict, struggle, and a clear

articulation of their differences), or their partner in learning (discoveries made "side by side" as they take on a new adventure or frontier together).

Parents not only learn about themselves—their values, priorities, temperament, and competencies—from their almost-grown children, but, just as importantly, their progeny also teach their parents to see them more clearly, to know them, to reckon with who they are and what they need. Sometimes the child is adamant and explicit, driving the lesson home again and again—often against parental inertia and resistance—until the parent finally looks, listens, and attends. Andrea Hunter, for example, talks about how her transgender son, Travis, spent months begging for a breast binder, turning up the heat with each request, desperate for his parents to recognize that he was their son, not their daughter, pleading with them to listen, asking for their respect. "This is who I am," he was insisting. Andrea admits that, "for the longest time," she did not listen to his pleas, which began to sound like "a broken record." She did not take him seriously, hoping his yearnings were transitory and "fleeting," perhaps a sign of his temperamental contrariness, a precursor of his adolescent rebellion. "It is as if my husband and I had earplugs on. We were so closed off . . . and Travis was trying to find a way to break the logjam." The irony, of course, was that when Andrea finally caved in—exasperated and defeated—and gave Travis permission to go online to order the breast binder, he did not follow through. What he wanted more than the binder was for his parents to finally listen to him, to recognize and honor his "true identity."

Over the years, Zoe, Simone Ray's daughter, now in her midthirties, has taken a more subtle but no less insistent approach than Travis, naming the contrasts—in temperament and style—between herself and her mother in an effort to claim her identity, hoping and trusting that one day Simone will be able to see her as a "separate person." The video that she takes of her mother sitting on the toilet is a poignant record of their different needs and personalities. Simone is so extroverted and out there that she allows her daughter to tape her urinating in the hotel bathroom. By contrast,

Zoe is saying, "I have a 'shy bladder' . . . I am the kind of person who needs my privacy. This is who I am."

Parents' narratives, then, largely refer to the insights they discover about themselves and the new understandings they develop about who their children are and who they are becoming. And parents' stories of learning refer to a pedagogy that is relational rather than didactic—a pedagogy that grows out of accumulated encounters between parents and their children, ordinary, often repetitive and ritualized moments of living together side by side and face-to-face.

Occasionally, and by contrast, the lessons feel surprising and momentous, arriving "like an epiphany" out of the blue, a sudden awakening, a noticeable shift of perspective or perch that seems to alter one's view of the larger universe. When Margo Lockwood chronicles many of the ways in which her two daughters, now in their thirties, have guided her in becoming a more "authentic" human being—more honest, open-hearted, collaborative, and respectful—she draws the distinction between the "slow learning" that accumulates over the years as she gets to know them each more deeply and begins to absorb aspects of their different temperaments, and the "fast learning" that "suddenly hits you like a "bolt of lightning." Margo describes these moments of epiphany as both specific and refracted, with ripple effects that extend way beyond the moment of impact. On the afternoon that she finds her fifteen-year-old daughter carving her lipstick into a sculpture after being sent to her room and refusing to do her homework despite her mother's harsh threats of reprisal, Margo is "bowled over" by her daughter's confident voice—"You do not have power over me"—and immediately "hears it and learns it." She turns on her heels, leaves the room, and cannot stop thinking about the implications of what her daughter has said—not only the ways it might have an impact on their mother-daughter relationship but also the ways she might handle misunderstandings with her new husband or collaborate with her colleagues at work.

Zarina Nielson describes one of these "shocking" moments of epiphany as she revisits the Christmas story from when her daughter Christina was eleven, now a family tale that has become iconic. When she discovered Christina's note to the Christmas elves under the tree, asking as nicely as she could for a Runway Barbie, she knew immediately that her offering of the handmade wooden barn was not about pleasing her daughter. It was about trying to fend off for one more year the American materialism that was seeping into her house; it was about satisfying her own needs for "high standards." Her daughter's note was a "wake-up call," one that Zarina could no longer resist or avoid, one that "hit her in the gut," and caused her to make the midnight run up to the mall in a desperate search for the Runway Barbie. But the story has become family legend because it represents much more than a poorly chosen gift. In that moment, facing the depleted shelves at Toys"R"Us, Zarina understood the folly of her ways: the impossibility of protecting her family from the influences of American society, the impossibility of controlling every aspect and morsel of her children's consumption, and the importance of revising her view of "good mothering."

Generational Ghosts and Echoes

The lessons that parents learn from their progeny reverberate with echoes from their own childhoods. At some point during all of my interviews, parents referred to the ways in which their experiences as children—as the daughters and sons of their own parents—not only influenced the ways they parent but also shaped their receptivity to the teachings of their children. Sometimes these generational echoes are conscious and described with great specificity and candor, drawing the connections to early autobiographical experiences that are now part of the family lore. At other times, the echoes resonate for the first time during our interviews, when parents hear themselves telling a practiced tale they have told many times before and, for the first time, recognize its powerful and surprising imprint on their own parenting. A story that has always felt uplifting feels—in the retelling and reinterpretation—strangely ominous; a simple, straightforward tale of valor becomes a confusing saga of moral uncertainty.

Some of these family ghosts are remembered as benign, even comforting. Steve Saltzman recalls the amazing trust that his father showed in him as he let him borrow the family car to drive with a bunch of his buddies to a jazz concert three states away, just three months after he got his driver's license at sixteen. Steve tries to mimic that sense of trust as he deals with the drama and chaos of his daughter's volatile adolescence. The trust—which he feels as "both an inheritance *and* a choice"—brings him some measure of distance and relief from the adolescent "madness." Choosing to trust does not spare him all of the worry and anxiety, but it does make him feel grateful for his father's powerful example, and it keeps him from "falling into the abyss of despair."

Steve also feels the ghost of his grandfather, who loved him unconditionally, who offered him a quarter for every A he did not get on his report card—proving that he loved him not for what he might achieve, not for his accumulated credentials, but for just being himself. That was enough. As Steve struggles to find a way to accept his son's mental illness and make peace with his daughter's lesbianism, he pictures his grandfather blinded by a degenerative eye disease but nevertheless always able to clearly see the goodness in his grandson. Steve works to achieve that vision, that kind of unconditional love for his own children.

Ryan Calabrese also feels the echoes of his father's generosity and love as he parents his adopted son Zach. He declares that his father has always been his hero and was the main reason that he always knew that he wanted to be a father himself. His dad was the one that Ryan finally came out to, after years of agony and hiding out within his family, and the person he most wanted to emulate as he endured the challenging times with his own son. His determination not to turn his back on Zach during their violent adolescent battles and his ability to see the "good and bad, side by side" in his son all feel like bountiful inheritances that he has received from his father. Most strikingly, Ryan's openness to letting his son "flip places" with him and become his "teacher and protector," he believes, grows out of experiencing the ways his own father shielded and supported him when he was growing up.

Just as Steve and Ryan live with the good ghosts hovering over their own parenting, so, too, several of the parents I interviewed spoke about the ways in which they worked to resist the generational echoes, the ways they were intentional in their efforts not to let the ancient encounters with their own parents distort their relationships with their own children. In a soft voice that still sounds uncertain, Hannah Fairchild discovers the ghosts of her authoritarian parents, as she tries to understand why it is so hard for her to give her own grown-up children the space they need to run their own lives and raise their own families. In our interview, she revisits and examines the haunts that she has inherited from her own upbringing in a fiercely controlling home where her parents' views and values went unquestioned; where there were strict gender roles carved out by her surgeon father and her homemaker mother; and where religious rigidities reined that inhibited generosity and emotional expressiveness. When Hannah's children draw clear boundaries—her daughter refusing to let her clean the bathroom sink when she arrives for a visit; her son refusing to let her pay for the groceries that he has brought to the family gathering—she feels the tug of "holding on" to decisions that should no longer be hers; she feels the tension of "letting go" of her parental control even as she begins to recognize the powerful and unwelcome echoes of her mother's quiet Quaker righteousness and her father's Presbyterian moral rigidity.

Simone Ray is even more adamant than Hannah about resisting the shrill and dogmatic voices of her Polish immigrant mother as she seeks to forge a loving and intimate relationship with her own daughter, Zoe. Tears spring to her eyes as she talks about how she always knew that, as a mother, she would need to battle the demons of the "mean-spirited" mother who raised her, who saw "love as ownership," who was always punitive, rigid, and rule bound. Simone wants her relationship with Zoe to be more embracing, more respectful, more reciprocal and fun. Redefining her mother-daughter bond with Zoe not only means doing the opposite of what she remembers her mother doing, it also means doing something harder: composing ways of being together that allow them to honor their differences and their similarities, that give them each the space to define the emerging meanings of love.

Difference and Deviance

The most powerful and enduring lessons seem to be taught by off-spring who are the most different from their parents, children who cause their parents confusion and consternation, children who feel like strangers or interlopers in the family, children who are hard for parents to read or understand, children who look different, think differently, have different temperaments, and make different life choices. It is in trying to span the abyss of differentness between them, in trying to learn how to love them despite — or because of — their differentness, that parents are forced to learn something crucial about their child and themselves. It is often out of the struggle to overcome their disappointments and frustrations with their child, and the suffering that comes with their own feelings of inadequacy and exhaustion, that parents discover new capacities within themselves, new qualities and resources in their children, and new understandings of the changing world around them.

Most of the parents I interviewed identified the difference in their child right from the beginning: seeing the early signs and patterns of behavior that did not align with their expectations and aspirations, struggling to get close, hoping to find reflections of themselves in the tiny person who felt like a stranger. Compared to his two siblings, Keith was always Steve Saltzman's most "different and difficult" child. The physical signs were clear from the beginning. At birth, Keith was small and sickly, always falling short when the pediatrician tracked his height and weight on the growth charts. When he began to talk, he stuttered badly; when he walked, his gait was strange and awkward; he was a fussy eater. His physical "defects" were layered with emotional struggles: a rage and defiance that smoldered just below the surface; a chronic depression that kept him alone and isolated; an incapacity to relate to, and read, other people. At the same time, Keith's intellect was huge and he had a prodigious capacity to recall and retrieve vast bodies of knowledge.

During Keith's childhood and adolescence, Steve and his wife would often exclaim to one another, "Whose child is this? Where did he come from?" They "got" their other two children, who were like them, whose reflections they saw in themselves, but Keith stood out as a stranger: difficult to know, hard to love. And now that he is in his midthirties, married, and employed by a fancy law firm, but still occasionally plagued by bouts of depression, his father looks back on their difficult journey together and claims that his son's differentness was "the greatest teacher." His voice is full of exhaustion and appreciation when he reflects on the ongoing learning. "I learned more from Keith than I did from the other kids. He was the most different from his mother and me. . . . With Keith, I am still on a learning trajectory . . . trying to move ever closer to understanding and acceptance."

Like Steve, Andrea Hunter observed the early signs of vulnerability in her son Travis, whose arrival in the world as a girl child came after a difficult twenty-four-hour labor that was compromised by "complications" and medical interventions, whose breast-feeding was difficult and painful, who was often sickly and inconsolable. On their first date six months after his birth, the babysitter called Andrea and her husband at the restaurant to report that Travis had stopped breathing and passed out four times. They rushed home and watched in horror as they saw it happen two more times that evening. The pediatrician gave the syndrome a name — "breath-holding spells" — and told Andrea that there was nothing they could do about it but that it would disappear on its own by the time the baby was eighteen months old. The passing out abated exactly as predicted, but the experience provoked a "crucial shift" in Andrea's views of parenting. "This was one of my first fundamental lessons as a parent," says Andrea, with lingering sadness, "that you cannot control everything no matter how diligent and protective you are." Those early signs of difficulty, and the anxiety and disequilibrium they caused her, were — Andrea believes — precursors to the long arc of learning that she traveled to understand and accept her transgender son.

Even though Naomi Sawyer has spent more than a decade and a half working with children with disabilities and helping their parents come to terms with the anguish and anger, the frustration, guilt, and disappointment—that so often plague their realistic assessment and understanding of their children's gifts and capacities and distort their ability to offer their full support and advocacy—she still sometimes struggles with wanting to "fix" her own autistic son. She still wishes that other people would see and appreciate Jonah's extraordinary intelligence, kindness, and creativity rather than assume that he is severely limited and compromised by his autism. She knows that even though Jonah was definitively diagnosed at age three, and even though his gifts shine out in his prodigious art and the loving relationships he has sustained for years with family, friends, and helpers, in retrospect, Naomi feels she has spent far too much time wanting to wish away the "deficits," and in the process, she has sometimes neglected to teach him the "life skills" that would make him more self-sufficient and independent, that would make his adaptation to the world somewhat smoother. She still struggles with deciding who her child is and whether his difference obscures Jonah's true self or is integral to it. More and more, she is finding peace with his differences; she is seeing them as "gifts," essential aspects of his identity and his worthiness.

Steve, Naomi, and Andrea all spotted the differences and difficulties in their offspring when they were very young—warning signs of trauma and trouble that would persist and evolve over the years, early evidence of the ways in which these children would become their primary teachers. All three of these parents also struggled with interpreting their children's behavior as deviant rather than merely different, moving ever closer to the latter as their offspring insisted that they give them space, honor their individuality and see them as "other"—not an alien other, but as another whose identity is separate and whole. Naomi Sawyer makes an important point when she refers to the tough emotional terrain that the parents of children with disabilities must travel. Their anxiety and disappointment, their guilt and their fears, she says, are not driven by rational calculations or objective data. "Even if they have a child who has a very mild form of dyslexia, it is as real to them as if their child had nonverbal autism. There is no metric to measure the pain. It hurts just as much." It is not the degree of difference, then, or the severity of the deviance, or the visibility of the disability that determine the parent's sense of vulnerability and helplessness; it is their perception of it. And it is how much this perception overwhelms and distorts their ability to see their child clearly.

The contrasts—in temperament, intelligence, values, allegiances, and demeanors—that parents experience between themselves and their children, that become sites of learning and acceptance, are not always muddled in the suspended space between illness and identity. For Zarina Nielson, for example, her daughter Christina's differentness felt "liberating" to her. Zarina always felt that there was no way that she could control or guide her daughter, who "came from such a different place . . . who marched to the beat of a different drummer." Christina's differentness defined a space between them that allowed for a growing recognition of their separateness and ultimately led to the development of their intimacy. Zarina remembers her daughter's utter contentment as she draped her grandfather in the colorful silk scarves while he slept in the rocking chair, or her deep, self-sufficient pleasure as she opened and closed the shutters of her dollhouse and softly sang a lullaby to the doll babies inside. Her daughter's joy, so essential to her being, was so different from the heavy sadness and chronic pain that Zarina lived with every day, and their differentness allowed Christina the space to carve her own path. Over the years, Zarina "learned to find joy in other people's joy" by honoring the contrasts with her daughter, by witnessing her daughter's "way of making whatever she found beautiful."

Like Zarina, Ryan Calabrese sees qualities in his son that surprise and delight him, differences in their characters that he wants to learn, absorb, and emulate. After the adolescent battling between them, Ryan notices a sturdy self-confidence in his son, who refuses to live by other people's measure, who does not worry about other's perceptions or judgments. Ryan watches Zach negotiate the separation and reunion with his girlfriend, and witnesses his maturity and respect, his decisiveness and clarity, his selflessness and self-protection, and he says to himself, "Who is this kid . . . how did this strength of character grow up in him?" Ryan's willingness to publicly come out of the closet to his colleagues and students, after years of hiding out, reflected not only his guilt at having let his son endure the ridicule and suspicions of having a father who was gay but also his efforts to become more like Zach, a person who believes in himself, who "has a strong sense of who he is and what he wants."

Almost-grown children who are different from their parents, then, tend to be particularly important in provoking their parents' learning. The differences seem to be spotted early — as things do not proceed as planned, as children do not measure up to the developmental targets and expectations, as vulnerabilities and disabilities are observed and diagnosed — and become written into the family script. The impact of the differences — often unwelcome, confusing, and frustrating but sometimes compelling and liberating — are not measurable by any metric. In *Far from the Tree*, Andrew Solomon makes a useful distinction between vertical identities and horizontal identities, the latter being defined by characteristics that the parents and child do not share. But as Naomi Sawyer reminds us, it is not merely the severity or intensity of the difference that causes the parents pain; it is their perception and interpretation of it. Even the most subtle and muted differences, not visible to others, may be experienced by parents and their children as boundaries and battle lines: significant sources of strain, separation, and suffering. Those small differences can make a big difference and can be sites of learning for parents whose children instruct them in their otherness and worthiness.

Culture and Context

The lessons that progeny teach their parents, of course, do not occur in a vacuum. They are shaped and framed by the broader

ecology, by the social, economic, and cultural context, by the physical and environmental setting, by the values and priorities that are
dominant in society, by the shifting public conversations about race
and class, gender and sexual orientation. When our children become our teachers, they are not only offering lessons on who they
are and what they believe, they are also drawing us closer to the
world they are living in. They are more likely than we are to feel the
contemporary beat of the cultural rhythms; and their teachings are
often focused on making their parents more current and relevant,
more flexible and adaptive, more hip and cool.

The narratives in this book that chronicle the growing intimacy
between immigrant parents and their progeny particularly underscore the power of context and cultural currency: young adult children helping their parents embrace the geographic and cultural
boundary crossing, begging their parents to release their "control
over their orifices," expanding their parents' horizons. The children
become their parents' mentors, guides, and translators, authority
relationships are recast, and the family curriculum has both prag-
matic and prophetic implications; it is about daily negotiating the
new societal realities, and it is about forging a blended cultural
identity.

Elvira Perez, who was born and raised in Barcelona and came to
the United States as a graduate student, is proud of the progressive
political heritage she inherited from her activist parents and passed
on to her son, Gabe, but she also sees the ways in which the changing contemporary context has allowed him to not only embrace the
liberal rhetoric but also live out and enact those values in his life.
"He builds the bridge from theory to practice," she says admiringly,
even as she recognizes that he has grown up in a cultural reality that
encourages a new kind of "inclusiveness and open-mindedness."
Gabe's pedagogy—more about "showing rather than telling," more
about "walking the walk than talking the talk"—is as much about
teaching his mother to appreciate the shifting cultural values as it is
about the ways he chooses to embrace them.

But shifts in the cultural context do not only have implications
for the trajectories of learning in immigrant families, they also

shape the learning of nonimmigrant parents. Ryan Calabrese, for example, understands that Zach's comfort with having a gay father is very much related to changes in the ways most of our society now views homosexuality: not as an illness or a choice but as a wholesome identity. Ryan startles when Zach strolls into the bedroom he is sharing with his boyfriend and feels relieved when his son casually lies down with them on the bed and watches the football game. Zach's friends who drop by the house feel the same level of comfort and nonchalance, barely seeming to notice the scene of two men living and sleeping together, fathering a heterosexual son. The world is changing around them, stereotypes are being assaulted, family structures and scripts are being rewritten, and parents look to their children to interpret the sometimes confusing, and occasionally threatening, social transformations.

When Andrea Hunter puts in her "earplugs" so she can avoid hearing the desperate pleas of her son Travis who is telling her he is transgender—a boy born in a girl's body—she knows intuitively that she is not only refusing to hear his voice, she is also resisting a cultural tide, one in which gender categories are much more fluid. And when Rachel—a woman in rabbinical training at their synagogue—calls to let Andrea know that Travis, who has slid into a deep depression, is in real danger and that she must "really listen" to him, she hears the voice of someone who calls herself "gender queer," someone "who is part of that generation for whom this is all much easier." The generational differences are important and instructive. Andrea listens to Rachel's admonition at two levels: at one level, she hears a diagnosis from a spiritual guide who is concerned about the soul and survival of her son; at another level, she is aware of the authority carried in Rachel's openness to the evolving cultural norms.

Later on, as Andrea reflects on the deep-seated prejudices she had a couple of decades ago, when one of her male coworkers came out as a transgender woman and would walk his children to school in dresses and high heels, her ignorance still causes her pain. She remembers feeling deeply annoyed and judgmental, thinking that her coworker was being an irresponsible, narcissistic parent, flaunting his eccentricities. Now, looking back, she sees it very differently. He was doing what he had to do; he was saving his life. "I now know," she says soberly, "that he would not have been alive today if he had not allowed himself to express his true identity . . . he would have committed suicide." Today, Andrea is learning to accept that Travis is a boy, and she has begun to see his male gender as a "permanent identity." But she also recognizes that Travis's sense of self is supported by changes in our cultural frames on identity, by the ways in which the circle of male dancers at the recent bar mitzvah the family attended quite naturally reached out their hands to him and drew him in.

Just as Andrea is able to identify—and appreciate—the cultural currents that have caused her to remove her earplugs and made her more open to Travis's teachings, so, too, Steve Saltzman sees clearly the ways in which the shifts in societal norms and legal precedents helped him accept his daughter's lesbianism. "Society and social change helped me," says Steve, a trial lawyer, as he first points to the *Goodridge* case written by his longtime colleague and friend Margaret Marshall, which allowed same-sex unions in Massachusetts. As he carefully studied Marshall's brief, he felt convinced by the logic and clarity of her argument and by the integrity of her ethical and legal stance. He also felt—in a not-so-litigious way—the broader shifts in the court of popular public opinion, the ways in which society was becoming more tolerant and accepting of gays. "It makes a difference," he admits softly, "when the world is not frowning on you so much . . . when you are not so worried about getting criticized or your child getting criticized."

In all of these stories of parental learning, the cultural context is a major force for change and reinterpretation: reframing the social landscape, rewriting the laws and policies, redefining boundaries and separations among groups of people, recasting the rhetoric and public conversations. The cultural surround is not only influential in reshaping parental attitudes, it is also often the focus of their progenies' pedagogy.

In reframing and enlarging our view of parental learning and growth, developmental psychologist Jack Demick critiques the stage theories that fail to account for the rapidly changing landscape of parenthood. His description of this landscape in 2002, focused primarily on rapid changes in the economic picture, rings completely true today:

> The declining prevalence of early marriage, increasing level of marital dissolution, and the growing tendency to never marry reflect changes in the relative economic prospect of men and women and support the conclusion that marriage is becoming less valued as a source of economic stability. These developments imply that relatively more children are born outside of marriage, spend at least part of their childhood in single-parent homes, and endure multiple changes in family composition. Paralleling these trends have been sharp changes in the economic stability of families, characterized most notably by a growing importance of women's income and increasing economic inequality among American families.[1]

Demick claims that parental development theories have to be able to contain the vast differences in parenting arrangements as well as the rapid changes in the social landscape. He argues for a "holistic, developmental, systems-oriented approach" to parental development and sees parents as embedded in a changing context.[2]

In developing his more holistic approach to parental development, Demick reviews the history of the psychological research on socialization, tracing the literature's shifting frames on learning. In the beginning, parents were seen as the "cause" or the originators of their children's socialization, solely responsible for the behaviors, beliefs, and values their youngsters acquired, the lessons always flowing from the parent to the child. By the 1950s, psychologists were beginning to view the parent-child relationship as "bidirectional," each one influencing and shaping the other's behavior and growth, each one initiating *and* responding. More recent views—including Demick's—have complicated the notion of bidirectionality and begun to refer to the concept of "transactionality," or the ways in which the two-way influences between parent and child are shaped as well by the social and economic context. The broad and shifting environment plays a large part, an active and dynamic role, in how parents and children grow each other up.

Demick's transactional model is helpful in reframing our view of parent-child influences into one that is two-way and dialectical, cumulative, and changing, and one that is embedded in, and shaped by, the sociocultural context. This book's narratives not only suggest the ways in which the pedagogy of children takes place within an evolving cultural frame but also point to the ways in which almost-grown offspring are likely to be the more sure-footed authorities on our rapidly transforming world. Their understanding, and translation, of the changing sociocultural context is written into the curriculum they teach their parents.

In the reflection that opens this book, I am sitting with my friend and colleague Mary Catherine Bateson, hoping to receive some parenting guidance and solace, trusting that she will have something useful to tell me about how to navigate my way through the adolescent struggles I am daily waging with my daughter Tolani. Bateson listens intently, letting me spew out my anguished saga, and then she offers a response that at first feels unsympathetic and facile. "Your daughter is living on another planet, and she has a lot to teach you about it. . . . Listen to her." Getting over my disappointment and defensiveness, I reflect, over the next week or two, on Bateson's spare response and discover the wisdom in her words. Now, after listening to the dozens of stories parents have told me about the focus and form of their children's pedagogy, I am even more convinced of the ways in which our progeny introduce us to the planet they inhabit—one that is different from the one we are living on. We can be informed and enlarged by their teachings if we are prepared to listen.

Suffering and Love

Bateson might have also been warning me that a deepening love, a growing intimacy and respect between my daughter and me, would not come without suffering, that the lessons our children teach us are often provoked by the pain and disequilibrium they experience, endure, or cause. In *Far from the Tree*, Andrew Solomon makes an important distinction in talking about the complex and hard-won love relationships, suffused with suffering, that parents develop with their children who are profoundly different from them. "Suffering does not necessarily imply love," he says, "but love implies suffering, and what changes with these children and their extraordinary situations is the shape of the suffering—and in consequence, the shape of the love, forced into a more difficult form."[3]

In this volume we hear stories of suffering and the changing shape of love, and the ways in which parents' learning from their children—from those with both horizontal and vertical identities—is more deeply etched when parents "believe their suffering has been valuable," when they see meaning, and even redemption, in their pain. Juliana Jordon tells perhaps the most painful story of parental love redefined, a story of betrayal, violence, and survival. When she and her husband Jake adopt three young siblings from a Russian orphanage, they have no idea that the children have been deeply scarred by unspeakable trauma. As soon as they land safely on this side of the ocean, all hell breaks loose at home: assaults with hammers and knives, running away and suicide attempts, drug and alcohol addictions, rapes and incarcerations. For sixteen years Juliana and Jake have learned to live with fear, loss, and chronic disappointment, learned to erect protective barriers, learned that in order to survive they need to go underground and hide out. Juliana, who has her black belt in karate, is beat up so many times by her older son that the nurse in the emergency room sees her coming and says, "not *you* again." As she deflects and absorbs this degree of suffering, her love is "forced into a more difficult form." When I ask Juliana whether she loves her children after all of these years of terror and trauma, her eyes are tearful but her voice is clear and certain. "I don't feel love for them. I feel responsible for them. Love is not always something you feel. But love is something that you do. It is my job to be relentlessly kind and interact in a way that makes me feel good about myself."

Love is also "forced into a more difficult form" as Andrea Hunter discovers that the path to knowing and accepting her transgender son is "letting go of the dream," learning to accept "what is" about Travis. But acceptance is a long, hard road, an ongoing disquieting question of deciding what is real and what is not, what should be allowed to grow and what should be tightly controlled (the breast binder is an apt metaphor), and what is permanent and what can change. When I ask Andrea whether she ever misses Emma, the daughter born to her, she admits that she misses her terribly but that the greatest suffering is her feeling of being suspended between two "mindsets": one that sees Travis's male gender as "permanent," another that hopes for "instability." She confesses that she is not managing the contradictory mindsets well, even though all those who counsel her—her rabbi, the doctors, the therapists and social workers, and the parents of other transgender children—tell her that she must embrace the idea of "permanence." That is the only way that she will ever find peace of mind, the only way that she will ever abandon her hopes for a "reversal," the only way she will truly accept Travis. But her haunting "reveries" lie just below the surface; Andrea admits that she still occasionally finds comfort in the "possibility of impermanence." She finds herself dreaming "that my son will grow up to be a girl, then a mother who will breast-feed his baby."

At the close of our interview Andrea is eager to sum up what she has learned from mothering Travis, the "big and difficult lessons" that she sometimes even rehearses to herself in times of uncertainty. One of them is a hard-won lesson—forged out of struggle and endurance—on maternal love. "I have learned," she says with finality, "that even if you don't feel love all the time, there is something stronger—an urge, a drive—that allows you to carry on and persevere through the struggle. It is a more primal instinct than love, the drive to protect your kid at any cost." Her voice, like Juliana's, is unsentimental but not defeated, truthful and unvarnished.

Several of the other parents whose voices fill this volume describe the ways in which their almost-grown children have taught them lessons on love—modeling a way of being—that they have tried to emulate in their own lives and relationships. Lessons learned through witness more than through suffering. Jacob Simon begins his interview with a simple, unadorned testimonial about his eighteen-year-old daughter Rebecca. "She has taught me about love and about how to love." He noticed that special capacity in his daughter from the time she was very small, remembering a tender, comforting moment during the burial of his father when Jacob was about to put the soil over the coffin as it was being lowered into the ground. Unbidden, three-year-old Rebecca walked up beside him, looked into his face, and held his hand. They clutched the shovel together. Over the years, Jacob has witnessed Rebecca's capacity for loving others, a love that is "nonjudgmental, gentle, tender, and nurturing." But he has learned most from the way in which her love is "layered and complex"; it is both tender and fierce; it combines a "vulnerability and a toughness." "She can let herself be wounded and still stay in the fray . . . she doesn't take shit from anyone." Occasionally, when Rebecca sees her father being "unloving and judgmental," she will call him on it; she seizes the "teachable moment." "Well, aren't you in a good mood today, dad."

The dance of intimacy Simone Ray has with her daughter Zoe is "full of lessons on love," as each tries to negotiate the space between them that will allow them to be both separate and together; that will accommodate their differences and similarities; that will nourish their mutual admiration. Their love grows out of subtle, daily calibrations — spoken and unspoken — as Simone learns that love is in part shaped by restraint and silence and as Zoe learns that love means speaking up and giving voice to her feelings. The lessons on love are ongoing, an ever-evolving dance of two woman discovering themselves and each other.

Steve Saltzman remembers the "unconditional love" he felt from his maternal grandfather, whose kindness and generosity were so different from what he received from his mother, whose "calculating and manipulative love" always seemed to come at a hefty price. As he has suffered through years of trying to love his own children, as he has come to terms with his daughter's lesbianism and volatile adolescence and his son's mental illness, Steve has tried to hold fast to the precious inheritance from his grandfather, who loved him without limit or judgment. He believes that through the years of struggle, and with the patient guidance of his offspring, he is getting closer and closer to his grandfather's evolved and loving vision. "It takes a long time to get there," he says wearily. But it is his last line, said in jest, which holds a fascinating truth. "Unconditional love comes immediately in the first week of life, and then it sort of disappears until much later." In between, there is suffering, the bedrock of "love forced into a more difficult form."

Acknowledgments

There is nothing more tender and treacherous than excavating the territory between parents and their children, nothing that is more likely to bring up ancient traumas, dated emotions, fierce loyalties, and layers of love. The parents who agreed to participate in this project, who willingly — even eagerly — offered their rich and resonant narratives about the life lessons taught by their children, were open-hearted, generous, and courageous. I am so thankful to them for their truth telling and authenticity, for their insights and revelations, for teaching me what they learned from their progeny.

As I listened to the stories of the dozens of parents I interviewed for this volume, I heard the echoes of the hard-won and essential lessons I have learned from my own children. During this project, I was once again face-to-face with the ways my research inquiries originate and how they are shaped by the puzzles and struggles, the questions and curiosities in my own life. I am grateful to my children, Tolani and Martin, for their masterful and wise teaching and for the lessons that deepen and ripen now that they have children of their own. My magnificent mother, Margaret, now one hundred one years old, is also connected to, and responsible for, the ideas embedded in this book. Over the years, she has always given her three progeny—now elders ourselves—credit for enriching who she is and who she is becoming, for expanding the ways she sees and gives to the world.

From the nascent beginnings of this project to the final moments of delivering the manuscript, two people were by my side, cheering me on and watching my back. Wendy Angus, my amazing assistant who has worked with me for over three decades and knows my every move and mood, brought her extraordinary skills, insights, and discernment to the work, offering me just the right balance of encouragement and challenge. My research assistant, Irene Liefshitz, was deeply and creatively engaged in all the phases of the work, from writing probing critiques of the literature to helping shape the narrative arc of the book. I am so thankful for her wise voice, her keen intelligence, her poetic provocations, and her steady loyalty.

With kindness and enthusiasm, my good friends encouraged me along the way . . . using their networks to help me find wonderful folks to interview, responding personally and with passion to the family stories in which they felt implicated, offering their insights on the ethical and empirical conundrums that are deep in the minefields of this research. I am grateful to Susan Berger, Maya Carlson, Andrea Fleck Clardy, Jessica Hoffmann Davis, Tony Earls, Howard Gardner, Kelli Kirshtein, Marita Rivero, Lisbeth Schorr, Mitra Shavarini, and Randy Testa. My sister Paula, my best and oldest friend, brought a rare perspective born out of our shared and ancient experiences in our family of origin—a perspective that complimented and challenged my own, a perspective imbued with reverence and love.

My agents, Ike Williams and Katherine Flynn, were strategic and patient in finding the perfect home for this book. By now they know me well; I trust them implicitly. Their spare interventions were always welcome and deftly timed. Their colleague, Hope Denekamp, runs the show with her perfect blend of organizational acumen and relational intelligence, her chutzpah and her humor. My editor Elizabeth Branch Dyson is a woman of deep intelligence and probing insight. Wise and gracious, her critiques were incisive and illuminating, her applause both measured and generous. It has been a great pleasure getting to know and work with her.

My man, Irving Hamer, was, as always, a force to contend with. Fierce in his love, tough in his challenges, staunch in his support, always encouraging the strength and amplification of my voice. My thanks are overflowing.

Notes

Introduction

1. For example: Robert S. Feldman, *Child Development* (Upper Saddle River, NJ: Prentice Hall, 2010) or Laura E. Berk, *Child Development* (Boston: Allyn & Bacon/Pearson, 2009).

2. Some literature that does consider parent learning and socialization by their children includes: Richard Q. Bell, "A Reinterpretation of the Direction of Effects in Studies of Socialization," *Psychological Review* 75, no. 2 (1968): 18 95; Richard Q. Bell and Lawrence Harper, *Child Effects on Adults* (New York: Halsted Press, 1977); Ester S. Bucholz, "Parenthood as a Developmental Stage," *Parenthood in America: An Encyclopedia*, ed. Lawrence Balter (Boulder, CO: ABC-CLIO, 2000), 2:440–42; Kelly E. Buckholdt, Gilbert R. Parra, and Lisa Jobe-Shields, "Intergenerational Transmission of Emotion Dysregulation through Parental Invalidation of Emotions: Implications for Adolescent Internalizing and Externalizing Behaviors," *Journal of Child and Family Studies* 23, no. 2 (2014): 324–32; Daphne Blunt Bugental and Joan E. Grusec, "Socialization Processes," in *Handbook of Child Psychology*, ed. N. Eisenberg (Hoboken, NJ: Wiley, 2006), 366–428; William L. Cook, "Interpersonal Influence in Family Systems: A Social Relations Model Analysis," *Child Development* 72 (2001):1179–97; Kirby Deater-Deckard, "Family Matters: Intergenerational and Interpersonal Processes of Executive Function and Attentive Behavior," *Current Directions in Psychological Science* 23, no. 3 (2014): 230–36; Jack Demick, "Effects of Children on Adult Development and Learning: Parenthood and Beyond," *Handbook of Adult Development and Learning*, ed. C. Hoare (New York: Oxford University Press, 2006), 329–43; James J. Dillon, "The Role of the Child in Adult Development," *Journal of Adult Development* 9 (2002): 267–75; Travis E. Dorsch, Alan L. Smith, and Meghan H. McDonough, "Parents' Perceptions of Child-to-Parent Socialization in Organized Youth Sport," *Jour-

nal of Sport and Exercise Psychology 31, no. 4 (2014): 444–68; Cherri Ho, "Intergenerational Learning (between Generation X & Y) in Learning Families: A Narrative Inquiry," *International Education Studies* 3, no. 4 (2010): 59–72; David Huh, Jennifer Tristan, Emily Wade, and Eric Stice, "Does Problem Behavior Elicit Poor Parenting? A Prospective Study of Adolescent Girls," *Journal of Adolescent Research* 21 (2006):185–204; Leon Kuczynski, Sheila Marshall, and Kathleen Schell, "Value Socialization in a Bidirectional Context," in *Parenting and Children's Internalization of Values: A Handbook of Contemporary Theory*, ed. J. E. Grusec and L. Kuczynski (Hoboken, NJ: Wiley, 1997), 23–50; Kurt Lüscher, Andreas Hoff, Giovanni Lamura, Marta Renzi, Mariano Sánchez, Gil Viry, and Eric Widmer, *Generations, Intergenerational Relationships, Generational Policy: A Multilingual Compendium* (Konstanz, Germany: Generationes, 2013); Josette Luvmour, "Developing Together: Parents Meeting Children's Developmental Imperatives," *Journal of Adult Development* 17, no. 4 (2010): 191–244; John F. Peters, "Adolescents as Socialization Agents to Parents," *Adolescence* 20 (1985): 921–33; Martin Pinquart and Rainer K. Silbereisen, "Transmission of Values from Adolescents to Their Parents: The Role of Value Content and Authoritative Parenting," *Adolescence* 39, no. 153 (2004): 83–100; Sue Tempest, "Intergenerational Learning: A Reciprocal Knowledge Development Process That Challenges the Language of Learning," *Management Learning* 34, no. 2 (2003):181–200.

3. For historical and social science literature on newly arrived immigrants, see, for example, Alan V. Brown, "Learning English on Her Own—Almost: The Facilitative Role of One Immigrant's Daughter," *Journal of Latinos and Education* 11, no. 4 (2012): 218–31; Susan Chuang and Catherine Tamis LeMonda, *Gender Roles in Immigrant Families* (New York: Springer, 2013); Rosalie Corona, Lilian Stevens, and Raquel Halfond, "A Qualitative Analysis of What Latino Parents and Adolescents Think and Feel about Language Brokering," *Journal of Child and Family Studies* (2012); Lisa M. Del Torto, "Once a Broker, Always a Broker: Non-Professional Interpreting as Identity Accomplishment in Multigenerational Italian-English Bilingual Family Interaction," *Multilingua: Journal of Cross-Cultural and Interlanguage Communication* 27, nos. 1–2 (2008): 77–97; Raymond Buriel and Christina Villanueva, "Children as Language Brokers: A Narrative of the Recollections of College Students," in *Language in Multicultural Education*, ed. Rumjahn Hoosain and Fari-

deh Salili (Greenwich, CT: Information Age, 2005), 255–72; Radosveta Dimitrova, Michael Bender, and Fons van de Vijver, *Global Perspectives on Well-Being in Immigrant Families* (New York: Springer, 2014); Lisa M. Dorner, Marjorie F. Orellana, and Rosa Jimenez, "'It's One of Those Things That You Do to Help the Family': Language Brokering and the Development of Immigrant Adolescents," *Journal of Adolescent Research* 50 (2008): 505–24; Cynthia Garcia-Coll, *The Impact of Immigration on Children's Development* (New York: Karger, 2012); Carol Kelley, *Accidental Immigrants and the Search for Home: Women, Cultural Identity, and Community* (Philadelphia: Temple University Press, 2013); Charles Martinez, Heather McClure, and J. Marc Eddy, "Language Brokering Contexts and Behavioral and Emotional Adjustment among Latino Parents and Adolescents," *Journal of Early Adolescence* 29, no. 1 (2009): 71–98; Marjorie F. Orellana, Lisa Dorner, and Lucilla Pulido, "Accessing Assets: Immigrant Youth's Work as Family Translators or 'Para-Phrasers'" *Social Problems* 50 (2003): 505–24; Guadalupe Valdés, *Expanding Definitions of Giftedness: The Case of Young Interpreters from Immigrant Communities* (Mahwah, NJ: Lawrence Erlbaum, 2003); Christina Villanueva and Raymond Buriel, "Speaking on Behalf of Others: A Qualitative Study of the Perceptions and Feelings of Adolescent Latina Language Brokers," *Journal of Social Issues* 66, no. 1 (2010): 197–210.

For literary accounts, see, for example, Tahar Ben Jelloun, *A Palace in the Old Village* (New York: Penguin Books, 2011); Anne Cherian, *The Invitation* (New York: Norton, 2012); Angie Cruz, *Soledad* (New York: Simon & Schuster 2011), and, *Let It Rain Coffee* (New York: Simon & Schuster (2005); Junot Díaz, *The Brief Wondrous Life of Oscar Wao* (New York: Riverhead Books, 2007); David Lee, *Yellow* (New York: W. W. Norton, 2005); Amit Majdumar, *The Abundance* (New York: Metropolitan Books/Henry Holt, 2013); Peter Malae, *Our Frail Blood* (New York: Black Cat, 2013); Elizabeth Nunez, *Not for Everyday Use* (New York: Akashic Books, 2014).

4. Oscar Handlin, *The Uprooted: The Epic Story of the Great Migrations That Made the American People* (1951; repr., Philadelphia: University of Pennsylvania Press, 2002).

5. Ibid., 226.

6. Sara Lawrence-Lightfoot, *The Third Chapter: Passion, Risk, and Adventure in the 25 Years after 50* (New York: Farrar, Straus and Giroux, 2009).

7. Benjamin Spock, *Baby and Child Care* (New York: Pocket Books, 1957).

8. Berry T. Brazelton and Heidelise Als, "Four Early Stages in the Development of Mother-Infant Interaction," *The Psychoanalytic Study of the Child*, 1979); Barry M. Lester, Joel Hoffman, and Berry T. Brazelton, "The Rhythmic Structure of Mother-Infant Interaction in Term and Preterm Infants," *Child Development*, 1985.

9. For example: Charles Brook, *All about Adolescence* (New York: Wiley, 1985); Gerald R. Adams and Michael D. Berzonsky, *Blackwell Handbook of Adolescence* (Malden, MA: Blackwell Publishers, 2003); Ian McMahan, *Adolescence* (Boston: Pearson/Allyn & Bacon, 2009); Laurence Steinberg, *Adolescence* (New York: McGraw-Hill, 2014)

10. Stanley G. Hall, *Adolescence: Its Psychology and Its Relations to Physiology, Anthropology, Sociology, Sex, Crime, and Religion* (New York: Appleton, 1928).

11. Erik H. Erikson, *Identity and the Life Cycle* (New York: W. W. Norton, 1959).

12. Kim G. Dolgin, *The Adolescent: Development, Relationships, and Culture* (New York: Pearson College Division, 2010).

13. Mary Levitt, Marcia Silver, and Jennifer Santos, "Adolescents in Transition to Adulthood: Parental Support, Relationship Satisfaction, and Post-Transition Adjustment," *Journal of Adult Development* (2007).

14. The quote is from Steve Sussman and Jeffrey J. Arnett, "Emerging Adulthood: Developmental Period Facilitative of the Addictions," *Evaluation and the Health Professions* 37, no. 2 (2014):147–55.

Some literature exploring emerging adulthood as a developmental phase includes: Jeffrey J. Arnett, "Emerging Adulthood: Understanding the New Way of Coming of Age," in *Emerging Adults in America: Coming of Age in the 21st Century*, ed. Jeffery Jensen Arnett and Jennifer Lynn Tanner (Washington, DC: American Psychological Association, 2006), 1–19; Sarah Coyne, Laura M. Padilla-Walker, and Emily Howard, "Emerging in a Digital World: A Decade Review of Media Use, Effects, and Gratifications in Emerging Adulthood," *Emerging Adulthood* 1, no. 2 (2013): 125–37; Ming Cui, K. A. S. Wickrama, Frederick Lorenz, and Rand Conger, "Linking Parental Divorce and Marital Discord to the Timing of Emerging Adults' Marriage and Cohabitation," in *Romantic Relationships in Emerging Adulthood*, ed. Frank D. Fincham and Ming Cui (New York: Cambridge University Press, 2011), 123–41; Christine T. Halpern and

Carolyn E. Kaestle, "Sexuality in Emerging Adulthood," in *APA Handbook of Sexuality and Psychology: Person-Based Approaches*, ed. D. L. Tolman, L. M. Diamond, J. A. Bauermeister, W. H. George, J. G. Pfaus, and L. M. Ward (Washington, DC: American Psychological Association, 2014), 487–522; Girija Kaimal and William Beardslee, "Emerging Adulthood and the Perception of Parental Depression," *Qualitative Health Research* 20, no. 9 (2010): 1213–28; Marion Kloep and Leo B. Hendry, "Letting Go or Holding On? Parents' Perceptions of Their Relationships with Their Children during Emerging Adulthood," *British Journal of Developmental Psychology* 28, no. 4 (2010): 817–34; Larry J. Nelson, Laura M. Padilla-Walker, Katherine J. Christensen, Cortney A. Evans, and Jason S. Carroll, "Parenting in Emerging Adulthood: An Examination of Parenting Clusters and Correlates," *Journal of Youth and Adolescence* 40, no. 6 (2011): 730–43; Annette M. C. Roest, Judith S. Dubas, and Jan R. M. Gerris, "Value Transmissions between Fathers, Mothers, and Adolescent and Emerging Adult Children: The Role of the Family Climate," *Journal of Family Psychology* 23, no. 2 (2009): 146–55; Judith A. Seltzer and Suzanne M. Bianchi, "Demographic Change and Parent-Child Relationships in Adulthood," *Annual Review of Sociology* 39 (2013): 275–90; Shirene A. Urry, Larry J. Nelson, and Laura M. Padilla-Walker, "Mother Knows Best: Psychological Control, Child Disclosure, and Maternal Knowledge in Emerging Adulthood," *Journal of Family Studies* 17, no. 2 (2011): 157–73.

15. Jeffrey J. Arnett, "Emerging Adulthood(S): The Cultural Psychology of a New Life Stage," in *Bridging Cultural and Developmental Approaches to Psychology: New Syntheses in Theory, Research, and Policy*, ed. J. J. Arnett and J. L. Tanner (New York: Oxford University Press, 2011), 255–75.

16. For more on the material support that parents provide their adult children and the phenomenon of college graduates moving back home, see Jessica Dickler, "Boomerang Kids: 85% of College Grads Move Home," CNN Money, November 15, 2010, http://money.cnn.com/2010/10/14/pf/boomerang_kids_move_home/index.htm.

17. For more on economic decline, employment and career change, and change in family composition, see National Center for Health Statistics, "Marriage and Divorce," Centers for Disease Control, last updated June 19, 2014, http://www.cdc.gov/nchs/fastats/divorce.htm; "Marriage and Divorce," U.S. Census Bureau, last revised May 23, 2012, http://www.census.gov/hhes/socdemo/marriage; Bureau of Labor Statistics, http://

www.bls.gov/oco; and Carl Bialik, "Seven Careers in a Lifetime? Think Twice, Researchers Say," *Wall Street Journal*, September 4, 2010, http://online.wsj.com/article/SB10001424052748704206804575468162805877990.html.

18. Sara Lawrence-Lightfoot, *Exit: The Endings That Set Us Free* (New York: Farrar, Straus and Giroux, 2012), 7.

19. For more on the relationship of trust and respect between the researcher and interview subjects, see Sara Lawrence-Lightfoot and Jessica D. Hoffman, *The Art and Science of Portraiture* (San Francisco: Jossey-Bass Publishers, 1997), 153–55 and 165.

20. For more on generalization, resonance, and validity, see ibid., 14 and 259–60.

Chapter One

1. Richard Wright, *Haiku: This Other World* (Anchor Books: New York, 1998), 29, 67, 81, 131, 166.

2. Ellen J. Langer, *On Becoming an Artist: Reinventing Yourself through Mindful Creativity* (New York: Ballantine Books, 2005), 188.

3. Sara Lawrence-Lightfoot, *Respect: An Exploration* (Cambridge, MA: Perseus Books, 2000), 206–8.

4. Atul Gawande, *Better: A Surgeon's Notes on Performance* (New York: Picador, 2007), 3, 8.

5. Ellen Galinsky, *Between Generations: The Six Stages of Parenthood* (New York: Berkeley, 1981).

Chapter Two

1. David Gutmann, "Parenthood: A Key to the Comparative Study of the Life Cycle," in *Lifespan Developmental Psychology: Normative Life Crises*, ed. Nancy Datan and Leon H. Ginsberg (New York: Academic, 1975), 167.

2. Jack Demick, "Stages of Parental Development," in *Handbook of Parenting*, vol. 3: *Being and Becoming a Parent*, ed. M. H. Bornstein (Mahwah, NJ: Lawrence Erlbaum, 2002), 390.

3. Therese Benedek, "The Family as a Psychological Field," in *Parenthood: Its Psychology and Psychopathology*, ed. E. J. Anthony and T. Benedek (Boston: Little, Brown, 1970), 131.

4. Erik H. Erikson, *Childhood and Society* (New York: Norton, 1950); Erik H. Erikson, *Identity: Youth and Crisis* (New York: Norton, 1968), and *The Life Cycle Completed* (New York: Norton, 1982).

5. Demick, "Stages of Parental Development," 391; Carolyn M. Newberger, "Time, Place, and Parental Awareness: A Cognitive-Developmental Perspective on Family Adaptation and Parental Care," in *Child Abuse and Neglect: Biosocial Dimensions*, ed. J. B. Lancaster and R. J. Gelles (New York: Aldine de Gruyter, 1987), 233–51; Daniel J. Levinson, "A Conception of Adult Development," *American Psychologist* 41 (1986): 3–13; Ellen Galinsky, *Between Generations: The Six Stages of Parenthood* (New York: Berkeley Books, 1981).

6. George Vaillant, *Aging Well: Surprising Guideposts to a Happier Life from a Landmark Harvard Study of Adult Development* (New York: Little, Brown, 2003), 131–33.

7. Buzz Bissinger, *Father's Day: Across America with an Unusual Dad and His Extraordinary Child* (New York: Houghton Mifflin Harcourt, 2012).

8. Ibid., 3.

9. Ibid., 62.

10. Ibid., 106.

11. Ibid., 139.

Chapter Three

1. Alan Shapiro, *Tantalus in Love* (New York: Houghton Mifflin, 2005), 84.

2. Sara Lawrence-Lightfoot, *Respect: An Exploration* (Cambridge, MA: Perseus Books, 2000).

3. Lisa M. Del Torto, "Once a Broker, Always a Broker: Non-Professional Interpreting as Identity Accomplishment in Multigenerational Italian-English Bilingual Family Interaction," *Multilingua: Journal of Cross-Cultural and Interlanguage Communication* (2008); Lisa M. Dorner, Marjorie F. Orellana, and Rosa Jimenez, "'It's One of Those Things That You Do to Help the Family': Language Brokering and the Development of Immigrant Adolescents," *Journal of Adolescent Research* (2008); Charles Martinez, Heather McClure, and J. Marc Eddy, "Language Brokering Contexts and Behavioral and Emotional Adjustment among Latino Parents and Adolescents," *Journal of Early Adolescence* (2009).

4. Rosalie Corona, Lilian F. Stevens, and Raquel Halfond, "A Qualitative Analysis of What Latino Parents and Adolescents Think and Feel about Language Brokering," *Journal of Child and Family Studies* (2012).

5. Alan V. Brown, "Learning English on Her Own—Almost: The Facilitative Role of One Immigrant's Daughter," *Journal of Latinos and Education* (2012).

6. Paule Marshall, *Brown Girl, Brownstones* (New York: Random House, 1959).

7. Gary Shteyngart, *Little Failure: A Memoir* (New York: Random House, 2014).

8. Ibid., 320–21.

9. Junot Díaz, *The Brief Wondrous Life of Oscar Wao* (New York: Riverhead Books, 2007), 55.

Chapter Four

1. Andrew Solomon, *Far from the Tree: Parents, Children, and the Search for Identity* (New York: Scribner, 2012), 42.

2. Ibid., 4.

3. Ibid., 15.

4. Ibid., 36.

5. Ibid., 42.

6. Jack Demick, "Stages of Parental Development," in *Handbook of Parenting*, vol. 3: *Being and Becoming a Parent*, ed. M. H. Bornstein (Mahwah, NJ: Lawrence Erlbaum, 2002), 402.

7. Solomon, *Far from the Tree*, 46.

Conclusion

1. Jack Demick, "Stages of Parental Development," in *Handbook of Parenting*, vol. 3: *Being and Becoming a Parent*, ed. M. H. Bornstein (Mahwah, NJ: Lawrence Erlbaum, 2002), 402.

2. Ibid., 403–4.

3. Andrew Solomon, *Far from the Tree: Parents, Children, and the Search for Identity* (New York: Scribner, 2012), 42.

Suggested Further Reading

SOME EXAMPLES OF PARENTS GROWING
THROUGH THEIR CHILDREN:

Bissinger, Buzz (2012). *Father's Day: Across America with
an Unusual Dad and his Extraordinary Child.*

To me, *Father's Day* reads like an extended example of a child growing
up his father. Buzz Bissinger recounts a cross-country road trip he took
with his twenty-four-year-old developmentally delayed son Zachary. Bissinger initiates the trip to try to "crack through the surface" into his son's
soul. As the trip goes on, however, Bissinger becomes more aware of *his*
own reality and the surfaces and depths of *his* own soul. The intimacy of
the hours on the road in the company of his adult son reveals his own
deficits and permits a process of healing and repair.

Solomon, Andrew (2012). *Far from the Tree:
Parents, Children, and the Search for Identity.*

In this moving book, Andrew Solomon writes about the experience of
families in which the children are very different from their parents, where
the degree of otherness tests parents' love, imagination, and own sense of
self and causes them to undergo a myriad of material, social, emotional,
and spiritual transformations. Solomon's interest in this relationship of
difference between parents and children is rooted in his own experience of being different. In dealing with his dyslexia, Solomon's parents
"trounced a neurological abnormality" by providing him with extra support with reading and writing so that he could succeed in school and
ultimately become a writer. But gayness — his other "abnormality" — was

different; it was an identity, not an illness. This dichotomy between disparaging a way of being by naming it "illness" and validating the same way of being by naming it "identity" is something that Solomon wishes all of us would examine more closely. In dealing with the distinctions and fusions of identity and illness in their children, parents often come to reassess their own personhood and identity as well, becoming different because of having a child with a difference.

THE DEVELOPMENTAL PSYCHOLOGY BEHIND THE BOOK:

Arnett, Jeffrey Jensen (2011). "Emerging Adulthood(s): The Cultural Psychology of a New Life Stage," in *Bridging Cultural and Developmental Psychology: New Syntheses in Theory, Research, and Policy*, edited by Lene Arnett Jensen

To understand and appreciate the concept of emerging adulthood, I found this chapter to be most helpful. In the field of cultural and developmental psychology, emerging adulthood is a distinct developmental period (ages eighteen to twenty-nine) that involves an extended duration of learning and experimentation before young adults settle into a career and stable relationships. Especially interesting is how this developmental stage correlates with the current social landscape: major shifts in demographic and economic trends and later entry into marriage and childbearing in industrialized Western societies have produced a cultural sphere in which young adults are neither adolescents nor independent adults. Another interesting feature of emerging adulthood is the change in intergenerational family relationships. Parent-child relationships now last much longer due to increased life expectancy, having fewer children, and young adults living at their parents' home for longer periods of time. Especially in coresidential situations, parents and their young adult children may give each other material, emotional, or moral support. In the parent–young adult relationship, issues of parental control, separation and individuation, and parental influence on the positive development of young adults are common themes. Arnett's chapter focuses on the emerging adult point of view, providing a welcome counterpoint to the parent perspective of this book.

Demick, Jack (2011). "Effects of Children on Adult
Development and Learning: Fifty Years of Theory and Research,"
in *The Oxford Handbook of Reciprocal Adult Development and Learning*,
2nd ed., edited by Carol Hoare

While most developmental research concerns parenting effects on children, there is growing interest on the developmental effect of children on their parents. In this area, Jack Demick's work is a must-read, helping us focus on the idea of parenthood as a mechanism of adult development. First, Demick gives a thorough overview of the evolution of parental development theory, starting with its first conceptualization in psychoanalytic theory by Benedek in 1959 through Gutmann, Erikson, Sameroff, and Feil; Newberger, Bronfenbrenner, Bucholz, Super, and Harkness; and Lerner. Through the frameworks of Benedek and Erikson, parenthood is conceptualized as a major life stage of some duration that has powerful potential for "parents' reorganization of self and environment." Demick, however, is critical of parental development theories for their inadequate account of the rapidly changing landscape of parenthood. He argues for a "holistic, developmental, systems-oriented approach" to parental development, suggesting that developmental processes occur within the complexity of everyday life, and that the central task of parenthood is attaining "equilibrium in the person-in-environment system." This holistic conceptualization of developmental changes can be a fruitful way with which to consider the lessons parents learn from their young adult children. Most importantly, Demick urges us to regard young adults as people who can "foster developmental transformations" in their parents.

Erikson, Erik (1959). *Identity and the Life Cycle.*

Erik Erikson's work on the stages of human development is not only a classic of developmental psychology but also a cultural touchstone. He defines the development of a healthy personality as the progression through critical psychological conflicts, from childhood to adulthood. Movement from one stage to the next is marked by a radical change in perspective or an exit from seeing and accepting things a certain way to seeing and acknowledging another way of being. Erikson's eight developmental stages are: (1) basic trust versus basic mistrust (infancy); (2) autonomy versus shame and doubt (early childhood); (3) initiative versus guilt (play age); (4) industry versus inferiority (school age); (5) identity versus identity diffusion (adolescence); (6) intimacy versus isolation (young adulthood); (7) generativity versus self-absorption (adulthood); and (8) integrity versus despair and disgust (mature age). These psychosocial crises occur within relationships with significant people and structures—with family, school, peer groups, and partners—and therefore are influenced by both biology and society. To more fully understand the developmental effect of young adult children on their parents, Erikson's work provides the background description of parents and children as developing individuals.

Galinsky, Ellen (1981). *Between Generations: The Six Stages of Parenthood.*

Ellen Galinsky's work is notable for the ways it builds on and deviates from Erikson's stage theory of development and for its emphasis on parenthood. Galinsky theorized that parental development progresses through six stages: (1) image-making stage, where prospective parents form images of parenthood; (2) nurturing stage, where parents become attached to their baby but also experience a conflict between expectations of what parenthood would be like and the reality; (3) authority stage, where the parent's central task is handling power; (4) interpretive stage, where the parent interprets the world to their children; (5) interdependent stage, where the parent interacts with a seemingly "new" child—who is an adolescent—and must reform and renegotiate most aspects of their relationship; and (6) departure stage, where the parent's key task is accepting their grown child's individuality and separateness while maintaining a connection and relationship. Perhaps the most significant aspect of Galinsky's stage theory of parental development is her focus on parental expectations and image formation. In addition, her writing is engaging and powerful. For example, she writes: "I realized that parents had pictures in their minds of the way things were supposed to go, and of the way that they as parents and their children were supposed to act. I came to think of these pictures as images . . . if an image has not been achieved in reality, it is seen as a loss and can cause anger and depression. If an image is realized, it brings joy." Parental development happens because of the disparity between image and reality, as parents have to change their own behavior or reconstruct their image of their children.

Levinson, Daniel (1986). "A Conception of Adult Development," from *American Psychologist*, vol. 4.

In contrast to most stage theories, Levinson was one of the first psychologists to place a greater emphasis on a more holistic understanding of adult development. His work helps us understand parenthood—and parental development—as a cohesive flow of transitions and changes. Levinson's theory of adult development was based on the concept of life structure, which he defined as "the underlying design of a person's life at a given time," within three connected contexts: the sociocultural level (the roles a person plays), the interpersonal level (the relationships a person has), and the intrapersonal level (a person's temperament and personality). Levinson theorized that adults create a series of life structures throughout the course of life and that although specific experiences may vary the life cycle common to all people includes some key aspects. These include the formation of independence, individualization and modification of relationships, an abundance of change, reevaluation of life choices, coping with sources of discord in one's life, amendment and rejuvenation, physical decline and decreasing responsibility, giving up of formal authority or power, and appreciation of one's wisdom and experience. These universal experiences of adulthood provide the changing background of parental development caused by children.

Vaillant, G. E. (2002). *Aging Well: Surprising Guideposts to a Happier Life from a Landmark Harvard Study of Adult Development.*

This book makes a very important point: how well we age depends on how much—and how well—we learn from our children. Drawing on data from three longitudinal studies of adult development, Harvard Medical School faculty member George Vaillant explored the physical, psychological, and social aspects of human maturation, concluding that social aptitude is the most salient determinant of successful aging. He distinguishes the "happy-well" from the "sad-sick" and identifies six factors as predictors of being in the "happy-well" category at age eighty: a stable marriage, a mature adaptive style, no smoking, little use of alcohol, regular exercise, and maintenance of normal weight. Concerning the adaptive style factor and building on Erikson's stage theory of adult development, Vaillant found that generativity—the task of sustaining life and work that will outlast the self—is achieved not only in parenting children but also in allowing the younger generation to inform the development of the older. In Vaillant's data, the septuagenarians who aged well and mastered generativity were overwhelmingly able to answer the question: "What have you learned from your children?" In allowing the familial role of giving to be reversed, adults were able to "take inside" the positive qualities and experiences their children offered. This reciprocity of learning between parents and children emerged as a strong predictor of successful aging.

And one more:

Lawrence-Lightfoot, Sara, and Jessica Hoffman Davis (1997). *The Art and Science of Portraiture.*

Though several of my books are close cousins to *Growing Each Other Up*—especially *Respect: An Exploration, The Third Chapter: Passion, Risk, and Adventure in the 25 Years after 50,* and *Exit: The Endings That Set Us Free*—I'd like to point readers interested in this kind of research and methodology to *The Art and Science of Portraiture.* Portraiture is a method of social science inquiry that is distinctive for its blend of art and science and the way it captures the complexity, dynamics, and subtlety of human experience and organizational life. This method has been used to document the culture of institutions, the life stories of individuals, stages of human development, essential relationships, processes, and concepts. Portraiture pushes against the constraints of ethnographic traditions in its explicit effort to combine empirical and aesthetic description, in its focus on the convergence of narrative and analysis, and in its goal of speaking to broader audiences beyond the academy. *The Art and Science of Portraiture* illuminates the origins, purposes, and features of this method, mapping it onto the broader terrain of qualitative research. The text describes the theory and technique of the method and provides ample illustrations from works of portraiture—both my own, and others'—to underscore the rigorous and creative aspects of this innovative method of social science inquiry.

Bibliography

Adams, G. R., and M. D. Berzonsky. (2003). *Blackwell Handbook of Adolescence*. Malden, MA: Blackwell Publishers.

Arnett, J. J. (2006). "Emerging Adulthood: Understanding the New Way of Coming of Age." In *Emerging Adults in America: Coming of Age in the 21st century*, edited by J. J. Arnett and J. L. Tanner, 1–19. Washington, DC: American Psychological Association.

———. (2011). "Emerging Adulthood(s): The Cultural Psychology of a New Life Stage." In *Bridging Cultural and Developmental Approaches to Psychology: New Syntheses in Theory, Research, and Policy*, edited by L. A. Jensen, 255–75. New York: Oxford University Press.

Bell, R. Q. (1968). "A Reinterpretation of the Direction of Effects in Studies of Socialization." *Psychological Review* 75:81–95.

Bell, R. Q., and L. V. Harper. (1977). *Child Effects on Adults*. New York: Halsted Press.

Benbassat, N., and Priel, B. (2012). "Parenting and Adolescent Adjustment: the Role of Parental Reflective Function." *Journal of Adolescence* 35 (1): 163–74.

Benedek, T. (1970). "The Family as a Psychological Field." In *Parenthood: Its Psychology and Psychopathology*, edited by E. J. Anthony and T. Benedek, 109–36. Boston: Little, Brown.

———. (1959). "Parenthood as a Developmental Phase: A Contribution to the Libido Theory." *Journal of the American Psychoanalytic Association* 7:389–417.

Ben Jelloun, T. (2011). *A Palace in the Old Village*. New York: Penguin Books.

Berk, L. E. (2009). *Child Development*. Boston: Allyn and Bacon/Pearson.

Bissinger, B. (2012). *Father's Day: Across America with an Unusual Dad and His Extraordinary Child*. New York: Houghton Mifflin Harcourt.

Brazelton, T. B., and H. Als. (1979). "Four Early Stages in the Development of Mother-Infant Interaction." *Psychoanalytic Study of the Child* 34:349–69.

Bronfenbrenner, U. (1979). *The Ecology of Human Development*. Cambridge, MA: Harvard University Press.

Brook, C. D. G. (1985). *All about Adolescence*. New York: Wiley.

Brown, A. V. (2012). "Learning English on Her Own—Almost: The Facilitative Role of One Immigrant's Daughter." *Journal of Latinos and Education* 11 (4): 218–31.

Bucholz, E. S. (2000). "Parenthood as a Developmental Stage." In *Parenthood in America: An Encyclopedia*, edited by L. Balter, 2:440–42 Boulder, CO: ABC-CLIO.

Buckholdt, K. E., G. R. Parra, and L. Jobe-Shields. (2014). "Intergenerational Transmission of Emotion Dysregulation through Parental Invalidation of Emotions: Implications for Adolescent Internalizing and Externalizing Behaviors." *Journal of Child and Family Studies* 23 (2): 324–32.

Bugental, D. B., and J. E. Grusec. (2006). "Socialization Processes." In *Handbook of Child Psychology*, edited by N. Eisenberg, 366–428. Hoboken, NJ: Wiley.

Butziger, R. (2006). "Another Look at the Expanding Nest." *Psyc CRITIQUES* 51 (36).

Cherian, A. (2012). *The Invitation*. New York: Norton.

Chuang, S., and L. C. Tamis. (2013). *Gender Roles in Immigrant Families*. New York: Springer.

Cook, W. L. (2001). "Interpersonal Influence in Family Systems: A Social Relations Model Analysis." *Child Development* 72:1179–97.

Corona, R., L. F. Stevens, and R. W. Halfond. (2012). "A Qualitative Analysis of What Latino Parents and Adolescents Think and Feel about Language Brokering." *Journal of Child and Family Studies* 21 (5): 788–98.

Coyne, S. M., L. M. Padilla-Walker, and E. Howard. (2013). "Emerging in a Digital World: A Decade Review of Media Use, Effects, and Gratifications in Emerging Adulthood." *Emerging Adulthood* 1 (2): 125–37.

Cruz, A. (2005). *Let It Rain Coffee*. New York: Simon & Schuster.

———. (2001). *Soledad*. New York: Simon & Schuster.

Cui, M., K. A. S. Wickrama, F. O. Lorenz, and R. D. Conger. (2011). "Linking Parental Divorce and Marital Discord to the Timing of Emerging Adults' Marriage and Cohabitation." In *Romantic Relationships in Emerging Adulthood*, edited by F. D. Fincham and M. Cui, 123–41. New York: Cambridge University Press.

Deater-Deckard, K. (2014). "Family Matters: Intergenerational and Interpersonal Processes of Executive Function and Attentive Behavior." *Current Directions in Psychological Science* 23 (3): 230–36.

Del Torto, L. (2008). "Once a Broker, Always a Broker: Non-Professional Interpreting as Identity Accomplishment in Multigenerational Italian-English Bilingual Family Interaction." *Multilingua: Journal of Cross-Cultural and Interlanguage Communication* 27 (1–2): 77–97.

DeMent, T., R. Buriel, and C. Villanueva. (2005). "Children as Language Brokers: A Narrative of the Recollections of College Students." In *Language in Multicultural Education*, edited by R. Hoosain and F. Salili, 255–72. Greenwich, CT: Information Age.

Demick, J. (2011). "Effects of Children on Adult Development and Learning: Fifty Years of Theory and Research." In *The Oxford Handbook of Reciprocal Adult Development and Learning*, edited by C. Hoare, 365–80. New York: Oxford University Press.

———. (2006). "Effects of Children on Adult Development and Learning: Parenthood and Beyond." In *Handbook of Adult Development and Learning*, edited by C. Hoare, 329–43. New York: Oxford University Press.

———. (2002). "Stages of Parental Development." In *Handbook of Parenting*, vol. 3: *Being and Becoming a Parent*, edited by M. H. Bornstein, 389–413. Mahwah, NJ: Lawrence Erlbaum.

Díaz, J. (2007). *The Brief Wondrous Life of Oscar Wao*. New York: Riverhead Books.

Dillon, J. J. (2002). "The Role of the Child in Adult Development." *Journal of Adult Development* 9:267 75.

Dimitrova, R., M. Bender, and F. van de Vijver, eds. (2014). *Global Perspectives on Well-Being in Immigrant Families*. New York: Springer.

Dolgin, K. G. (2010). *The Adolescent: Development, Relationships and Culture*. New York: Pearson College Division.

Dorner, L. M., M. F. Orellana, and R. Jimenez. (2008). "'It's One of

Those Things That You Do to Help the Family': Language Brokering and the Development of Immigrant Adolescents." *Journal of Adolescent Research* 23 (5): 515–43.

Dorsch, T. E., A. L. Smith, and M. H. McDonough. (2014). "Parents' Perceptions of Child-to-Parent Socialization in Organized Youth Sport." *Journal of Sport and Exercise Psychology* 31 (4): 444–68.

Erikson, E. H. (1950). *Childhood and Society.* New York: Norton.

———. (1968). *Identity: Youth and Crisis.* New York: Norton.

———. (1982). *The Life Cycle Completed.* New York: Norton.

Feldman, R. S. (2010). *Child Development.* Upper Saddle River, NJ: Prentice Hall.

Field, J., H. Lynch, and I. Malcolm. (2008). "Generations, the Life Course, and Lifelong Learning." Learning Lives Summative Working Paper no. 3. http://www.tlrp.org/project%20sites/LearningLives/papers/working_papers/Generationsandthelifecourse.pdf.

Galinsky, E. (1981). *Between Generations: The Six Stages of Parenthood.* New York: Berkley Books.

Gawande, A. (2007). *Better: A Surgeon's Notes on Performance.* New York: Picador.

Garcia-Coll, C. (2012). *The Impact of Immigration on Children's Development.* New York: Karger.

Gutmann, D. (1975). "Parenthood: A Key to the Comparative Study of the Life Cycle." In *Lifespan Developmental Psychology: Normative Life Crises,* edited by N. Datan and L. H. Ginsberg, 167–84. New York: Academic.

Hall, G. S. (1928). *Adolescence: Its Psychology and Its Relations to Physiology, Anthropology, Sociology, Sex, Crime, and Religion.* New York: Appleton.

Halpern, C. T., and C. E. Kaestle. (2014). "Sexuality in Emerging Adulthood." In *APA Handbook of Sexuality and Psychology: Person-Based Approaches,* edited by D. L. Tolman, L. M. Diamond, J. A. Bauermeister, W. H. George, J. G. Pfaus, and L. M. Ward, 487–522 Washington, DC: American Psychological Association.

Handlin, O. ([1951] 2002). *The Uprooted: The Epic Story of the Great Migrations That Made the American People.* Philadelphia: University of Pennsylvania Press.

Hardy, D. (2010). *The Solution Room.* Unpublished. Available online at http://file1.wcfbooks.top/?pid=243.

Ho, C. (2010). "Intergenerational Learning (between Generation X & Y) in Learning Families: A Narrative Inquiry." *International Education Studies* 3 (4): 59–72.

Huh, D., J. Tristan, E. Wade, and E. Stice. (2006). "Does Problem Behavior Elicit Poor Parenting? A Prospective Study of Adolescent Girls." *Journal of Adolescent Research* 21:185–204.

Kaimal, G., and W. R. Beardslee. (2010). "Emerging Adulthood and the Perception of Parental Depression." *Qualitative Health Research* 20 (9): 1213–28.

Kelley, C. (2013). *Accidental Immigrants and the Search for Home: Women, Cultural Identity, and Community*. Philadelphia: Temple University Press.

Kins, E., B. Soenens, and W. Beyers. (2012). "Parental Psychological Control and Dysfunctional Separation-Individuation: A Tale of Two Different Dynamics." *Journal of Adolescence* 35 (5): 1099–1109.

Kloep, M., and L. B. Hendry. (2010). "Letting Go or Holding On? Parents' Perceptions of Their Relationships with Their Children during Emerging Adulthood." *British Journal of Developmental Psychology* 28 (4): 817–34.

Kuczynski, L., S. Marshall, and K. Schell. (1997). "Value Socialization in a Bidirectional Context." In *Parenting and Children's Internalization of Values: A Handbook of Contemporary Theory*, edited by J. E. Grusec and L. Kuczynski, 23–50. Hoboken, NJ: Wiley.

Langer, E. J. (2005). *On Becoming an Artist: Reinventing Yourself through Mindful Creativity*. New York: Ballantine Books.

Lawrence-Lightfoot, Sara. (2012). *Exit: The Endings That Set Us Free*. New York: Farrar, Straus & Giroux.

———. (2000). *Respect: An Exploration*. Cambridge, MA: Perseus Books.

———. (2009). *The Third Chapter: Passion, Risk, and Adventure in the 25 Years after 50*. New York: Farrar, Straus and Giroux.

Lawrence-Lightfoot, S., and J. H. Davis. (1997). *The Art and Science of Portraiture*. San Francisco: Jossey-Bass Publishers.

Lee, D. (2001). *Yellow*. New York: W. W. Norton.

Lerner, R. M. (2006). "Developmental Science, Developmental Systems, and Contemporary Theories of Human Development." In *Handbook of Child Psychology*, edited by R. M. Lerner and W. Damon, 1:1–17 New York: Wiley.

Lester, B. M., J. Hoffman, and T. B. Brazelton. (1985). "The Rhythmic Structure of Mother-Infant Interaction in Term and Preterm Infants." *Child Development* 56 (1): 15–27.

Levinson, D. J. (1986). "A Conception of Adult Development." *American Psychologist* 41:3–13.

———. (1978). *The Seasons of a Man's Life.* New York: Ballantine Books.

Levitt, M. J., M. E. Silver, and J. D. Santos. (2007). "Adolescents in Transition to Adulthood: Parental Support, Relationship Satisfaction, and Post-Transition Adjustment." *Journal of Adult Development* 14 (1–2): 53–63.

Lüscher, K., A. Hoff, G. Lamura, M. Renzi, M. Sánchez, G. Viry, and E. Widmer. (2013). *Generations, Intergenerational Relationships, Generational Policy: A Multilingual Compendium.* Konstanz, Germany: Generationes.

Luvmour, J. (2010). "Developing Together: Parents Meeting Children's Developmental Imperatives." *Journal of Adult Development* 17 (4): 191–244.

Majdumar, A. (2013). *The Abundance.* New York: Metropolitan Books/ Henry Holt.

Malae, P. (2013). *Our Frail Blood.* New York: Black Cat.

Martinez, C. R., Jr., H. H. McClure, and J. M. Eddy. (2009). "Language Brokering Contexts and Behavioral and Emotional Adjustment among Latino Parents and Adolescents." *Journal of Early Adolescence* 29 (1): 71–98.

McMahan, I. (2009). *Adolescence.* Boston: Pearson/Allyn & Bacon.

Mizumoto, M., and R. Yamane. (2011). "Mother-Daughter Relationships in Emerging Adulthood: Development Of A Mother-Child Psychological Independence Scale and Proposal of a Four-Category Model of Mother-Child Relationships." *Japanese Journal of Educational Psychology* 59 (4): 462–73.

Negru, O., C. Haragâş, and A. Mustea. (2014). "How Private Is the Relation with God? Religiosity and Family Religious Socialization in Romanian Emerging Adults." *Journal of Adolescent Research* 29 (3): 380–406.

Nelson, L. J., L. M. Padilla-Walker, K. J. Christensen, C. A. Evans, and J. S. Carroll. (2011). "Parenting in Emerging Adulthood: An Examination of Parenting Clusters and Correlates." *Journal of Youth and Adolescence* 40 (6): 730–43.

Newberger, C. M. (1987). "Time, Place, and Parental Awareness: A Cognitive-Developmental Perspective on Family Adaptation and Parental Care." In *Child Abuse and Neglect: Biosocial Dimensions*, edited by J. B. Lancaster and R. J. Gelles, 233–51. New York: Aldine de Gruyter.

Nunez, E. (2014). *Not for Everyday Use*. New York: Akashic Books.

Orellana, M. F., L. Dorner, and L. Pulido. (2003). "Accessing Assets: Immigrant Youth's Work as Family Translators or "Para-Phrasers." *Social Problems* 50:505–24.

Peters, J. F. (1985). "Adolescents as Socialization Agents to Parents." *Adolescence* 20:921–33.

Pinquart, M., and R. K. Silbereisen. (2004). "Transmission of Values from Adolescents to Their Parents: The Role of Value Content and Authoritative Parenting." *Adolescence* 39 (153): 83–100.

Robinson, S. A. (1987). *Child Development*. New York: Holt, Rinehart & Winston.

Roest, A. M. C., J. S. Dubas, and J. R. M. Gerris. (2009). "Value Transmissions between Fathers, Mothers, and Adolescent and Emerging Adult Children: The Role of the Family Climate. *Journal of Family Psychology* 23 (2): 146–55.

Sameroff, A. J. and L. A. Feil. (1985). "Parental Concepts of Development." In *Parental Belief Systems: The Psychological Consequences for Children*, edited by I. E. Siegel, 83–105. Mahwah, NJ: Lawrence Erlbaum.

Schaffer, H. R. (2007). "The Mutuality of Parental Control in Early Childhood." In *Childhood Socialization*, edited by G. Handel, 45–64. New Brunswick, NJ: Aldine Transaction.

Seltzer, J. A., and S. M. Bianchi. (2013). "Demographic Change and Parent-Child Relationships in Adulthood." *Annual Review of Sociology* 39:275–90.

Shapiro, A. (2005). *Tantalus in Love*. New York: Houghton Mifflin.

Shteyngart, G. (2014). *Little Failure: A Memoir*. New York: Random House.

Solomon, A. (2012). *Far from the Tree: Parents, Children, and the Search For Identity*. New York: Scribner.

Spock, B. (1957). *Baby and Child Care.* New York: Pocket Books.

Steinberg, L. D. (2014). *Adolescence.* New York: McGraw-Hill.

Stepanova, G. S. (2014). "Problems of the Socialization of Today's Young People." *Russian Education and Society* 56 (4): 90–98.

Super, C. M., and S. Harkness. (2002). "Culture Structures the Environment for Development." *Human Development* 45:270–74.

Sussman, S., and J. J. Arnett. (2014). "Emerging Adulthood: Developmental Period Facilitative of the Addictions." *Evaluation and the Health Professions* 37 (2):147–55.

Tempest, S. (2003). "Intergenerational Learning: A Reciprocal Knowledge Development Process That Challenges the Language of Learning." *Management Learning* 34 (2):181–200.

Urry, S. A., L. J. Nelson, and L. M. Padilla-Walker. (2011). "Mother Knows Best: Psychological Control, Child Disclosure, and Maternal Knowledge in Emerging Adulthood." *Journal of Family Studies* 17 (2): 157–73.

Valdés, G. (2003). *Expanding Definitions of Giftedness: The Case of Young Interpreters from Immigrant Communities.* Mahwah, NJ: Lawrence Erlbaum.

Vaillant, G. E. (2003). *Aging Well: Surprising Guideposts to a Happier Life from a Landmark Harvard Study of Adult Development.* New York: Little, Brown.

Villanueva, C., and R. Buriel. (2010). "Speaking on Behalf of Others: A Qualitative Study of the Perceptions and Feelings of Adolescent Latina Language Brokers." *Journal of Social Issues* 66 (1): 197–210.

Wright, R. (1998). *Haiku: This Other World.* New York: Anchor Books.

Index

Names of interviewed parents are indexed under surname and also under first name.